The In-Between People

Language and Culture Maintenance and
Mother-Tongue Education in the
Highlands of Papua New Guinea

**SIL International
Publications in Language Use
and Education**

Publication 3

Publications in Language Use and Education is a serial publication of SIL International. The series began as a venue for works covering a broad range of topics in sociolinguistics and has been expanded to include topics in education, including mother-tongue literacy, multilingual education, and nonformal education. While most volumes are authored by members of SIL, suitable works by others will also form part of the series.

Series Editors

Gloria E. Kindell
Graduate Institute
of Applied Linguistics

Stephen L. Walter
Graduate Institute
of Applied Linguistics

Volume Editor

Rhonda Hartell Jones

Production Staff

Bonnie Brown, Managing Editor
Karoline Fisher, Compositor
Hazel Shorey, Graphic Artist

The In-Between People

Language and Culture Maintenance and Mother-Tongue Education in the Highlands of Papua New Guinea

Dennis L. Malone

SIL International
Dallas, Texas

© 2004 by SIL International
Library of Congress Catalog No: 2004-102308
ISBN: 1-55671-147-6
ISSN: 1545-0074

Printed in the United States of America

Copies of this and other publications of the SIL International
may be obtained from

International Academic Bookstore
SIL International
7500 W. Camp Wisdom Road
Dallas, TX 75236-5699

Voice: 972-708-7404
Fax: 972-708-7433
Email: academic_books@sil.org
Internet: http://www.ethnologue.com

Contents

List of Tables

List of Figures

Acknowledgments

I am almost overwhelmed at the length of my list of people whose questions, suggestions, help, support and encouragement have contributed significantly to whatever is worthwhile in this research project, which formed the basis for my doctoral dissertation (Malone (1997) and this revision of it. To start at the beginning, I thank God for His gracious provision of good health, good family, good mentors, and the good neighbors without whom I would surely still be muddling through heaps of data.

I thank the members of my dissertation committee—Professor Larry Mikulecky, whose incisive questions and suggestions provided much needed direction for this study, Professor Linda Mabry, whose knowledge and experience in case study methodology and constant encouragement through the "dry days" provided psychic energy for completing this project, Professor Carmen Simich-Dudgeon, whose knowledge of issues and sources for language planning, sociolinguistics, and bilingual education opened many new paths of exploration for me, and Professor Carlos Ovando, whose knowledge of, experience in, and enthusiasm for minority group education provided ongoing motivation for this project.

I am equally grateful to my Kaugel colleagues and neighbors who helped and befriended me throughout my field research period. I especially thank Rambai Keruwa and Apé Kolowa for their willingness to share with me their extensive knowledge and insights into Kaugel language, life, and culture. I am also grateful to the Kaugel vernacular preschool teachers and community school teachers who readily shared their classrooms and their thoughts with me.

I thank Steve Walter, former International Literacy Coordinator for SIL International, through whose efforts I was able to secure grants for my field research from special SIL funds.

I also thank Rambai and his wife Nalli and Rob and June Head, SIL colleagues, for their generous hospitality during my six months of field research in the Tambul Basin.

I thank Rita Barsun for her voluntary and expert database searches on topics of special concern for this case study.

I thank my four children—Sharon, Jim, Dan, and Steve—for their faithful support and love, and their tolerance for endless discussions about "the dissertation."

Finally, I thank my wife Susan for her sacrifice of time and energy and for her indefatigable patience, hope, and encouragement (which I sorely tried in the final month of writing). Where she lives is—to steal a phrase from Victor Hugo—"the address of my soul."

List of Acronyms and Abbreviations

ACE	Accelerated Christian education
AIDA	Alberta International Development Agency
BE	Bilingual education
BICS	Basic interpersonal communication skills
BOM	Board of management
BTA	Bible Translation Association of PNG
CALP	Cognitive/Academic Language Proficiency
CIDA	Canadian International Development Agency
CS	Community school
EBM	Evangelical Bible Mission
EHP	Eastern Highlands Province
ENBP	East New Britain Province
ERU	Educational Research Unit
GLGC	Giluwe local government council
KNFEA	Kaugel Non-Formal Education Association
KRS	Kaugel Reading Series
KTPPS	Kaugel *Tok Ples Pri Skul* (Kaugel Mother-Tongue Pre-School)
L1	First language (mother tongue)
L2	Second language
LARR	Linguistic Awareness and Reading Readiness test
LAS	Literacy and Awareness Secretariat
LGC	Local government council
LWC	Language of wider communication
MT	Mother tongue (vernacular)
MTE	Mother-tongue education

NDOE	National Department of Education
NFE	Nonformal education
NGO	Nongovernment organization
NSP	North Solomons Province
PLC	Provincial Literacy Coordinator
PNG	Papua New Guinea
REU	Research and evaluation unit
RLS	Reversing language shift
SIL	SIL International
SHP	Southern Highlands Province
STEP	Supervisors' Tokples Education Program
TPNG	Territory of Papua and New Guinea
TPPS	Tok Ples Pri Skul (mother-tongue pre-primary class)
UNICEF	United Nations Children's Education Fund
UNESCO	United Nations Educational, Scientific, and Cultural Organization
UPNG	University of Papua New Guinea
VSD	Division of Village Services, Department of Village Services and Rural Development
VTPS	*Viles Tok Ples Skul* (Village Mother-Tongue School)
WHP	Western Highlands Province

1

Introduction

I was just beginning school here [at Tambul Bible Mission]. It was a few months into school and so I was around about twelve, thirteen, in between there. I was called to live on the mission station. And, I think I might have lived there for some weeks. The men had done their selections here in the village, in the clan [regarding] who should do this, who should be taken from each haus man, liklik haus man[1]—Sakalem, Kikuwa, Pombol, Purare, all these [place names]. And then for Kikuwa, they have somehow chosen me, and asked Karoma to go pick me, take me out of the school....And I can remember [the] time. I was in [the] classroom, and it was the afternoon when we finished these lessons and came out. And here Karoma was just beside the classroom door. And he didn't say any words, he just pulled me by the hand. I thought, oh, I think he must have something for me, or he wants to give me something in secret so others cannot see. So he pulled me out away from the classroom, and we walked some distance, and he said, I've come to take you. I want you to leave school. There's something worthwhile going on in our village you have to learn....And he said, all the men want you to come. And I said, who, who are the men? All the Aika men, he said. And, you know, I kept on asking and I thought, in the first, I thought, I must have got into trouble. And he said, no, the men are going to teach you something. Out of all Aika, for our Kikuwa clan, he said, they chose the names of Karoma, him and me, only two of us. Not others. And he said,

---

[1]Literally, 'man's house, small man's house'. The reference here is not to a building but to a small subgroup of cousin/brothers who in traditional culture would have slept in one house with older boys separate from the women and small children. I will use the term *haus man*, which is commonly used by Tambul people to refer to the social group to whom they are most loyal and obligated. The term rarely refers to an actual building, as brothers now customarily sleep with their wives and children in a single *haus lain* (group house).

1

This is special. You have got to leave your school and come. (Rambai
Keruwa, interview, July 29, 1995, T2B:98–134)[2]

Karoma had come to the Evangelical Bible Mission school at Tambul in
the Western Highlands of Papua New Guinea to get the 12-year-old
Rambai for a male youth initiation called *sandallu.* This episode drama-
tizes the intersection of cultures that gave rise to this case study. It also illustrates one of the study's key assertions: that Rambai and his generation
of Kaugel speakers—the *namel manmeri* 'the in-between people'—live in a
unique time period, touching the old and the new in a way that will never
again be duplicated for this ethnolinguistic community. They are argu-
ably the most critical players in the maintenance of Kaugel language and
culture.

In a sense, all parents stand between two generations—their own parents' and their children's—and in times of rapid change tend to feel that
they straddle an ever-widening gap between the past and future. Among
the Kaugel, Rambai's generation is unique; they are the last to have experienced the before-and-after of a seismic sociocultural event in Kaugel history: their people's first contact with European civilization in the early
1950s.

Although limited to a relatively small ethnolinguistic community, this
case study of the Kaugel Tok Ples Pri Skul (KTPPS) program includes the
multidimensions of the social, political, economic, and spiritual context
in which the program takes place. It allows the reader to view how members of one community are addressing the social and educational needs of
their children in a time of rapid change.

Language and Education in Kaugel

Around the world, societies educate their children so that the children can
fully employ their talents and energies for their own and their society's
benefit. Education (as a societal institution) can become distorted in one
of two ways. It can so encumber the children with unnecessary information that they are too inhibited to learn, or it can so thoroughly enthrall
them—while simultaneously removing or obscuring their points of reference—that they are unable to know who they are or what their role is in
the society.

---

[2]References to taped sources include the number of the tape (1, 2, 3,...), the side (A or B),
and the respective page numbers of the printouts of the transcripts of the tape.

In 1991, the Papua New Guinea (PNG) National Department of Education (NDOE) conducted an Education Sector Review in which the existing education system was characterized as providing limited access (enrolling only 73 percent of potential students), as having "an appalling attrition rate between grades 1 and 6" (almost 45 percent), and as alienating students "from the way of life of the people," while doing little "to equip them with the knowledge, skills, and attitudes necessary to contribute positively to community or national development" (Department of Education 1991a:3).

In this study, I focus on a mother-tongue pre-primary school in the Western Highlands Province, an educational innovation that is an attempt to minimize the negative effects of the dysfunctional formal education system in one ethnolinguistic community.

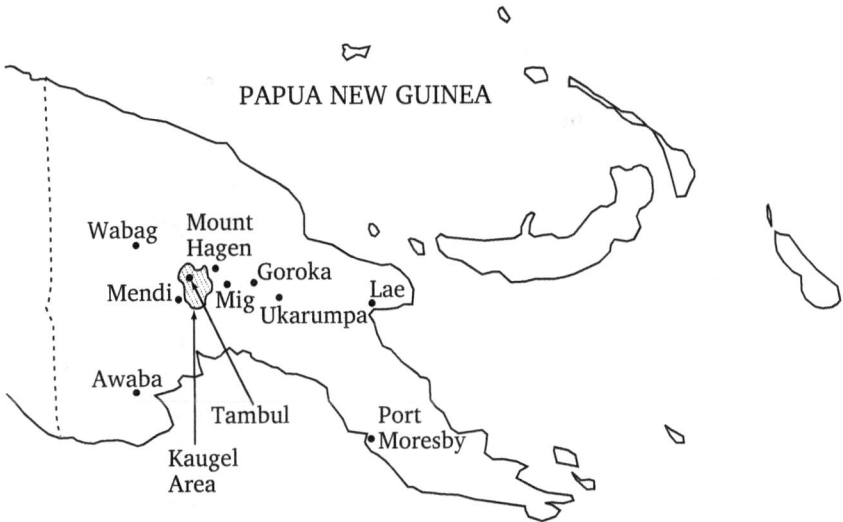

Figure 1.1. Kaugel area in Papua New Guinea.

One of many community-based pre-primary education programs emerging around the country in the mid-1980s, the Kaugel Tok Ples Pri

Skul (KTPPS)[3] program was initiated in 1985 with assistance from SIL.[4] By 1994, the KTPPS program had expanded from one pilot class to fourteen "preschools" enrolling in excess of five hundred children (Rambai Keruwa, personal communication, January, 1995).

Although the use of the learners' mother tongue as medium-of-instruction has been promoted as generally (although not necessarily) beneficial in the early years of formal education, short-term small-scale efforts, such as the one-year KTPPS program, are generally considered inadequate[5] for achieving the government's goals: "(1) to enable children to develop close ties to the local community and (2) to prepare children for successful participation in the formal education system" (Department of Education 1990:1).

The expansion of the KTPPS, therefore, raises questions of theoretical and practical significance for this case study: Can a pre-primary education program that is meant to prepare children for a successful experience in an English-language formal education system simultaneously enable them to develop firm attachments to their own language and culture? How do the tensions inherent in an enterprise with conflicting goals affect the attitudes and actions of parents, teachers, program administrator, and the children themselves?

My purpose in this study was threefold: (1) to understand, in a general way, how the KTPPS program has been maintained and expanded since its inception in 1986; (2) to understand the ways in which the *namel manmeri*—like Rambai and Karoma in the vignette that opened this chapter—work within the community to effect a beneficial education for their children, and (3) to describe how community members attempt to resolve the tension between the children's culture and language maintenance on the one hand, and their academic success in an English-language formal education system on the other.

---

[3]The term, *tok ples* [lit., 'talk-place'] is from the PNG national creole and refers to local languages. It will be used interchangeably in this study with vernacular. The Tok Pisin and Umbu-Ungu transliterations of the term preschool—*pri skul* and *piri sukuli*, respectively—have caused major misconceptions about the nature of these schools. Umbu-Ungu speakers frequently do not distinguish between [p] and [f], which, in this case, renders *pri skul* 'preschool' as the phonological equivalent of *fri-skul* 'free school', this latter a concept being promoted at the time by politicians throughout the country. The effort to rename these schools prep schools to emphasize their function as preparatory to entrance into the formal system's grade 1, never caught on with the local people. Therefore, I have retained the use of *pri skul* throughout this study, with the misconception echoing within it.

[4]SIL International is an international, nonprofit organization committed to linguistic, translation, literacy, and community development projects among the ethnolinguistic minorities of the world.

[5]See Cummins 1981, 1984, 1986; Hakuta 1986; Skutnabb-Kangas and Cummins 1988; Hornberger 1988; Ovando 1990; Ramirez, Yuen, and Ramey 1991; Krashen 1991; Dolson and Meyer 1992; Watson 1994; Romaine 1995; Baker 1996.

The assumption that tension exists between the goals of maintaining minority language and culture and of achieving success in a dominant-language formal education system rests on a large and growing body of literature addressing issues in education in multilingual contexts throughout the Third World (Spolsky 1972; Modiano 1973; Afolayan 1984; Benton 1986; Phillipson, Skutnabb-Kangas and Africa, 1986; Smolicz 1986; Hornberger 1988; Harris 1990; Akinnaso 1989, 1991; Smalley 1994; McLaughlin 1994). This tension is a focal point of the analysis in chapters 5 and 7.

As the issues of language shift and language death (cf. Crystal 2000; Dorian 1981; Fishman 1991, 2001; Grenoble and Whaley 1998; Krauss 1992) and the education of minority language groups (cf. Cenoz and Genesee 1998; Cummins 2000; Cummins and Danesi 1990; Harris 1990; May 1999; Ovando 1994; Paulston 1986; Rubagumya 1994; Skutnabb-Kangas 1986, 2000) have gained an international hearing, relatively few studies have been done from the perspective of the ethnolinguistic communities themselves (cf. Hornberger 1988, Davis 1994, *Peabody Journal of Education,* Winter 1994). This case study provides a grassroots view of minority language education in Papua New Guinea, the world's most multilingual nation.

The goals of PNG's vernacular pre-primary schools to improve student success in the formal system and to develop closer ties between the children and the community are contested issues in the literature. Based on his study of Aboriginal education and culture in Australia, Harris (1994:141) suggests the two goals are "mutually exclusive." This case study examines the tension between these goals and extends the knowledge about the complex relationships existing among language, culture, and education in ethnolinguistic minority communities.

The study also provides ethnographic detail regarding the role of mother-tongue education in preparing children for formal primary education and in combating cultural discontinuity, a feature lacking in much of the literature on vernacular and bilingual education (cf. Engle 1975; Larson and Davis 1981; Dutcher 1982; Delpit and Kemelfield 1985; Fafunwa, Macauley, and Sokoya 1989. See Hornberger 1988 for a notable exception).

Nor have recent studies considered the effect of parents' perceptions of mother-tongue pre-primary programs on their children's formal education (cf. Delpit and Kemelfield 1985). This lacuna in mother-tongue education research is especially significant in the PNG context because the national government, through the Department of Education, is implementing a three-year mother-tongue elementary program as part of a general restructuring of the formal education system (Department of Education 1991a; discussed in detail in chapter 3).

From the viewpoint of government and nongovernmental organizations (NGOs) involved in mother-tongue education around the world, a qualitative, in-depth analysis of a single local program provides empirical evidence of those aspects of mother-tongue education programs—the perceptions and activities of the people involved in them—that are especially resistant to quantification. This case study should provide a point of reference for comparison with similar mother-tongue education projects in other contexts and provide insights into the factors that influence their sustainability. In addition, this study responds to criticism by social scientists like Mühlhäusler (1990) and Topping (1992), who question whether vernacular literacy actually serves to promote and maintain indigenous cultures (cf. Franklin 1975; Bernard 1992; Watson 1994).

Finally, this case study provided the research participants with an opportunity to consider the issues of language and culture in their own speech community at a time when community awareness and action can still be effectively utilized for maintenance.

Language and Education in Traditional Societies

The conceptual framework for this case study of the Kaugel Tok Ples Pri Skul program in Papua New Guinea grows out of several interrelated theoretical perspectives drawn from the literature. These are the relationship between language and identity, concerns for language and culture maintenance among the world's many ethnolinguistic groups, concerns about the introduction of print literacy into traditionally nonliterate societies, conflicting views of the effects of bilingualism and the various models of bilingual education involving ethnolinguistic groups, and concerns for language and education in multilingual societies, particularly in Papua New Guinea.

Language and identity

For the past fifty years, sociolinguists have debated whether or not there exists an isomorphic relationship between language and culture and, by extension, between language and individual and group identity.

Although Edwards (1985, 1992) and others contend that no isomorphic relationship exists between language and ethnic identity, Fishman (1991) and others argue that the loss of the ethnic language profoundly alters the cultural content, if not the boundaries, of an ethnic group. Romaine (1995) finds that group identity with the ancestral language does not guarantee its maintenance while Jordan (1988) and Lal (1995) suggest that the emic perceptions of the group members themselves are what matter most in language and identity issues.

In some countries (e.g., Ireland, Spain, New Zealand) concerns for the loss of language have led to the development of language planning as a corrective to the *laissez-faire* approaches to language and culture maintenance in the past.[6]

Language planning and language shift

The need for language planning

In the language planning literature, PLANNING refers to deliberate efforts to influence the way people acquire, structure, and allocate their languages (Cooper 1989). As such, language planning involves STATUS PLANNING (concerned with raising a language's profile and prestige; addresses the uses of language), CORPUS PLANNING (concerned with spelling, grammar, vocabulary, and standardization issues; addresses the language itself), and ACQUISITION PLANNING (concerned with promoting language spread by increasing the number of users; addresses the speakers of a language) (cf. Hornberger 1994; Baker 1996).

Language planners frequently refer to language shift and language maintenance (Fasold 1984; Paulston 1986; Hornberger 1988, 1994; Baker 1996). LANGUAGE SHIFT involves a gradual decrease in the number of speakers and uses of a language and in language proficiency. LANGUAGE MAINTENANCE refers to a state in which a language is not necessarily gaining members or uses, but is stable in terms of the number of speakers and domains and proficiency of use. Cooper (1989) coined the term LANGUAGE SPREAD to identify languages that are demonstrably expanding in terms of numbers of speakers and geography and also in the domains in which the language is used by speakers of other languages.

Ruiz (1984) finds that planners in multilingual settings adopt one of three "orientations" to languages and their role in society: language-as-problem, language-as-right, and language-as-resource. Language planners holding the "language-as-problem" orientation view a multiplicity of

---

[6]On the other hand, motivation for language planning can also encompass concerns for maintaining the status quo (e.g., English-only in the U.S.), for improving the socioeconomic and political positions of some groups over others (e.g., Yoruba, Hausa, Igbo in Nigeria), and for promoting national or regional languages over ethnic languages (e.g., Kiswahili in Tanzania, Telegu and Hindi in India).

minority languages as an impediment to the integration of minority groups[7] into the larger national society. Those holding a "language-as-right" orientation view language as an inherent individual and group right that must be ensured and protected by the national government. Those holding a "language-as-resource" orientation view languages as social and cultural resources not only for their speakers, but for the society as a whole.

Compare this with Williams (cited in Baker 2001:53–54), who describes three attitudes toward language minorities[8]: evolutionist, preservationist, conservationist. The "preservationist" and "conservationist" categories correlate closely with language-as-right and language-as-resource orientations, respectively. The "evolutionist" attitude differs from a language-as-problem orientation in that its Darwinian language policy of natural selection leads to laissez-faire language planning, whereas the language-as-problem orientation frequently stimulates active promotion and support of a lingua franca, national, or international language to the detriment of minority languages.

For the past quarter century, sociolinguists and others have studied language shift, language spread, language maintenance, and language death in industrialized as well as in Two-Thirds World societies in order to facilitate language planning and policy formation, as well as to present rationales for the need to plan in multilingual settings (Haugen 1972, 1985, 1987; Fishman 1972, 1991; Edwards 1981, 1985; Dorian 1981, 1993; Fasold 1984; Paulston 1986, 1992, 1994; Smalley 1994).

In an issue of *Language* (Hale 1992) that devoted a substantial section to a set of essays regarding "endangered languages," Krauss (1992) presents data from several catalogs of world languages to argue that the potential exists for 90 percent of the estimated 6,000 languages currently in use to become extinct during the twenty-first century unless action is taken to reverse the

---

[7]I use "minority" in reference to all nonmajority languages including—but not limited to—indigenous languages.

[8]The World Conference on Linguistic Rights, held at Barcelona, Spain in June 1996, had the over-all objective of providing an intergovernmental protocol on linguistic rights that

> would become a point of reference to be used by nongovernmental organizations and other institutions and bodies which work towards the recognition of linguistic rights in the pursuit of research and in the formulation of requests and demands. (World Conference on Linguistic Rights, Barcelona, June 1996, Information Summary [on-line] p. 1. Available: http://www.partal.com/ciemen/conf/english.html)

The conference objectives included increasing awareness among international public opinion of the concept of linguistic rights, assessing legal, sociolinguistic, and demolinguistic information to determine current status of language rights issues, and establishing a collaboration among NGOs and other institutions to organize an inter governmental conference on linguistic rights.

process of language shift. His argument is based on an analytical process that distributes languages among three categories: MORIBUND, ENDANGERED, and SAFE. Moribund refers to languages in which children are no longer taught the mother tongue (cf. Paulston 1986; Fishman 1991). Endangered languages are those in which children are currently learning the L1 but the conditions for the cessation of that practice are essentially in place. Safe languages are those which enjoy both official state support and proportionately large numbers of speakers. With only three languages in PNG exceeding 100,000 speakers, the implications are dire.

In response to these essays, Ladefoged (1992) raises the issue of the right of endangered language communities to decide *against* the preservation of their languages. He argues that intervention is unprofessional in many cases and even unethical when those efforts enter the political arena and compete for the limited funds available to Two-Thirds World governments. The implication here is that to deny indigenous groups the right *not* to maintain their language—if such is their collective desire—merely constitutes a subtler form of paternalism.

Dorian (1993) counters Ladefoged's warning to linguists to "be wary of arguments based on political considerations" (p. 575), by pointing out that passive acquiescence to a state government's efforts toward national unity (as per Ladefoged's example of Tanzania) is as much a political act as active opposition to the government's efforts to stamp out tribalism. Dorian also makes a strong point that the generation of speakers that decides not to transmit the ancestral language to their children—usually in order to get out from under the socioeconomic burdens of a stigmatized tongue—is very likely to experience the eventual resentment of the later generation which, now secure in their social position in the dominant society, "yearn after the lost language" (p. 577). Thus, she argues, the right of a minority group to linguistic self-determination is a simple and uncomplicated exercise only if they disregard their posterity and the difficulties such groups have customarily experienced in trying to retrieve what has been left for dead by a previous generation.

In regard to language death, Edwards (1985) questions whether the cause is suicide rather than murder. While there are numerous languages (e.g., Scottish Gaelic, various Native American, and Australian Aboriginal) that one could argue have been "murdered," cases of language groups consciously choosing to give up their language are more difficult to document. Often the choice is so stark in socioeconomic terms as to be no real choice at all.

The predominance of social and economic forces as decisive factors in language shift situations is also argued by Edwards (1981, 1985) and Paulston

(1986, 1992, 1994). Heath (quoted in Paulston 1986) concludes from her study of language policy in Mexico "that language decisions are primarily made on political and economic grounds and reflect the value of those in political power" (p. 118).

Not all language decisions, however, are made by policy makers, and not all decisions are based on social and/or economic factors. Individual members of speech communities make choices daily and for a variety of reasons (Fishman 1991). As Fasold (1984) notes, some languages are maintained under the same socioeconomic conditions in which other languages shift (p. 240).

Language shift and language maintenance

Language shift

In the search for causes of change in language use, Paulston (1986) focuses on Cooper's distinction between language spread and language shift. Language spread refers to the adoption of a given language or dialect to perform "a given communicative function," usually in the form of a lingua franca. Language shift occurs when the lingua franca ceases to be *added* to the L1 and instead *becomes* the mother tongue. Language shift that occurs within ethnolinguistic minorities without a territorial base somewhere else results in language death (p. 120). Language spread, language shift, and language death are processes taking place within a larger social, economic, and political context.

In Paulston's theoretical framework (1986, 1992, 1994), the key to useful language and education planning is a clear and "disinterested" understanding of the social, cultural, political, and economic forces contributing to language shift. Those forces are articulated as four types of "social mobilization" in table 1.1 forming a continuum from the vulnerable to the strong: ethnicity, ethnic movement, ethnic nationalism, and geographic nationalism (adapted from Paulston 1986:131–141).

Table 1.1. Four types of social mobilization

Ethnicity	Ethnic movement	Ethnic nationalism	Geographical nationalism
shared biological past, common ancestors, identify personally with group, self-ascribed [e.g., Kaugel]	militant ethnicity, concern to maintain boundaries, engages in power struggle with dominant group [e.g., Maori]	separatistic, feels entitled to independent statehood [e.g., Kurds, Quebecois]	similar to 'ethnic nationalism' but isomorphic with the nation-state [e.g., France, Japan]

The most vulnerable of Paulston's four types—ethnicity—is most descriptive of the Kaugel community that is the focus of this study. The clans that comprise the community tend to stress their roots in "the place," their shared ancestors, and their shared biological and cultural history. Their members describe themselves in terms of their ethnic group, hold in common a set of cultural values and beliefs, and feel relatively "comfortable with the past and future" (p. 134). Paulston contends that minority groups in this category, living in a multilingual setting, will not maintain their language if the dominant group allows assimilation and provides access to the L2 through a set of contributing social conditions: e.g., universal schooling, exogamy, access to mass media, access to roads and transportation, urban migration. That virtually all of these conditions pertain to the Kaugel situation requires, at the least, a sociolinguistic perspective for this case study, and raises questions regarding the extent to which Paulston's "dominant group" exists in the socioeconomic and political realities of PNG.

Sociolinguists have been trying for decades to determine why language shift takes place. Table 1.2 lists factors that have been identified as contributing to language shift and is adapted from Fasold (1984), Paulston (1986), and Baker (1996).

Table 1.2. Factors contributing to shift from L1 to dominant language

Socio-political factors	Cultural factors	Linguistic factors
Small number of scattered speakers	Lack of mother-tongue institutions	Widespread bilingualism
Long, stable residence in dominant L2 area	Cultural and religious activity in dominant L	L1 is nonstandard; not in written form
Homeland remote	Ethnic identity defined by nonL factors	Use of L1 writing system which is expensive to reproduce, difficult to learn
L1 home community losing vitality	Few nationalistic aspirations	L1 of little or no international importance
Shift to urban occupations	Mother tongue not the only homeland language	L1 considered inferior to L2
Military service in L2	Self not defined by shared L1	Little or no L1 literacy
Easy travel out of L1 area	High emphasis on individual, low emphasis on family, community ties	No tolerance of new terms from L2; conversely, indiscriminate lexical borrowing from L2 resulting in L1 loss
Employment requires L2	Emphasis on education in L2	
Social, economic mobility	Acceptance of L2 education	
Access to L2 mass media	Culture and religion similar to that of L2	
Social institutions in L2 open to L1 speakers (e.g., education)	Bilingual parents transmit only L2 to children	
Exogamy allowed		
Potential community leaders alienated from L1 group by education		
Social and economic discrimination leads to denial of ethnic identity		

Awareness of the factors in table 1.2 will benefit language planners working on strategies to control language spread and/or language shift but the presence or absence of the factors do not necessarily predict the shift or maintenance of any particular language (cf. also Baker 1996: 44–46). Fasold (1984) suggests that the later stages of language shift are easier to detect, but more difficult to reverse, than the early stages. Characteristics of later stages include the denigration of the L1 and its speakers, a marked imbalance in the use of L2 loan words by L1 speakers, holding religious services in L2 that were traditionally the sole domain of L1, and the discontinuation of what Fishman (1991) terms "intergenerational transmission" of the language from parents to children. By the time these characteristics are observable to language planners and to the people themselves, the optimum time for taking action to reverse the trend may long since have passed. For language planners with an evolutionist perspective, such an occurrence merely constitutes a case of ethnolinguistic natural selection—the survival of the fittest. To others, it is a potential loss that merits serious preventative efforts.

Reversing language shift

In *Reversing Language Shift* (1991), Fishman provides both a rationale and a method for combating the loss of language and culture by ethnolinguistic minorities. The motivation for this case study presupposes a degree of threat to the language and culture of the Umbu-Ungu speech community. Therefore, "Why should we be concerned?" and "What can we do?" are cogent questions.

Fishman's rationale for investing the effort and resources needed for reversing language shift (RLS) recognizes the social, cultural, and political complexities involved but contends that a view of ethnolinguistic minorities as irreplaceable "encapsulations of human values" leads naturally to an effort to plan for their maintenance:

> The languages and cultures of a nation are among that nation's most precious resources. Affirming and seeking to retain them would not imply resistance to change or particularism at the expense of national identity. It is possibly even an ethical obligation to affirm people's right to retain their most deeply held societal values. (Fishman 1990:32)

However, acknowledging that most RLS efforts will have to begin in minority groups that are already in a state of weakness and decline, Fishman (1990:18) posits an eight-stage RLS model (table 1.3 from Fishman 1991) that describes a progressive movement back from the "weak side" (stages 8 to 5) to the "strong side" (stages 4 to 1). The eight stages present an ordered set of priorities with regard to reversing language shift, not a prescription for language planners to apply in any endangered language situation.

Table 1.3. Graded Intergenerational Disruption Scale for threatened
languages

Weak side

Stage 8	Stage 7	Stage 6	Stage 5
So few fluent speakers that the community needs to re-establish language norms; requires outside experts (e.g., linguists).	Older generation uses language enthusiastically but children are not learning it.	Language and identity socialization of children takes place in home, community.	Language socialization involves extensive literacy, usually including L1 schooling.

Strong side

Stage 4	Stage 3	Stage 2	Stage 1
L1 used in children's formal education in conjunction with national or official language.	L1 is used in workplaces of larger society, beyond normal L1 boundaries.	Lower governmental services and local mass media are open to L1.	"...cultural autonomy is recognized and implemented" (Fishman 1990:18); L1 used at upper government level.

Within Fishman's RLS framework, the Umbu-Ungu speech community
falls somewhere between stages 6 and 4, at the point where Fishman sees the
school as the bridge between the "weak side" and "strong side"
(1991:410–411). A modified version of stage four is, in fact, being implemented through the PNG Education Reform that proposes a new pre-primary
elementary level for the formal education system. The medium of instruction
in the three-year elementary program is the children's mother tongue (see
"Educational Context," chapter 3). The Kaugel elementary schools, however,
differ from Fishman's schools, in that the latter are proposed for ethnic minority languages in industrialized nations (e.g., Navajo in the U.S., Irish in
English-speaking Ireland, Basque and Catalan in Spain, Frisian in the Netherlands, Maori in New Zealand, Aboriginal groups in Australia, and French in
Canada). In each of those situations, the ethnic minority exists within a

larger, clearly dominant language and culture. Thus, the issues involved in Fishman's RLS approaches need to be reconsidered in view of a Kaugel community that exists in a nonindustrialized society whose myriad ethnocultural groups are *all* language minorities.

In summary, some linguists and sociolinguists contend that unless serious interventions are undertaken, as many as 90 percent of the world's languages will become extinct by the end of this century. Others consider language death an unfortunate but nevertheless inevitable consequence of dynamic and irreversible socioeconomic forces. Paulston (1986), for one, acknowledges ethnic group language maintenance as a "self-evident" right, but contends that that does not necessarily obligate the state to provide economic support for language maintenance efforts. She cautions language planners in education against setting policies that are "doomed to failure if they go against the prevailing social forces, especially the economic situation" (p. 141–142).

A knowledge of the factors that contribute to language shift, an understanding of the social and economic forces that affect language-related decision making, and a familiarity with the process of reversing language shift, all shed light on the language context of the KTPPS program.

The Umbu-Ungu speaking people of the Tambul Basin are currently in a position of *apparent* choice in terms of preserving their mother tongue. The mother tongue is dominant in the community. The PNG government has set the goal of achieving universal primary education, but its achievement is still in the distant future. I discuss the sociological findings of this case study in greater detail in chapter 5. It is worth noting at this point that in the Kaugel community, complex and multilayered sociolinguistic factors are at work that have already set in motion a language shift. My data demonstrate that local-level language planning efforts are clearly warranted.

Literacy and traditional societies

Fishman's (1991) emphasis on L1 literacy as a major component in strengthening minority languages and the central role that mother-tongue literacy acquisition plays in the KTPPS program call for a discussion of the issues surrounding the introduction of print literacy to traditional societies.

The effects of the introduction of literacy into traditional societies have been vigorously debated for the past thirty years. Goody and Watt (1988, 1968), reacting to what they call the "diffuse relativism and sentimental egalitarianism" that reject cognitive distinctions between "primitive" and "civilized" peoples, laid the groundwork for what has become known as the

"Great Divide" theory by tracing Western literacy back to the Greek adaptation of Semitic syllabaries into a phonetic writing system. According to Goody and Watt, the development of writing influenced the essential nature and direction of Hellenic culture and, by extension, Western civilization. They argue that more than any other single factor, alphabetic writing (and, consequently, literacy) accounts for "the intellectual difference between simple and complex societies" (p. 27).

Responding to the "consequences of literacy" literature (i.e., Goody and Watt 1988; Olson 1988 (1977); Ong, 1982), Street (1984) developed two models of literacy: the autonomous and the ideological. His AUTONOMOUS model considers literacy a neutral but powerful technological innovation with specific, predictable consequences. The IDEOLOGICAL model describes an approach to literacy which concentrates on "specific social practices of reading and writing," understanding that they are integrally linked to the culture in which they are observed and are, therefore, products of differing world views (p. 2).

A perception of literacy as an autonomous technology leads to one of two positions: literacy is viewed as a necessary, if not sufficient, component in the development of all people, regardless of their social and cultural context or it is just another Western technology imposed on unwilling or defenseless traditional societies that results in irreversible cultural damage (cf. Mülhäusler 1990, 1996; Topping 1992).

Street (1993), however, contends that an understanding of literacy as a set of social practices embedded in the culture of its participants, with implicit ideological ramifications, leads to a more modest view of literacy's impact. In fact, Slack (cited in Finnegan 1988) argues that to speak of literacy as having *any* impact independent of its human agency is misleading and obscures the probability that the neoliterates are active, not passive participants in their acquisition of literacy (cf. Kulick and Stroud 1993). Like any technology, literacy is shaped, adapted, and used by people for achieving certain goals, according to their own world views, which may be helpful or harmful, depending on a host of social, economic, political, and cultural conditions.

The debate over the nature of literacy and its supposed effects—autonomous versus ideological—had its Melanesian version as well. Basing much of his argument on theories promoted by Goody and Ong, Mühlhäusler (1990) submits ten "theses" suggestive of dire consequences to indigenous ethnic groups in the Pacific region as a result of vernacular literacy (cf. also Topping 1992).[9] Two of his propositions are particularly relevant to the purpose of this case study:

> (ii) The most general long-term effect of literacy in the vernacular has been language decline and death....
>
> (v) The role of literacy in vernacular education has been an ambivalent one. In many instances languages were literally 'reduced' to writing. (p. 190)

Responses to these assertions by members of SIL suggest a complex of socioeconomic and political forces (not simply literacy) as contributing to the language shift Mühlhäusler observed. SIL members argue that no empirical evidence has been uncovered that demonstrates that written language forms have ever replaced or displaced oral language forms. This latter argument is also made by Finnegan (1988) in reference to her study of orality and literacy in South Pacific indigenous societies:

> Does this mean that the use of writing is now driving out oral literary forms? ...In one way, perhaps the extensive use of writing does mean some decline in the relative position of oral literature.... But in another sense, oral literature shows no signs of disappearing. Songs...continue to be composed and performed, oratory is a constant feature of the Pacific scene, and stories are still exchanged based on recent events as well as old traditions.... All in all, it is hard to see a quick death for oral literature in the Pacific, or any inevitability about its "decline." (p. 121)

Mühlhäusler's contention that literacy negatively transforms Pacific area villagers' ways of thinking and speaking is also questioned by Kulick and Stroud (1990), whose study of literacy in Gapun village in PNG's East Sepik Province revealed that villagers conceive and use literacy in the same way they conceive and use oral language:

> Rather than literacy "taking hold" of Gapun, Gapuners have taken hold of those dimensions of literacy for which they consider they have the most use.... The villagers have not been "transformed" by literacy. If anything, they themselves have "transformed" it. (p. 301)

Gapun village is not an isolated instance of the manner in which members of traditionally oral societies adapt literacy to their own uses. Besnier (1993) writes that in the Pacific, Nukulaelae Islanders dismissed all the "functional" uses of literacy and focused on the potential of letter writing

---

[9]Topping (1992) presents similar conclusions but offers little empirical evidence for his many assertions with regard to the introduction of literacy as a cause for the demise of oral societies in the Pacific.

as vehicles for expressions of feeling that accorded with their own cultural values. Literacy uses in a remote community on the island of Madagascar are determined by villagers' understanding of what constitutes knowledge (Bloch 1993). The Mende people of Sierra Leone use literacy as a vehicle for secrecy, restricting its use to initiated cult members, rather than as a medium of general communication for the whole community, valuing it "not *in spite* of the difficulty of attaining it, but *because* of it" (Bledsoe and Robey 1993:131; emphasis in original).

In fairness to Mühlhäusler (1990) and Topping (1992), Duranti and Ochs (1986) present findings, based on their research in Samoa, supporting the view that, at least in some circumstances, literacy does have independent and apparently unavoidable negative consequences. They report effects that they attribute to the introduction of literacy and Western schooling—effects that include reorientation of children toward "task accomplishment" in a way that differs markedly from traditional views. That this is a "consequence" of literacy is argued by the authors, but the data they provide is open to multiple interpretations, as when they report that "writing is not a common activity" but admit that it is used for letter writing (cf. Besnier 1993) and for "some books in which older men keep family genealogies and ceremonial greetings..." (Duranti and Ochs 1986: 215), an instance that suggests strongly the adaptation of literacy by Samoans for their own purposes (cf. Scribner and Cole 1981).

The debate over the cognitive and societal affects of literacy has led to a rejection of literacy as a process defined simply as "reading and writing." Literacy, like language, cannot have "effects" apart from its human agency. Rather than an autonomous technology with transformative powers, literacy is now more frequently portrayed as a complex process inextricably linked to its social, economic, political, and cultural contexts. Members of traditionally oral societies into which literacy is introduced are not passive recipients upon whom the effects of print literacy work their inevitable consequences. Rather, numerous studies have demonstrated the active roles villagers take in adapting literacy to their own world view and their own uses.

Bilingual and bicultural education

The introduction of vernacular literacy and the use of the mother tongue as the medium of instruction in the Kaugel pre-primary education program raise questions in another theoretical area, namely, bilingual and bicultural education. Throughout the world, bilingual education has become a strategy for educators concerned with the failure of majority language educational programs to meet the needs of minority-language students. However, wide-ranging disagreement prevails in regard to the kind of bilingual education that is best.

Bilingual education

The success of language-immersion education projects, in which children enter an L2 medium-of-instruction primary education program, depends to a large degree on the socioeconomic status (SES) of the students' families.

In their study of an English-French program in Canada, Lambert and Tucker (1972) report that mother-tongue English children immersed in a French-language primary education program developed reading, writing, and calculation skills in French while, virtually simultaneously, developing them in English. A key feature of this program is that the English-speaking students were mainly children from the middle socioeconomic class and from the nation's dominant language, whose parents considered their acquisition of bilingualism in French to be advantageous.

Cummins (1979, 1981) subsequently studied language-minority children in the U.S. who were immersed in English-medium instruction but who, unlike the children in the Lambert study, had achieved neither language proficiency nor academic success. Based on that research, Cummins (1981) formulated a "threshold hypothesis" that proposes minimum levels of linguistic proficiency which bilingual children must reach in order to benefit cognitively. According to the hypothesis, a child who does not reach the "threshold" for L1 proficiency is not likely to reach proficiency in the L2, resulting in what Cummins called "semilingualism": facility but not proficiency in two languages.

Cummins (1979, 1981, 1986) also proposes an "interdependence hypothesis,"[10] which asserts,

> To the extent that instruction through a minority language is effective in developing academic proficiency in the minority language, transfer of this proficiency to the majority language will occur given adequate exposure and motivation to learn the majority language. (1986:20)

---

[10]I am aware of several critiques of this hypothesis (Genesee, in Baker 1996; Canale 1984; Troike 1984), but agree with Marcel Danesi's opinion that despite the critiques, the hypothesis still provides a useful framework for researching, assessing and understanding all kinds of linguistic and cognitive behaviours as they manifest themselves in educational contexts that involve minority children (in Cummins and Danesi 1990:66).

The implications of Cummins' hypotheses[11] for bilingual education programs focus primarily on the issue of length of time given to minority language development. Late-exit transitional and enrichment (or two-way, or balanced) bilingual education program models are preferred because they allow a more complete development of the students' first language and, by inference, a better chance of achieving proficiency in the majority L2 on which the school curriculum is based (Hakuta 1986; Skutnabb-Kangas 1988; Krashen 1991; Cazden 1992; Dolson and Meyer 1992; Cummins 1993). Cummins concludes that virtually all the research data done in the intervening twenty years confirms the truth of the Interdependence Hypothesis, but that research on the Threshold Hypothesis, "remains speculative and is not essential to the policy-making process" (2000:75).

Cummins' interdependence hypothesis cannot be applied unmodified to the Kaugel context because it assumes that the L1 and L2 are in a minority/majority relationship, respectively, which is not the case in Papua New Guinea. As stated above, PNG's linguistic diversity is such that all the language groups are minorities. English enjoys a position of high prestige and power, but Kaugel children living in their ancestral communities hear it only rarely.

Bicultural education

Harris (1990), writing out of many years of experience with Aboriginal bilingual schools in Australia, raises another serious concern about the interdependence hypothesis. As is, the hypothesis views bilingual education more as a vehicle for academic achievement than for cultural maintenance. Harris uses data from several studies of the Northern Territory bilingual program to support a theory of cultural domain separation, an idea drawing on Fishman, Gertner, Lowy, and Milan's (1985) assertion that an "ethnocultural compartmentalism" must be maintained if an ethnolinguistic minority is to experience stable bilingualism.[12] Harris argues that using Aboriginal languages to teach what are basically Western academic components may actually inhibit cultural maintenance.

---

[11]This is an admittedly cursory treatment of Cummins' research; he has developed his hypotheses into a theory of language use by bilingual students that distinguishes between basic interpersonal communication skills (BICS) and cognitive/academic language proficiency (CALP). The theory tries to account for the difficulties minority language students have in majority language schools (in the U.S. and elsewhere) by demonstrating that a sufficient level of BICS in the L2 does not ensure an adequate level in CALP to succeed in the classroom (cf. Baker 1996: 151–156; also, pp. 159–160 for critique of this theory).

[12]That is, a diglossic relationship: one in which both languages function in specific, complementary domains. If both languages are being used in the same domains, the dominant language will eventually take over (cf. Fishman 1980a, 1991, 1999, 2001b).

The crux of the dilemma for Harris is that bilingual education—even a two-way, maintenance model of bilingual education—may not necessarily result in bicultural education. In other words, teaching nontraditional subjects in the mother tongue may lead to improved success in school and even to language maintenance, while simultaneously eroding the traditional culture. To Harris, a knowledge of what is legitimately traditional and what is not—a knowledge generally held only by members of the speech community—will be necessary in developing a curriculum that is bicultural as well as bilingual (p. 116ff.).

> Other researchers, exploring the relationship between schools and communities with respect to language minority education argue that language and cultural maintenance cannot be achieved by a single social institution but rather by collaborative and mutually supportive efforts.

Moll (1992) reports on several studies of bilingual education that searched the minority children's communities for insights into how an understanding of the children's social and cultural milieu can improve classroom instruction. Drawing on the cognitive development theories of Vygotsky (1978), Moll promotes a sociocultural approach to bilingual instruction that makes use of the resources available in the children's community—what he terms "funds of knowledge" (p. 21). Education is viewed as a social and cultural activity that helps to mediate a child's intellectual growth, especially the way he or she uses essential "cultural tools" (e.g., reading, writing, mathematics). The local community becomes a resource and community knowledge is valued, along with "school knowledge," as legitimate content for bilingual curriculum (p. 23).

Community knowledge plays a significant role in efforts to reverse Maori language shift in New Zealand. A key strategy for this RLS program is the "language nests" movement in which Maori parents who have lost proficiency in their mother tongue enroll their children in *kohanga reo* 'language nests' where only Maori is spoken to the children, usually by older people enlisted from the community who are still fluent in Maori (Benton 1986; cf. also Athapaskan in Ovando 1994). The Maori RLS effort, and its counterpart in Ireland, emphasize the major role of the formal education system in preserving indigenous languages. However, the degree to which the formal system directs children's attention and learning away from the home raises questions regarding the likelihood of intergenerational transmission taking place primarily in formal education classrooms (as in the Irish case) or in language nests (as per Maori). Already in the mid-1980s, Maori parents could see the erosion of their *kohanga reo* by an English-only school system and

were lobbying for the introduction of some kind of on-going bilingual education program (p. 70).[13] But RLS "cannot be delegated to one social institution, the school, with any reasonable hope of long-term success" (Benton
1986:72; cf. Hornberger 1988; also compare Lipka 1994 and Harris 1994 regarding need for community control of school curriculum).

> Although the language cannot survive without the help and
> co-operation of the schools, a bilingual society will come into being
> (or remain in being) only if the efforts of the schools are supported
> in the homes and by many other social institutions. (Benton
> 1986:73)

On the basis of an extensive interview survey of a wide range of
ethnolinguistic minority families, Wong Fillmore (1991) summarizes the
need for educational systems to work with, rather than against, the homes
and communities of language minority students they serve. She points out
the implications for children who lose their home language.

> What is lost is no less than the means by which parents socialize
> their children: When parents are unable to talk to their children,
> they cannot easily convey to them their values, beliefs, understand-
> ings, or wisdom about how to cope with their experiences.... Talk is
> a crucial link between parents and children: It is how parents im-
> part their cultures to their children and enable them to become the
> kind of men and women they want them to be. When parents lose
> the means for soicalizing and influencing their children, rifts de-
> velop and families lose the intimacy that comes from shared beliefs
> and understandings. (p. 343)

This type of strategy accords well with Fishman's (1991) RLS priorities of
community initiative and intergenerational transmission of the language,
provided the participants are highly motivated, and the critical L1 domains
can be retained. If Fishman is correct, the school plays a critical, perhaps decisive, role in moving a minority language from the weak side of his continuum to the strong side, but the home and community are the decisive arenas
for maintaining the language and culture.

With respect to the KTPPS program, mutually supportive efforts point
to the need to identify which institutions are being utilized to promote
language and culture maintenance and which are contributing to its potential shift. The solutions to many of the classroom problems may well be
in the Kaugel community itself.

---

[13]Bilingual education programs were subsequently developed, including a Maori immersion program *(Kura Kaupapa Maori)*. However, of the 13.2 percent of Maori elementary students enrolled in bilingual education classes, only 0.4 were in the immersion
program (Waite, cited in Cummins 1993:52).

Language and education in multilingual settings

Questions regarding the relationship between language and culture and between language and education are being investigated throughout the world. Their findings provide an important reference point for the study of the KTPPS program. This section reviews relevant research projects from multilingual settings in the Third World and presents research and evaluation studies specifically from Papua New Guinea.

Language and education in Third World multilingual settings

Bilingual education and language maintenance in Peru

Hornberger's (1988) case study of a bilingual education program in two Quechua-speaking communities in highland Peru grew out of a concern for Quechua language maintenance. The purpose of her study was to describe language use in the two communities and in the schools situated in each, to understand and interpret language use in regard to the bilingual education program in the schools, and to predict the long-term survival of Quechua as the language of those communities.

One of Hornberger's main conclusions is that language and education planners and policy makers need to learn about community attitudes toward the use of the local language in formal education prior to implementing a bilingual education program. By all indications, the program in question improved the students' academic success and their ability to use Spanish (the L2). However, she found that the community members rejected the use of Quechua in the school because they consider Quechua to be the home/community language and Spanish the school language. To the community, mixing the two domains was not acceptable. Other reasons for rejecting Quechua as a medium of instruction were that the children already know Quechua—school is for learning Spanish—that using Quechua confuses the children's learning of Spanish, and that any projects perceived as being imposed from the outside are to be resisted.

Hornberger's conclusion raises the same dilemma that is identified in this study.

> In the present national circumstances, community members might accept bilingual education in their schools if they were convinced that bilingual education more successfully taught their children Spanish; but in that case, the schools would not be agents for language maintenance. (1988:236)

The Kaugel situation is similar with respect to people's perception of themselves as being active players, not docile, passive recipients of other people's decisions relating to their language and culture. The two programs differ in that the Kaugel mother-tongue education program is the result of a community-generated effort that has involved community members in key decision-making roles with initial help and support from a nongovernmental organization whereas the Quechua program was implemented from outside the community.

A further point of comparison relates to mother-tongue speakers' attitude toward their own language. The Quechua are, by Hornberger's estimation, clearly attached to their language and interested in its maintenance, but they do not perceive their language or culture to be endangered (1988:224), in spite of the presence of several indicators generally associated with language shift (e.g., constriction of L1 domains, expansion of L2 domains). Hornberger's suggestion to interviewees that Quechua might cease to be was regularly met with disdain. Thus, despite the demonstrable success of mother-tongue instruction in their children's formal education, the Quechua communities involved rejected the bilingual education program. Her conclusion: "Schools cannot be agents of language maintenance if their communities, for whatever reason, do not want them to be" (p. 229). Like the Quechua, most Kaugel people are strongly attached to their language and want their children to attend Tok Ples Pri Skuls. But, most of them perceive the classes more as a means for easing their children's transition to the formal school system than as an additional way of enculturating them (cf. chapters 5 and 6).

Mother-tongue education in Nigeria

With over 400 indigenous languages and a mother-tongue education (MTE) policy since the late 1970s, Nigeria represents a language and education setting even more complex than Peru's. Akinnaso (1991) contends that the current MTE policy resulted from a struggle against the use of a colonial language, especially in early literacy acquisition, and a desire to foster linguistic pluralism and cultural diversity. Nigeria mirrors PNG's situation, with one significant exception: Nigeria has three dominant indigenous languages (Hausa, Igbo, and Yoruba), while PNG has none. The result is an ambivalence toward MTE by Nigeria's other language minorities.

> Although language minorities are happy that their languages may at last be used as media of instruction in the schools, they are anxious to ensure that the MTE policy is not a political design to expand the

influence of the major languages at the expense of the minor ones. (1991:90)

Another difference between the Nigerian MTE project and the PNG situation is the almost complete absence in Nigeria of any reference to positive effects that mother-tongue education might have on the children's appreciation of and facility in their own culture and community. According to Akinnaso, "the MTE policy is a transitional, bilingual education policy in which the increasing use of English is accompanied by the decreasing use of the mother tongue" (p. 93). Thus, the orientation of the project is toward language-as-problem (Ruiz 1984), with linguistic assimilation as its long-term goal. In PNG, there is a strong emphasis in the nation's formative documents on preserving its multiple languages and cultures. However, the Education Reform, initiated by the government in 1995, resembles an early transitional model of bilingual education more than an enrichment or maintenance type of program.

Language maintenance in Melanesia

In a study that touches close to Papua New Guinea's linguistic and cultural issues, Schooling (1990) addresses language maintenance and shift among indigenous language groups in New Caledonia where French is the language of wider communication. Schooling cites Tabouret-Keller's study of language maintenance and shift in Europe, reporting that she found that "children from poor nonliterate communities often do not benefit from education in a language which is not their mother tongue" (p. 70). Schooling adds that his own findings confirmed the limited value that New Caledonian children received from formal education in French, which did not accelerate a shift from vernacular to the language of wider communication (LWC).

However, with respect to this study, Schooling's most noteworthy conclusion is related to the social networks of which the participants in his study were members, which he characterized as "dense" (specific, clearly-defined relationships) and "multiplex" (varied and multiple relationships). These social networks tend to have strong regulatory mechanisms which aid the communities in resisting change from the outside. The introduction of French has resulted, not in language loss, but in an increase in the indigenous linguistic repertoire (p. 125).

> Apart from the school years, however, the occasions when rural villagers need to function in [French language] domains is [sic] quite limited. Most verbal activity in a rural environment centers around

family and communal life, and the vernacular is totally appropriate
and adequate for such domains. (1990:126)

In addition, as Hornberger found that educated Quechua professionals
were in the forefront of language maintenance activities in their communities, Schooling concludes that the more educated New Caledonians get,
the more they identify with their sociocultural heritage, and the more ea-
ger they are to preserve the language.

Language and education in Papua New Guinea

Mother-tongue education innovation in North Solomons Province

Delpit and Kemelfield (1985) evaluated the North Solomons Province (NSP)
mother-tongue pre-primary education project (*Viles Tok Ples Skuls*, VTPS) in
PNG during 1982 and 1983. The two-year VTPS scheme grew out of a situation of social unrest in which the Provincial Government and the University
of Papua New Guinea Education Research Unit (UPNG-ERU) provided a forum for community concerns regarding the formal education system. The
VTPS scheme was the result of actions taken to address those concerns.
Three benefits were anticipated: educational, social, and cultural. After two
years of operation (1980–1982), the evaluation of the educational benefits
revealed that the VTPS children were acquiring distinct educational advan-
tages that the nonVTPS children did not have.

In late 1982, Downing (1984) conducted a related study of metacognitive
readiness for learning literacy among NSP children. Administering his Linguistic Awareness and Reading Readiness (LARR) test to three groups of children—VTPS grade 1 students, non-VTPS grade 1 students, and children who
had no school experience—Downing found that non-VTPS grade 1 students
scored lower on the test than VTPS grade 1 students. However, even the children who had had no schooling scored higher than the non-VTPS grade 1
students who had been learning to read in English. Downing speculated that
learning to read in a language they did not understand had caused "cognitive
confusion" (p. 370).

As Downing points out in his report, not only were the grade 1 students
trying to learn in a foreign language, they were learning from a teacher
who did not speak their mother tongue and who, like the children, spoke
English (the language of instruction) as a foreign language.

Assessing the social and cultural benefits of the VTPS scheme was more
difficult. Relying mainly on interviews with parents and teachers and on
observation at larger community meetings at which parents and community members spoke out on their views of the program, the evaluators

concluded that a valid assessment could not be done until the VTPS graduates had completed community school (i.e., grade 6). Unfortunately, the follow-up evaluation was not done and since 1989, civil unrest on the island of Bougainville have rendered such a study impossible.

Evaluation of PNG's national literacy and awareness program

Ahai and Bopp (1993), in a UNICEF-funded evaluation of the national Literacy and Awareness Program, stated specifically that their evaluation would not include "vernacular literacy programmes for children" as "Tok Ples Skuls constitute a vast domain for evaluation in their own right" (p. 19). They indicate that a separate evaluation of the children's vernacular literacy programs would be conducted by the National Research Institute and that a proposal submitted jointly with the National Department of Education (NDOE) was awaiting funding. However, if such an evaluation has been done, it has not yet been reported.

Despite their disclaimer on evaluating Tok Ples Pri Skuls (TPPS), Ahai and Bopp do make some observations and forceful recommendations on the NDOE's proposed Elementary Education level. Briefly, the authors consider the TPPS programs to be quite successful and argue that much of that success is due to the program being rooted in the communities, with provincial and community control over curriculum and teacher selection. They view the proposed restructuring plan as an NDOE attempt to take over this community initiative (p. 57). They also find that the "proposed amalgamation of Tok Ples Skuls into the formal system is fraught with risks, dangers, and unanswered questions" and they "therefore recommend that the NDOE does not carry out the amalgamation until completion of a thorough evaluation of Tok Ples Skuls" (p. 59).

Ahai and Bopp's concerns seem warranted. Wari and Roakeina (1994) conducted a limited evaluation of the Milne Bay Province trial Elementary School Program and found many of Ahai and Bopp's concerns realized. Communities had not provided the additional classrooms needed for the new elementary level. Selection of teachers had shifted from the communities to the Provincial Literacy Coordinator. Teacher training was lacking, and the stated need for community awareness of the program was repeated numerous times, usually a clear sign that the community has not been involved in the planning and implementation stages.

Both the Ahai and Bopp and the Wari and Roakeina reports raise issues about the restructuring of the formal education system which forms at least part of the language and education policy context in which the KTPPS program is operating. The degree to which these issues are affecting Kaugel

community attitudes toward the KTPPS program, if at all, is a secondary focus of this study.

Organization of the Study

The *namel manmeri*—the generation of Kaugel parents struggling to provide their children with the benefits of two cultures and two languages—provide the focus of this study of a mother-tongue, pre-primary
education program in the Highlands of Papua New Guinea. The study consists of seven chapters.

Chapter 2 presents the qualitative research methodology used for se-
lecting the site for the study, the data collection, and data analysis.

Chapter 3 provides a background for an understanding of the KTPPS
program, describing the national, regional, and local aspects of the geographical, historical, social, and educational contexts. Discussion of the
educational context features a comparison of traditional and nontraditional education in the Kaugel community.

Chapter 4 narrows the presentation of essential background and context by describing the KTPPS program itself, its development, and especially the key persons involved in its inception and sustainability as a
community-based education program.

Chapter 5 includes an analysis of community attitudes toward Kaugel
language, culture, and identity and of parents' attitudes toward their children's formal education in English. Also in chapter 5 is a discussion of bilingualism in the community as a conscious community goal and an
analysis of individual and community activities as they relate to issues of
language and culture maintenance.

Chapter 6 examines language use in the KTPPS classroom, the extent of
code-switching and lexical borrowing, and the ways in which local culture is, or is not, affirmed. It then analyzes the problems teachers have
with the KTPPS curriculum and instructional method and takes a close
look at the key role played by the primary literacy materials for the
KTPPS: the seventeen-volume Kaugel Reading Series.

The study concludes in chapter 7 with a discussion of the ways that
community leaders and other community members are attempting to resolve the inherent tensions in their aspirations for their children. It includes a set of recommendations for action that arises from the concerns
already voiced within the community that have emerged through analysis
of the current situation. Generally speaking, the *namel manmeri* occupy
not only a unique historical position from which to effect a bridge for

their children from the past to the present, but also possess a predisposition to accept that responsibility and take what they deem to be necessary actions. Hopefully, this study will provide them with a tool that will help them achieve their goals.

Definition of Terms

Community-based education programs are those that are planned, implemented, and supervised by members of the communities for whose benefit they have been introduced. The term implies the primary use of local personnel and materials but does not preclude assistance from outside the community. By this definition, the KTPPS program is community-based, but the National Department of Education's community schools are not.

Elementary level, in PNG and other Commonwealth nations, refers to a level of formal education preceding a child's usual entry into the primary level of the education system, the community school. Within PNG's restructured national education system (see "Education Reform" below), elementary or elementary level refers to the three-year, mother-tongue pre-primary education program that includes elementary prep (EP), elementary one (E1, equivalent to grade 1), and elementary two (E2, equivalent to grade 2) which have been added to the formal system.

Education reform refers to the restructuring of the formal education system from elementary (pre-primary) grades through high school. Following the three-year elementary component (see "Elementary level," above) the primary level (formerly grades 1–6) begins at grade 3 and ends with grade 8. The process of adding grades 7 and 8 (formerly known as lower secondary) to the primary level is referred to as **"top-up."**

Ethnolinguistic is a term used by sociolinguists and others to refer to language minority groups in multilingual settings. It is used here because it recognizes lexically the integral connection presumed, in this study, to exist between language and culture (Fishman 1990; cf. Paulston 1986 and Edwards 1985).

European, unless otherwise stated, is used generically to refer to all Caucasians and to things Western. Other terms used similarly are whites, whiteskins, *waitskin* (Tok Pisin), *kondoli* ('red' Umbu-Ungu), expatriate/expat, or *masta* (Tok Pisin).

Kaugel refers to (1) the river and valley located along the northern and eastern slopes of Mount Giluwe, (2) the name given by outsiders to the people sharing one language who live in the upper Kaugel River Valley

and in the Tambul and Sinsipai basins, and (3) the name previously given
to the language of the Kaugel people. Since the people themselves refer to
their language as *Umbu-Ungu* 'indigenous talk', that is the primary term
used for their language in this study; however, the phrase "Kaugel language and culture" is used when the two terms—language and culture—are used together.

Mother tongue refers to the first language (L1) acquired as a child, although it may or may not be the first language of the mother. In fact, since
families in Kaugel and other Highland societies usually reside in the fathers' clan areas, in the case of interlanguage marriages, children are
more likely to learn the father's language than the mother's. Other terms
that are used interchangeably with mother tongue, in this study (although
not by all researchers) are "local language" and "vernacular" and the Tok
Pisin term *tok ples* 'native language, mother tongue'.

Pri skul is a Tok Pisin transliteration of 'preschool' and refers to schooling
prior to entry into the formal education system. Not to be confused with
common Western usage referring to pre-kindergarten programs for children
five-years-old and under, the PNG *pri skuls* frequently enroll no children
younger than six years old and promote the children's acquisition of
mother-tongue literacy prior to their entry into the formal education system.

Tok Pisin refers to the national lingua franca spoken throughout the
country, but especially in the Highlands, Momase, and Island regions (but
not as extensively in the Southern [Papuan] Region). Also known as Melanesian Pidgin, Neo-Melanesian, or, colloquially, Pidgin or Tok Pisin, it is
spoken and understood by many, but certainly not all, mother-tongue
Umbu-Ungu speakers. A best guess would be about 50 to 60 percent of the
men under fifty and perhaps 20 to 30 percent of the women under fifty.

Tok ples is the Tok Pisin term meaning 'local language', 'native language', or 'mother tongue'. Umbu-Ungu, therefore, is the *tok ples* of the
people living in the Tambul Basin and Kaugel River Valley.

Research Questions

The research questions which have given direction to this case study both
preceded and emerged from the process of data collection and analysis.
The relevant questions are presented below and are addressed specifically
in the chapters that follow.

The over-all question is, How do Kaugel community members attempt
to resolve the tension inherent in the pursuit of twin educational goals for

their children: their success in the formal English-language system and their appreciation for and adherence to community language and culture?

Sociological questions are, To what extent do community members express concern that their language and/or culture may be lost? Conversely, to what degree do community members express confidence in the strength of their language and culture (see chapter 5)? What are the parents' goals for their children's participation in the KTPPS program and how do they compare to those stated by the KTPPS director and teachers (see chapter 5)? How do the parents, the teachers, and the KTPPS director perceive their roles in sustaining the KTPPS program (see chapter 4)?

Educational questions include, How are children in the KTPPS program being prepared to participate in the formal education system (see chapter 6)? How and to what degree are the language and culture of the community valued and promoted in school-related activities, curricular and extracurricular (see chapters 3 and 6)? What evidence is there that children in the KTPPS program are forming closer ties to the Kaugel language and traditional culture? Also, what evidence is there that children in the KTPPS program are being prepared for English-language schooling (see chapters 4 and 6)?

2

Research Methodology

There is plenty of time. We may stand here in front of it, and watch it, so long as it may please us to; watch its wood: move and be quiet among its rooms and meditate what the floor supports, and what is on the walls, and what is on shelves and tables, and hangs from nails, and is in boxes and in drawers: the properties, the relics of a human family; a human shelter: all in the special silence and perfection which is upon a dwelling undefended of its dwellers, undisturbed; and which is contracted between sunlight and a human shell; and in the silence and delicateness of the shame and reverence of our searching.—James Agee, from Let Us Now Praise Famous Men *in Rodman (1949:172)*

A qualitative case study approach was appropriate for this research project because its purpose is to understand a particular phenomenon—a pre-primary mother-tongue education project—in its natural setting, not to test an hypothesis or experiment with a new approach to early childhood education. The need "to understand" draws not only from my estimation of a gap in the knowledge base of mother-tongue educators, but also from my past personal involvement in this particular community. It is quite possible to live and work very intensely, with great personal satisfaction, among a unique society of people, quite different from one's own, yet not understand what has happened (to have the experience but miss the meaning, as T. S. Eliot suggests).

Simplified, the methodological question is: "What's going on here?" Yet, even that simple question needs to be interpreted to include the researcher in the term "here." What is being interpreted in the "natural setting" of the phenomenon is also being channeled through a human being engaged in "a garrulous, overdetermined, cross-cultural encounter, shot through with power relations and personal cross purposes" (J. Clifford, quoted in Van Maanen 1988:1).

So we stand "in the silence and delicateness of the shame and reverence of our searching," aware simultaneously, viscerally, of the tension inherent in an enterprise that presents the possibility of subjecting holy and sacred beings to a profane and objectifying scrutiny, to favorable or disfavorable judgments that must be made on the basis of only partial evidence. The expatriate researchers are also a *namel manmeri.*

Rather than relying on methodological procedures and precautions to neutralize my own biases in order to gain "objectivity" (because I do not believe it to be possible), I, as a researcher using qualitative approaches, take pains to expose my subjectivity as best I can.

> My subjectivity is the basis for the story that I am able to tell. It is a strength on which I build. It makes me who I am as a person *and* as a researcher, equipping me with the perspectives and insights that shape all that I do as a researcher, from the selection of topic clear through to the emphases I make in my writing. Seen as virtuous, subjectivity is something to capitalize on rather than to exorcise... By means of my subjectivity I construct a narrative, but it must be imaginable by others, and it must be verifiable by others. The worth of my narrative cannot rest on its goodness or rightness in some private sense. It cannot be illusion or fantasy that has no reality outside my own mind. (Glesne and Peshkin 1992:104)

Having been involved with the KTPPS program from its inception, I have tried to make a particular effort to be alert to my own predisposition and prejudices (see "The Researcher" below). However, I have taken consolation in Glesne and Peshkin's suggestion that researchers who investigate "their own 'backyards'" may be better situated to overcome problems of defining research focus, developing collaborative groups, and knowing when and how to leave a project—problems that tend to plague "outsider" researchers (1992:12).

Qualitative research is often contrasted with quantitative research, a false dichotomy which leads Erickson (1990) to prefer the term "interpretive" to "qualitative" because "it avoids defining these approaches as essentially nonquantitative...since quantification of particular sorts can often be employed in the work" (p. 78). However, "qualitative" persists as a cover term (Eisner 1991; Bogdan and Biklen 1992; Glesne and Peshkin 1992; LeCompte and Preissle 1993) and will be used here interchangeably with "interpretive."[14]

---

[14]I will, however, include Erickson's provision that a central focus of the qualitative/interpretive approach is including "the meanings of actions from the actors' point of view" (1991:78).

Eisner (1991) contends that a qualitative case study can provide a dual benefit by understanding a particular learning situation in a way that is useful to other learning situations, as well as understanding a particular learning situation in a way that is useful to the participants themselves (p. 12). Such is the intent of this case study.

In addition to the above reasons for taking an interpretive approach, the nature of the Kaugel pre-primary mother-tongue education project seems to me clearly to call for one. An experimental design in the Kaugel situation—with its inherent requirement for control over variables in a cross-cultural setting that is not readily known to the outside researcher—echoes Bronfenbrenner's contention that such manipulation often results in *"the strange behavior of children in strange situations with strange adults for the briefest possible periods of time"* (quoted in Lincoln and Guba 1985:191; emphasis in the original).

Thus, researching the researcher seems to be an appropriate place to begin a presentation of the qualitative methodology employed in this case study.

The Researcher

Stake (1995) describes several roles that the case study researcher can assume: as teacher, advocate, evaluator, biographer, interpreter. Although these roles are in some instances overlapping, the researcher role I tried consciously to fill is that of interpreter. I do not presume to place myself in the position of interpreting the experience of Kaugel people for them. In that respect, I am sensitive to Harris's observation regarding educational research in Australia's Northern Territory where Aboriginal people "have come to openly resent whites speaking on their behalf or telling them what's best for them educationally" (1990:xiii). Rather, the role of researcher as interpreter includes that of "gatherer of interpretations" (Stake 1995:99) which is at the heart of interpretive research (Erickson 1986; cf. Geertz 1973).

According to Spradley (1980), interpretive inquiry (i.e., ethnography) is not *studying* people, it's *learning* from people (p. 3). The role of researcher as learner is one I was able to assume more easily than any other as I am already a confirmed "language learner"—*Na Umbu-Ungu pilimbu tekero.* 'I am trying to learn/hear Umbu-Ungu'. This role is critical, not only because it is literally true, but because the people themselves perceive me—and any other outsider—as such, no matter how extravagant their praise of our language abilities or of our "profound" knowledge of their ways.

The fact that I had lived and worked among these same Kaugel people as a literacy specialist between 1982 and 1987 and on-and-off between 1989 and 1991, virtually assured me additional "roles" in the eyes of my neighbors and colleagues (some of which only they are aware of). My participant observer activities allowed me to fill my various "established" roles (educational advisor, small-time financier, resource linker, language learner, friend) as well as "researcher as interpreter."

Lack of native-like facility with the Umbu-Ungu language, one of my admitted limitations as a "researcher-as-research-instrument," provided a window into the complexities of my researcher subjectivity. Hoping to "jump-start" my re-entry into the Kaugel speech community after an absence of four years, I had written to Rambai Keruwa, director of the KTPPS program, suggesting that he look around for some families with KTPPS-age children with whom I could live during the research period. Below is an excerpt from field notes inscribed after my first visit with Rambai following my arrival in PNG.

> I mentioned also my thoughts about perhaps staying with a different family, whose child(ren) have attended KTPPS, in order to work on my Kaugel. In his gentle, diplomatic way, his explanation went something like this (from Tok Pisin):

> If you had not built a house at Purare and had not slept in it, and had not given it to Suku, then sleeping at someone else's house would not be a problem. But, if you sleep somewhere else now, then leave and go to America, or elsewhere, people will think and say, 'O, Dennis returned, and Suku would not let him stay in his house, and Rambai would not let him stay with him, and so he had to wander around looking for somewhere else to sleep, and, therefore, became upset and that is why he has left.' Therefore, if you don't stay at Suku's house, or at mine, we will have a *hevi* [i.e., a problem].

> I acknowledged his wisdom and said I'd not put them in that position. So I'll have to find another way of spending time with people while sleeping at the Purare house. (Field notes 1. 26)

My researcher role was but one of several. The others will appear as the story of the case study unfolds. In brief, they include: co-founder of the KTPPS (along with Rambai and my wife, Susan), liaison to SIL and to the

National Department of Education (NDOE), member of the Christian community, Aika clan's whiteskin,[15] and curriculum writer for the KTPPS.

Each of the previous roles presents its own difficulties for the data gathering and analysis process. As cofounder of the KTPPS program, I made notes that accompanied the interviews that were spattered with comments like, "I think he/she is buttering me up." Although those "spatterings," however sincere they may have been, were easy to spot and disregard, they left behind a residue of apprehension that some other favorable comment was actually a subtler, more obscure offspring of the same impulse to "butter me up." Thus, in addition to looking for disconfirming evidence with respect to such comments, I have tried to indicate my apprehensions and suspicions in the analysis of those interview data in which they occur.

In my role as liaison/consultant with SIL and NDOE, I found that my oft repeated declamation that I had not come to evaluate the KTPPS program but to *understand* it, did not so much fall on deaf ears as on an already existing desire by participants to get assistance with problems and questions they had previously identified. My very slow realization of this fact led to several missed opportunities for participatory research that I would subsequently regret (see "Limitations" below).

As a member of the Christian community, I occasionally felt the need to make data collection decisions on the basis of how my actions would be perceived and interpreted by other Christians. The decisions were as wide ranging as whether or not to leave a worship service in order to follow one of the children I had been observing during the Sunday school hour, to passing up an opportunity to talk to some card players, to attending a showing of videos at the Kalapolo *haus piksa* 'picture house', a place to show videos. The latter two occasions point up a further complication of this role because Aika clan members are divided between two Christian affiliations, Lutheran and PNG Bible Church, the former a mainline denomination and the latter a more conservative, fundamentalist group.

In order not to appear to be approving behavior that a large number of local Christians considered unacceptable, I passed up the opportunity to observe Sunday morning card players (I could observe them anytime as card playing is a daily activity) but did not pass up the opportunity to

---

[15]This possessive designation is not uncommon in PNG, and works both ways. In fact, expatriates are frequently criticized for "paternalistic" references to "our people" or "our language group." However, I recall an incident when members of Purare lineage group, who were talking with people passing through our area on their way home from market, responded to the assertion that "Whiteskin Dennis belongs to all of us," by vehemently announcing that "Dennis belongs to the Aika clan," at which point our landlord asserted "Actually, he belongs to the Purare *haus man* [i.e., lineage]." This was followed by the lineage resident comic's announcement that "Incontrovertibly, Whiteskin Dennis belongs to me!" followed by raucous laughter by all.

observe the video show (which was a recurring topic of concern voiced by a wide range of people). Thus, I was constantly weighing the relative merits of activities in terms of their value in understanding a particular phenomenon for the study on the one hand, and their potential for offending my fellow Christians on the other. Frequently, I found that I had overestimated the research value of the activity and under-estimated my friends' and neighbors' tolerance for *kondoli*[16] curiosity.

My previous role as trainer and curriculum writer forced me to make other critical decisions with regard to my data collection. The KTPPS supervisor, Rambai Keruwa, requested that I revise the KTPPS *Teacher's Guide* which had been in use since the pilot class in 1986. My quandary revolved around the time required for this type of "participation" and the opportunity the request presented for me to involve the KTPPS teachers in a curriculum development process. Rambai and I planned and carried out a three-day curriculum development workshop in which we presented, in abbreviated form, the curriculum development process that the NDOE Education Reform Office was using to prepare teachers for the new elementary level, pre-primary schools. The teachers, however, found the process too complicated and suggested that if I wrote the curriculum they would have no trouble teaching it. After much thought, I agreed to help with the clearly needed teacher's guide revision provided Rambai and Apé Kolowa, my research colleagues, help with developing the curriculum components. As it turned out, I spent the final two weeks of my data collection time, writing the teacher's guide with Rambai and Apé.

I include all this under the rubric of "Researcher Role," not as a model for action research but as a brief look at the logistical and ethical problems this "backyard" case study presented for me. I doubt that any "insider" researcher ever resolves all these problems satisfactorily.

Research Colleague

I had asked Rambai to look for someone in the clan who could help me with the data collection and translation aspects of the research project. He chose Apé Kolowa. Because of my own limitations with the language, my research colleague's credentials take on added significance. I am, therefore, providing

---

[16]*kondoli* is the Umbu-Ungu term for Caucasians, which I translate as 'whiteskin'. The term means, literally, "red" and is also applied to Papua New Guineans with light (therefore, reddish) skin color, e.g., *Kondoli Oke okomo* 'Red Oke is coming'. As far as I can determine, the term has no pejorative connotations.

an extended account of Apé's personal background and of his growth and value as a researcher.

Apé is in his mid-40s, a member of the Aika clan, of the Purare lineage, a mother-tongue Umbu-Ungu speaker who also speaks fluent Tok Pisin and English and knows Melpa, the largest Western Highlands Province (WHP) language located in the Mount Hagen provincial capital area. He is married to Kundembo with whom he has four children: Mark, Lenda, Kerolin, and Magaret. Both Mark and Lenda are graduates of the KTPPS at Purare. Mark attended grade 6 and Lenda grade 2 of the Tambul Community School during my field research time. Kerolin is a 5-year-old and has not yet attended the KTPPS at Purare, and Magaret is an infant, about a year old. Their house sits midway up the nearest hill, a five-minute walk from Suku's house where I slept.

Apé's grasp of the research purpose and his skills as a researcher became apparent very early in the data collection. Below is an excerpt from a parent interview that illustrates his ability to probe beneath a superficial response (underlined passages are Apé's rephrasings, explanations, or probes):

AK: *Manda kinie talo sipe ya [reads title of interview guide again with reference to Part II] "Yambomane Ou Uluma Ningindo Nambulka Ningu Pilikimili?" [Now reads Part II, item #1] "Yambo marene ningulie kangambola marene enenga umbu ungu kinie yambomanga ou uluma komu siku munduku kelkemele nilimele…[corrects his miscue] nikimili. Akumu nuni nambulka konopu lekeno?"* <u>*Sukuli tengi pungindu ou ulu pulu akuma munduku kelkemele nilimele, yambo marene. Aku nuni kinie nambulka ningu pililtu?*</u>

Okay, now the second [reads title of interview guide again with reference to Part II]: "What do people think about the old customs?"…[Reads] "Some people say that some children are forgetting and abandoning the language and the customs of our ancestors? What do you think about that?" Some people say that the children go to school and [as a result] abandon the traditions. What do you think about that?

SD: *Akuline okunduli munduku kelkolie kinie wi kondenga lo komindili lingi pulimele aku siku niku piliku nilimili.*

They're saying that because they're abandoning the old ways in favor of the good new ways.

AK: *Nakolo nuni pe kinie nambulka ningu pililtu?*

But what are you thinking about?

SD: *Pe nane aku nimbu pililuka.*

I think the same way.

AK: *Ou ulu puluma munduku kelkolie….*

Abandon all the traditional ways….

SD: Ou ulu puluma keri, pe kinie ulu   The traditional ways are not good. The
*sukuli tepa **Inglis** pilipe ulu teli akuli*   good way is to go to school and learn
komindi nimbu pilipulie nane akulika   English, and that's the way I support.
paka tolio konopu akuli pekemo.   That's my firm conviction.

(Parent, interview, August 31, 1995, T22A.14)[17]

Later in the same interview, after the parent talked about the success of his two older sons (one a university graduate and the other completing a baccalaureate degree in Australia), Apé presents his own hypothetical situation to the interviewee which probes a central cultural issue: where will you die, in your place or with your emigrated children?

The results of this particular probe, in a topic area not included in the interview guide but of importance to the sociocultural context of the case study, are discussed in detail in chapter 5. The point I am making here is that, with only on-the-job training, Apé became quite adept at eliciting thoughtful responses and explanations from interviewees that give the data a truly emic dimension. That I credit, in part, to his own growing interest in the research topic.

> Apé needed kerosene for his pressure lamp yesterday. RH [Rob Head] gave him a liter. (He'll need more!) This morning he brought the first book back with RK's [Rambai Keruwa] whole interview recorded [i.e., transcribed].... He'd stayed up until [well-past] midnight. He said he was tired but that Rambai's ideas were so good he'd just kept writing. (Field notes 1.34)

Apé provided key observer comments,[18] did all but two of the Umbu-Ungu transcriptions (writing marginal notations that were helpful to my later analysis), and provided a valuable tape recording of a spontaneous encounter with pre-school age children in a natural language setting.

---

[17]Words in bold in texts written in Tok Pisin or Umbu-Ungu signify loan words (English if the majority of text is in Tok Pisin; Tok Pisin and/or English if the text is mostly Umbu-Ungu.) these words in **bold** can then be distinguished from words that are underlined to display speakers' emphasis.

[18]Two examples will suffice. On one occasion, I was puzzled when one of the brightest *pri skul* students had trouble recognizing his name when the teacher had written it on the chalkboard ["Matyu"] as his "exit visa" for recess. He hesitated for about ten seconds, then left. Later, when Apé transcribed the tape recording of that classroom interaction, he included a marginal note stating that he had observed the same hesitation and that it was probably because the boy was comparing the chalkboard version with the version on his name card on which his name was spelled "Metyu." On another occasion, while we were observing a "maths" lesson, I told Apé about a small boy I had seen using "stones" (circles drawn on his small chalkboard) as counters to unerringly calculate his "sums." Apé replied that he had observed a girl using her fingers in the same way but she would either forget her count or become distracted, then shake her hands violently, as if to throw off her confusion, and start over.

Site and Context

The Tambul Basin, where most of the data collection took place, lies in the southwestern corner of the Western Highlands Province of Papua New Guinea at the head of the Kaugel River Valley. The site was chosen because I had lived there with my family from late-1982 to mid-1987; the KTPPS program began there in 1986; Rambai Keruwa, the KTPPS program supervisor, lives there; I was at home with and familiar to the people of the Aika and Korika-Kengelka clans who live on the northern side of the Basin; and the area provided most of the traditional and nontraditional features of a typical Kaugel community, including the original KTPPS school and several others, three community schools (i.e., English language schools of the formal education system), and road access to other key sites in the case study area.

Data Collection

The three most common sources of data in interpretive, ethnographic research—observation, interview, and documents—were used extensively in this study. To these three I added a miscellany of taped activities ranging from classroom interactions, to cultural events, to end-of-year school closings, and a Board of Management meeting. Below is a brief summary of each data collection technique.

Direct and participant observation

Table 2.1 summarizes the sites of the two observation techniques I used for data collection and the rationale for distinguishing between them.

Table 2.1. Direct and participant observation sites

Observation technique	Sites (representative)	Rationale
Direct: I did not take an active part in the actual activity(ies) being observed; passive observation	Preschool,* Community School,** and ACE classrooms, public hearings/trials, Karoma's compensation, grade 6 teacher's funeral	Because I was most interested in why the KTPPS program was being maintained and did not want to affect directly the classroom interactions, or, in the case of public events, because I had no role to play.
Participant: I take part in the activity(ies) being observed; active observation***	Church services, Sunday school, Board of Management meeting, video "theater," end-of-year school closings, community days at community school, local family related activities (meals, market, travel to provincial capital)	I already had a participant role in most of these activities. The video show was new but lent itself to an active role (questioning viewers, choosing a video when asked to).

*On one occasion (August 2, 1995) I did participate in the KTPPS program at Purare by arranging for Apé and three other flute players to play and sing for the children.

**I also participated briefly in the classroom at the request of the Grade 6A teacher, explaining to the children the general nature of my research and my interest in their language and culture.

***I regret most my decision to adopt a passive observer role in the Purare KTPPS classroom. I wanted to view the teacher and children interacting without a new input of ideas or a review of past training. By adopting a passive role I felt that the teacher would be revealing either what he usually did or what he thought I expected him to do. I did not want the children responding to instruction that they had not had before. I had no illusions that my passive presence would not alter the situation (a fact reinforced for me when the teacher remarked to Apé and me that the boys were behaving quite well, compared to usual, probably because they were afraid of us). I was merely attempting to minimize the influence. I did not offer advice because I had gone out of my way to assure and reassure him that I was not there to evaluate his teaching but simply to try to understand what was going on in the classroom. In retrospect, I should have confined mostly observing to the first week, and then become more participative thereafter.

Prior to the field work, I had familiarized myself with Spradley's (1980) participant observation matrix[19] and with Dell Hymes mnemonic for observing speech events (SPEAKING)[20] used by Hornberger (1988) in her case study of bilingual education among the Quechua in Peru. Although I did not intend to do in-depth linguistic analysis as part of the case study, portions of the data lend themselves to such analysis and SPEAKING has proved helpful ex post facto (chapters 5 and 6).

Interviews

Interviews formed the basis for a large portion of the data collection. As detailed above, Apé Kolowa served as the primary interviewer. His expertise made it possible to leave the choice of interview language up to the interviewee, most of whom chose Umbu-Ungu, thus avoiding the irony of inquiring after a person's attitude toward their own language in a foreign one (that is, Tok Pisin). His increasing ease with the interview guide and skill in probing for expanded expression on the part of the interviewee(s) is evidenced by the in-depth data his interviews provided for analysis in chapters 5 and 6.

Questions

A key feature of the interview guide (appendix A4) was the use of four types of interview questions suggested by Strauss, Schatzman, Bucher, and Sabshin (cited in Merriam 1988): (1) hypothetical, (2) devil's advocate, (3) ideal position, and (4) interpretive. A HYPOTHETICAL QUESTION begins with a "what if" or "suppose" equivalent and proceeds to describe a particular situation and asks interviewees to respond. The DEVIL'S AD-VOCATE QUESTION challenges the interviewees to consider an opposite viewpoint. An IDEAL POSITION QUESTION asks respondents to describe an

---

[19]The matrix proved more law than gospel for me. I found that its vision of observational scope and depth did not impart the strength and presence of mind to ensure its fulfillment, but did provide a wonderful post-observation judgment on the inevitable empty cells where I had not gotten the necessary information.

[20] This acronym represents a device for describing speech acts, events, etc.

    S = setting/scene
    P = participants
    E = ends (outcomes/goals)
    A = act (form and content of message)
    K = key (tone, manner)
    I = instrumentalities (language/dialect, variety, code, style)
    N = norms (interaction and interpretation)
    G = genres (poems, myth, talk, lecture, prayer)

ideal situation. The INTERPRETIVE QUESTION probes a possible explanation of the issue or phenomenon, then seeks a reaction from the respon-
dent (Merriam 1988:80). The hypothetical questions—along with the
devil's advocate questions—proved very helpful in avoiding "why" questions, which in the Kaugel community can be impolite, as well as threat-
ening, and which have the potential, according to Patton, for an "infinite
regression of why, why, why" (quoted in Merriam 1988:80). Apé became
adept at formulating his own hypothetical questions to get at the more
deeply held convictions of the interviewees.

The original selection process for the interviews sought to represent a
cross-section of a KTPPS community. However, the distribution represented in the grid of community member interviewees in table 2.2 demonstrates that such was not the case:

Table 2.2. Community member interviewee profile

Age group*	Children		Youth		Adults		Total	
Clan/ Sex	M	F	M	F	M	F	M	F
Aika	2	3	1	2	9	7	12	12
Korika					2		2	
Kengelka					1		1	
Other	5	5					5	5
Total M/F	7	8	1	2	12	7	20	17
Total	15		3		19		37	

*Children: ages 6–12; Youth: ages 13–20; Adults: ages 21 and over (married)

The selection of community members (primarily parents) for interviews did not allow for a generational analysis of responses, and sixteen
of the nineteen parents interviewed were from the Aika clan. When I
raised this issue with Rambai and Apé, they responded that the Aika and
Korika-Kengelka axis provides a relatively homogenous set of experiences
and opinions, and they considered it unlikely that responses would differ
significantly between them. In fact, one person suggested that narrowing
the community research participants to the *haus man* at Purare would provide me with data that could be generalized to all of the communities in
the Kaugel River Valley. At that point, however, I decided against such a
radical refocusing of the research due to time constraints and to the fact
that my principal research colleague was a member of the Purare lineage
making it more difficult for him, in my estimation, to deal with the issue

of subjectivity than it was for me. Nevertheless, I find the suggestion intriguing as a possible strategy for examining the intricate networks of relationships that affect attitudes and actions at play in educational decisions made by parents for their children.

As the research progressed, I began to focus more and more on the various tensions and concerns expressed by parents in regard to their children's education with respect to language and culture (see table 2.3). The trial interviews with children and youth were largely unsuccessful in eliciting responses to open-ended questions, primarily because the formal interview process was culturally strange to the children who were too shy or frightened to respond to a set of hypothetical situations. Even in a group interview of six high school students, only one male and one female student responded, the others, reticent and uncomfortable as a result, I assume, of not being able to understand our purpose in talking with them. Children and youth are not traditionally questioned extensively by adults unless some trouble involving them has occurred. The interview format, however, yielded excellent responses from the parents.

Table 2.3. Aika clan interviewee profile

Age group*	Children		Youth		Adults		Total	
Place / Sex	M	F	M	F	M	F	M	F
Kikua					2	1	2	1
Sakaleme		1			2	3	2	4
Purare	2	2		2	2	1	4	5
Pombol			1		3	2	4	2
Total M/F	2	3	1	2	9	7	12	12
Total	5		3		16		24	

*Children: ages 6–12; Youth: ages 12–20 (unmarried); Adult: ages 21 and over (married)

The low number of children interviewed formally does not take into account extensive observation and about 450 minutes of taped classroom interaction, two hours of taped Sunday school interactions, Apé's tape of his daughter and nephew narrating their "stolen berries" story, and a tape of children singing nontraditional tunes with Umbu-Ungu lyrics.

Others involved at some level with the implementation of the KTPPS program were also interviewed. Table 2.4 represents the distribution of interviewees for this aspect of the data collection.

Table 2.4. Education-related interviews

Position	Male	Female
KTPPS teacher	10	1
CS teacher	7	4
CS head teacher	1	1
CS inspector	1#	0
KNFEA member	1	0
Education Reform Coordinator	1	0
REU* research officer	1#	0
KTPPS director§	1§	0
ACE principal**	0	1#
Total M/F	23	7
Total	30	

*REU: Research and Evaluation Unit; **ACE: Accelerated Christian Education;
§Represents about five hours of taped interviews; #Not recorded.

With respect to the scope of these interviews, the Research and Evaluation Unit (REU) is a section of the National Department of Education; the
WHP Education Reform Officer represents a province-level viewpoint;
and the Community School Inspector provides a Tambul-Nebilyer District
perspective. All the remaining interviewees are from the KTPPS area.

With respect to their representation of the relevant population: there are a
total of fourteen KTPPS teachers (eleven interviewed), twenty-one community school teachers (ten interviewed), two Community School head teachers
(two interviewed), one Community School school inspector (one interviewed), one provincial Education Reform coordinator (one interviewed),
three REU officers (one interviewed), one KTPPS director (one extensively
interviewed), one Tambul ACE principal (one interviewed), and seven members of the Kaugel Non-Formal Education Association (KNFEA; one interviewed). This last group was not meeting regularly (did not meet at all
during my field work time). Thus, I interviewed one of the KNFEA members
who had a son at the Purare KTPPS as part of a parent interview.

Transcription

The transcription of interviews warrants mention here because it became
a process which simultaneously helped and limited interpretation. Apé

Kolowa did all but two of the transcriptions from Umbu-Ungu[21] and subsequently did dynamic translations of them into Tok Pisin, a national lingua franca. Five tapes were not transcribed. One of the tapes Apé and I agreed would be unethical to transcribe as it involved children whose parents were not informed about our research, and four could not be completed before I left the field, and Apé was unable to complete them after I left.

Table 2.5. Transcriptions of taped material in three languages

Transcribers	Umbu-Ungu	Tok Pisin	English
Apé Kolowa§	43	2	1§
Dennis Malone	0	4	14
Petrus Pes	2	0	0
Not transcribed#	5	0	0
Total*	50	6	14

§ Apé interviewed his daughters in Umbu-Ungu and his son in English and transcribed the entire tape, which is listed as an Umbu-Ungu transcription.

Not all the tapes could be transcribed during the period of field work. As a result twelve of those tapes were left with Apé to be completed after my departure. When, for various personal reasons he was unable to complete the entire set, the most important ones were prioritized, completed, and returned to me.

* The total does not equal the number of tapes (63) because several of the transcripts contained responses in two or three languages and, therefore, had more than one transcriber.

Activities (Taped)

Classroom

To investigate the teacher-student interactions in the preschools and community schools that might reveal how language and culture were being used, I taped approximately 450 minutes of KTPPS classroom activities and about 180 minutes of community school classroom activities. This was done in addition to direct and participant observation in both domains. The transcripts from these sessions have proved helpful in understanding the interplay of language and culture and the subtle—and not-so-subtle—ways the former

---

[21]The only Umbu-Ungu interview tapes not transcribed by Apé were the two from the Pomboli Lutheran Church Sunday school and the morning worship service. These were done by Petrus Pes, a young man who was present at both. I felt he was in a good position to understand what was going on. His grasp of Kaugel orthography was not as sophisticated as Apé's, but many of his invented spellings are of interest (and perhaps value) for future orthographic development.

can influence the latter (see chapter 6). The majority of the taped classroom activities took place at one KTPPS site. Two other KTPPS classrooms were also taped.

Classroom activities taped and/or observed at the three community schools in the Tambul Basin provide an important backdrop to the KTPPS experience since almost all of the children leaving the KTPPS program enter one of these three schools.

Religious

Tape recordings of Sunday school and morning worship services at two churches provided data on the use of language in a domain that figures strongly in the life of the community as a whole. Transcripts from these recordings, coupled with extensive participant observation, provided data on how members of two different Christian denominations use language and culture in worship and educational settings.

Cultural

Two cultural events were recorded that relate to KTPPS children's language and culture maintenance. The first was Karoma's *makali* (a traditional wealth exchange involving live pigs) with another clan over the death of his son-in-law. Karoma's younger daughter was a Purare KTPPS student at the time of my field work. Although an interpretation of this type of event requires an experienced anthropologist's knowledge and skills (which I do not possess), the prominence and timing of the event in the life of the Aika and Korika-Kengelka communities, the involvement of a parent of one of the KTPPS students in the study, and the forum the event presented for highlighting perceived social problems in the area warranted its inclusion, even if it provided only a descriptive dimension to the over-all presentation of the case and context.

The second cultural event was a flute-playing evening. Staged for my benefit, the event lacked the intrinsic interest and, probably, spiritual significance a flute-playing session traditionally had.

Meetings

Three meetings were recorded, the most productive of which was the Purare Community School Board of Management meeting at which many issues of significance to this study were raised. The participants at the meeting represented an interesting cross-section of community leaders involved in the oversight of the Purare Community School.

Children

Several attempts were made to tape record children in natural speech settings. The first involved a father teaching *pilkano teli* "string games" to his 12-year-old son. The second was a session of children singing Umbu-Ungu language songs to nontraditional tunes (see chapter 5). Kaugel people clearly love to sing and have modified the traditional practice of improvising lyrics for specific occasions, by using nontraditional "melodies" and Kaugel stanzas littered (or spiced, according to one's sociolinguistic perspective) with lexical borrowings. These are discussed at greater length in chapter 5. Although there were too few samples for a thorough analysis of the impact of Tok Pisin and English on the music of Kaugel children, taping this activity was meant to help confirm or disconfirm parental fears that the younger generation was forgetting their traditional culture.

Data Analysis

The tension inherent in "the shame and reverence of our searching" becomes most apparent in the process of data analysis. In essence, the analytic process requires the researcher to begin theorizing about the data s/he has collected, a burdensome endeavor heavy with the implications of the very complexities the qualitative researcher eagerly sought out during data collection. Goetz and LeCompte note that

> "going beyond the data into a never-never land of inference" is a difficult task for most qualitative researchers because they are too close to the data, unable to articulate how the study is significant, and unable to shift into a speculative mode of thinking. (Goetz and LeCompte, in Merriam 1988:141)

Faced with such a predicament—I confess to a personal experience of the phenomenon—the alternative danger is to oversimplify a complex problem. Thus, during my attempt to analyze a large amount of ethnographic data in a way that yields understanding while, at the same time, avoiding a reductionism that forfeits the complexities present within the case study boundaries, I became alert to the tension that participants in the KTPPS program would necessarily be experiencing as they pursued two educational goals that are, seemingly, contradictory. These goals are expressed in the

overall research question: Can a one-year mother-tongue pre-primary education program that endeavors to prepare children for academic success in the
formal English-language education system also provide a context for
mother-tongue and local culture maintenance?

In addition to a sensitivity to the dialectic of cross-cultural minority education, I became aware of the local Kaugel community leaders'—the parent
generation—self-perception as *namel manmeri* 'the in-between persons'.
Since their children attend the KTPPS program as well as the English education institutions in the Kaugel area, I began to focus on them in order to learn
how they attempt to resolve the tensions inherent in their children's education, informal and formal alike. The analysis of interview data in which the
subjects express their own views and data from community events and interactions, coupled with extensive participant observation of classroom and
community activities yielded a kind of Venn diagram of what people say and
what they do with regard to language and culture, where the intersection
represents a coherence of words and acts, if not a resolution of tensions.

Since the presence of a language/culture maintenance goal for the
KTPPS program presupposes a certain amount of language shift, I focused
my participant observations on discovering the presence of language shift
indicators. The indicators of language shift are numerous but relative
(Fasold 1984; Paulston 1986; Romaine 1995; Baker 1996). Conditions
that clearly have contributed to language shift in some speech communities have existed for centuries in others without causing irreversible shift
(e.g., Yiddish, Hebrew, Frisian, Catalunya).

To check my observations of classroom and community language activities, after the field work period, and to verify the presence of language
shift indicators I had observed in the community, I used the transcripts of
tape recordings of these activities to analyze the actual language being
used (not just my observation of the language used). For this analysis I
adapted a sociolinguistic approach, searching the transcripts for occurrences of code-switching. The search yielded numerous examples of lexical borrowing and code-switching.

LEXICAL BORROWING, as discussed in chapter 5, refers to the use of terms
or phrases from one language in utterances of another. The types of lexical
borrowing identified through analyzing transcriptions of recorded events are
loanwords, nonce borrowings, and loanshifts. In this study, loanword refers
to what Poplack, Sankoff, and Miller (cited in Romaine 1995:62) call "established loanwords"—words that are so widely borrowed from the L2 and consistently used by L1 speakers that they are often considered indigenous terms
to monolingual L1 speakers. I distinguish between isolated and integrated
loanwords. An ISOLATED LOANWORD is one that has been borrowed from the

L2 in toto, and has not been altered to conform with L1 grammar. An INTE-GRATED LOANWORD refers to a borrowed item that has been altered to conform with L1 grammatical conventions (e.g., the Tok Pisin *long skul* 'in school' becomes *skulna* 'in school' in Umbu-Ungu). For the purposes of this analysis, I also categorized as isolated loanwords those that may be integrated phonologically but not grammatically.

LOANWORDS are contrasted with what Poplack et al. call NONCE BORROWINGS: single, ad hoc use of an L2 lexical item that may be temporarily integrated. The presence of nonce borrowings are considered to be more indicative of the individual's discourse style than of a movement in societal language use.

LOANSHIFTS are indigenous L1 terms that acquire expanded meaning through contact with an second language and culture, e.g., *pirimu* in Umbu-Ungu originally referred to 'thorn' but now is used primarily for 'nail' as in *yuni **ama** kini ambolopa **pirimu** tomba* 'he's going to hit the nail using the hammer he's holding'.

CODE-SWITCHING is "the juxtaposition within the same speech exchange of passages of speech belonging to different grammatical systems or subsystems" (Gumperz, in Romaine 1995:121). The types of code-switching identified in my analysis are tag-switching, intersentential switching, and intrasentential switching. TAG SWITCHING involves words or phrases (tags) often added to utterances as signals or fillers, e.g., in English, 'you know', 'I mean', 'okay'. The bilingual speaker may frequently borrow a tag for the L2, e.g., ***Okay**, olio pamili pai!* 'Okay, let's get going!' (T8A.2). INTERSENTENTIAL CODE-SWITCHING refers to changes from one language or variety to another between clause boundaries. Poplack's classic example: "Sometimes I'll start a sentence in English *y terminó en español*" (quoted in Romaine 1995:123). The ease with which speakers move intersententially between L1 and L2 is indicative of their fluency as bilinguals. INTRASENTENTIAL CODE-SWITCH, although common, is much more difficult to execute fluently because of risk to the syntax of either or both languages, e.g., *ol bai lusim **providing suppose the tribal system** bilong yumi em i **fade away*** 'they will forsake [*the language*] if our tribal system fades away' (T42B.18).

This search for multiple examples of what people say about language and how they use it provided a third perspective with many examples, opening observations and interpretations to further confirmation and disconfirmation.

Limitations

Due to the length of time required for the interview guide using open-ended questions, the "language attitude and use survey" was administered to only seven respondents. The absence of data from the broader range of respondents that a widely administered survey would have yielded removes one source of triangulation for the interview data. However, the extensive classroom observation and the participant observation of community events, along with the analysis of most relevant documents (the Kaugel Reading Series), provided an alternative means for confirming and disconfirming data.

No systematic testing of the KTPPS children was done to determine their ability to read and write Umbu-Ungu. The ad hoc testing that was done targeted former KTPPS students who were then in the community schools. Also, I had assured the KTPPS teachers that I was not observing the classrooms to evaluate them as teachers, but that my purpose was merely to understand what was going on in the classroom. I suspected that a test of any sort would be perceived as breaking my promise. However, I realized as soon as my analysis of the classroom data began in earnest that evaluation was a necessary, inevitable component of a qualitative case study. I have, therefore, endeavored to illuminate as much of the extra-classroom context and conflict as possible so that whatever weaknesses in classroom pedagogy appear in the presentation of data can be seen in that light.

A third limitation was the result of my attempt to assume a non-participatory researcher role in certain contexts, namely, the KTPPS classroom. I chose not to become actively involved so that teachers would follow their normal routine of activities (rather than doing activities that I had helped them plan). A participatory role would have provided the KTPPS teachers and me an opportunity to share ideas about instruction and learning that would have provided needed help to the teachers. It could also have served as an opportunity for me to confirm and/or disconfirm my interpretations of what was happening in the classroom and in the community. I attempted to overcome the first limitation by helping Rambai and the teachers develop a new curriculum for the TPPS classes. The second limitation was overcome, to a degree, by my out-of-class interviews with the teachers.

A final limitation was my inability to converse at a deep level in Umbu-Ungu. I could not effectively interview most participants by myself. Nor could I transcribe most language tapes alone. My primary transcriber also had to serve as my primary interviewer, thereby cutting his time at both tasks in half. However, Apé became a skilled transcriber and interviewer which, in turn, ensured that his emic perspective would be heard. The process of checking interpretations with participants became a necessity and a source of much insight.

3

Kaugel Tok Ples Pri Skul Context

The Kaugel Tok Ples Pri Skul program operates within a context of local, provincial, national, and international events and processes. To provide a basic understanding of its contextual complexity, this chapter presents a brief, panoramic view of the national and provincial geographical, historical, political, socioeconomic, sociolinguistic, and educational factors that affect the program. Following the broad overview of each category, I "zoom in" on the immediate case study area in the Kaugel area of the Western Highlands of Papua New Guinea.

Geographical Context

Papua New Guinea

Lying in the western Pacific north of Australia, east of Indonesia, south of the Philippines, and west of the other Melanesian island nations (Solomons, Vanuatu, New Caledonia, Fiji), Papua New Guinea occupies the eastern half of the island of New Guinea and hundreds of outlying islands. The country is commonly divided into four, mainly geographic regions: Islands, Momase,[22] Southern (or Papuan), and Highlands.

---

[22]Momase is a combination of the first two letters of each of the provinces of PNG's North and Eastern coastal area: Morobe, Madang, Sepik.

The Highlands

The Highlands region occupies the center of mainland Papua New Guinea, lying south of the lowlands and swamps drained by the Sepik and Ramu rivers and north of the Papuan lowlands that stretch a hundred kilometers southward to the Gulf of Papua. The five provinces that make up the Highlands are, from east to west, Eastern Highlands, Simbu, Western Highlands, Enga, and Southern Highlands.

Kaugel-speaking people live in the southwestern corner of the Western Highlands, a province that features the large, fertile, and heavily populated Wahgi Valley, about 1,600 meters above sea level, checkered with traditional sweet potato gardens and, since the 1950s, with large green swatches of coffee and tea plantations. The Wahgi Valley is bounded on the south by the Kubor Range, on the west by the Hagen Range and on the north by the Sepik-Wahgi Divide. At the western end of the valley is Mount Hagen, the provincial capital and market center for vegetable growers. Southwest from Mount Hagen, across the Murmur Pass lies the Kaugel River Valley and the Tambul Basin.

The Tambul Basin

The Tambul Basin is a part of the larger Kaugel-language area that includes the Kaugel River Valley, the Sinsipai Basin, and the Upper Mendi community in the Southern Highlands along the Old Mendi Highway.

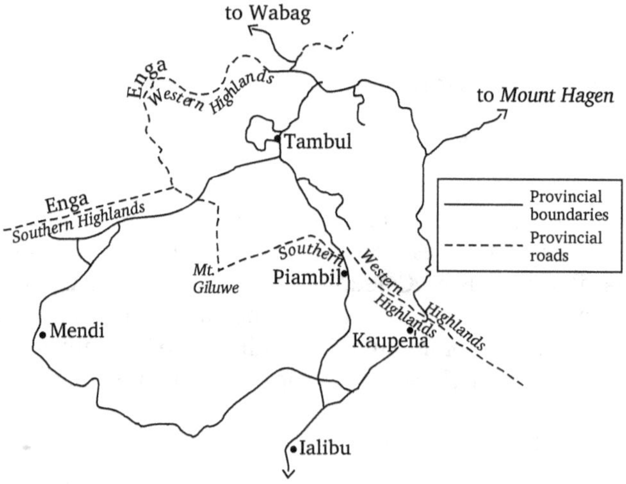

Figure 3.1. Kaugel area.

Standing on the Tambul Basin Road beside the Tok Ples Pri Skul at Purare, you can look down the Kaugel River Valley and, on a clear day, see the conical shape of Mount Ialibu (3,500 meters above sea level) forty kilometers to the southeast. Due south, and less than ten kilometers away, the dark green tree-covered slopes of Mount Giluwe (4,368 meters above sea level) rise to about 3,100 meters, then yield to the pale green kunai grass plateau. The semicircle of craggy peaks that cap this extinct volcano are not visible from Purare. To the west, *Mulu Laimindi* (the Umbu-Ungu name for a mountain that is rarely named on maps) rises like an isosceles triangle to over 3,120 meters. The remainder of the Basin "ring" is made up of a series of hills and ridges increasing in altitude northward, reaching about 3,075 meters somewhere beyond eyesight.

According to a weathered sign at the Tambul High Altitude Experimental Agriculture Station, the altitude at the Purare *pri skul* classroom is approximately 2,240 meters and, according to the Rand McNally *Cosmopolitan World Atlas* (1994), roughly 144° E. longitude and 6° S. latitude. These are abstractions that figure materially in the lives of the people in the Basin, if not in their consciousness. The high altitude tempers the tropical temperatures one might expect from the Basin's close proximity to the equator and provides the specter of killing frost each dry season when the absence of an insulating cloud cover lowers night temperatures to below freezing, a geographical reality that requires a compensating horticulture. One of the first things the observer notices about nearby gardens is the mounds of mulch and soil into which sweet potato vines have been planted, so that the tubers can grow in the ferment of the decaying grasses, protecting them from the cold nights. The success of the mulching technique in providing needed warmth to the growing tubers is easily observed at sunrise on a cold morning, as plumes of condensing vapors rise from the mounds like smoke.

Normally, PNG's location in the western Pacific, between the equator and the Tropic of Capricorn, combines with monsoonal wind patterns to deliver up to 4,000 millimeters of rain a year to the Tambul Basin. Standing beside the *pri skul* classroom during the rainy season, the observer's reverie may well be interrupted by the roar of a six-wheel flatbed diesel truck vainly trying to extricate itself from the cavernous depressions that pass for potholes on the rain-drenched Basin Road. The rain and the waterlogged and pot-holed roads affect the ability of Rambai Keruwa, the director of the KTPPS program, to supervise the fourteen KTPPS schools scattered around the Basin and throughout the Kaugel Valley. The resulting lack of adequate supervision was a concern mentioned by several KTPPS teachers (chapter 4).

The altitude and terrain, which in pre-European contact times provided Kaugel people a measure of protective isolation, is also ideal for growing marketable vegetables (broccoli, cauliflower, carrots, cabbage) that do not grow well at lower elevations. But, the high altitude renders the area unfit for the major cash crops (coffee, tea, copra, cocoa) that are a source of income at lower altitudes. Relatively few wage-earning jobs exist in the Kaugel area and, as a result, Kaugel young people frequently migrate to towns, attracted by the chance of wage employment and the excitement of urban life.

The geography of the Tambul Basin and Kaugel Valley contributes to the mix of influences shaping the people who live there, including the community members who have been recruited as KTPPS teachers. The amount of time required to prepare a series of gardens to provide for a family's year-long subsistence with enough remaining to allow the family to participate in the community's corporate activities exceeds the amount of time left after a Kaugel teacher has devoted three to four hours each morning to instructing pre-primary children in the local language. If the teachers do not receive material compensation that permits their families to purchase trade store supplies when their own gardens run low, as is frequently the case, then they and their families struggle, as expressed by one teacher.

*Kou **mone** silimili ulu kundu mere* The way they are reducing our
***tulopo kina, pipitin** nimbe pulumu* pay—twelve or fifteen
*ululinga kinie **stowana pras** kepe* kina[23]—while all the prices of the
melema omba olando olando things in the store are going up, up
pukumulu ululinga nanga mere causes me anguish [lit., makes me
konupu kundu we laiyare kuru sick]. I'm saying I teach school,
*tolemo. **Sukul** tenjikiruka nimbu* coming in the morning and then
ipulali ou olio, pulio, kongono ulke going back home [lit., my work
kolia kongono te naa telio, ulu place] but I can't work. Because of
*akulinga we **amamas** naa telio.* this I am not happy.

(KTPPS Teacher, interview, October 12, 1995, T14B.12)

There is obviously more going on here than geography, but the teacher's reference to his need to be able to work in his gardens and care for his pigs when he's finished teaching is a function of a climatic reality that makes

---

[23]The standard pay for KTPPS teachers, prior to 1993, was K20 per fortnight; the decrease in pay, and its unpredictability, was exacerbated by the devaluation of the kina, a roughly 25 percent devaluation with respect to the U.S. dollar, with which it had been on parity. This is discussed in more detail under "Educational Context" in this chapter.

maintaining a series of sweet potato and vegetable gardens at varying stages of growth a necessary hedge against the times when food is scarce.

Historical Context

Papua New Guinea

"Discovered" by Portuguese and Spanish explorers in the sixteenth century, the island of New Guinea was not colonized until the nineteenth century when the Dutch took over the western half. The remainder was divided between the Germans and the British, the British ceding their southern portion to Australia in 1906. After the First World War, the League of Nations mandated that Australia administer the entire eastern half of the island as a single entity, which it did until the Japanese invasion of the Territory in 1942. Following Japan's surrender in 1945, the Territory of Papua and New Guinea became a United Nations Trusteeship, with the Australian administration eventually granting self-government to the Territory in 1973 and full independence in 1975 (Hunter 1994:985).

A relevant historical note, hidden in the brief chronology above, is that the central Highlands, initially thought by Europeans to be largely uninhabited, were discovered to be heavily populated when aircraft began flights over the central cordillera in the late 1920s. Highlanders, however, would not see their first Europeans until miners and Australian patrol officers climbed into the high valleys in the early 1930s in search of gold and populations, respectively (Connolly and Anderson 1987).

The Highlands

Accounts of Highland society prior to the appearance of Europeans generally portray the agricultural base of community life as a feature dating back some 9,000 years. Although Merlan and Rumsey (1991) argue that archeological data provides convincing evidence that the cultivation of tubers has been part of Highland life for at least the past seven millennia, Strathern (1979) and others believe the current staple, sweet potato, is a much more recent innovation, perhaps "only a few hundred years ago." Citing work by Watson, Strathern suggests that the introduction of the sweet potato

> must have triggered off something like a revolution in agricultural practices, leading to increased population, increased colonisation of high mountain slopes, and an intensification of pig-herding and of

competition between groups by means of both warfare and elabo-
rate practices of ceremonial exchange: in other words, to the
pattern of Highland life observed by the first Europeans to enter the
whole area in the early 1930s. (1979:xiii)

An equal, if not greater, "revolution" occurred with the advent of Europeans, whom Strathern groups into three general categories: business, in
particular, gold prospecting by the Leahy brothers, colonial administration, and Christian mission, in that chronological order though the latter
two may have been reversed in the Mount Hagen area. The effect on all aspects of Highlander life by this first and all the subsequent contact with
European civilization has been pervasive.

An airstrip was constructed at Mount Hagen in the 1930s, and thus began the influx of steel implements (axes, bush knives, spades) along with
the coastal shells so highly valued by the Highlanders.[24] By the early
1950s, Australian business men had begun the large coffee and tea plantations that now are found throughout the Wahgi Valley.

The Tambul Basin

The colonial administration of what are now two separate provinces, Western Highlands and Enga, established a subdistrict patrol post at Tambul in
the early 1950s. Soon after, Evangelical Bible Mission, Lutheran, and Catholic missionaries established stations at Tambul, Alkena, and Kiripia, respectively. Airstrips were constructed at Tambul and Alkena in the early 1960s,
and by the early 1970s, a government road had been constructed that connected Tambul with other Highlands localities.

Gold had already been discovered in the Enga area to the west. To meet
the transport needs of the Enga mine and the large coffee and tea plantations in the Wahgi Valley, the "Highlands Highway" was constructed in
the 1970s, connecting Highland provinces with the eastern port city of
Lae. The ease of travel on this road greatly increased both material and
human commerce between Lae and the central highlands, stimulating an
urban migration that included many people from the Tambul area.

The period of time from the establishment of the Tambul patrol post until independence in 1975 was one of relative peace for the Kaugel people.
Following independence, tribal conflicts in the entire Highlands area became more and more common. One conflict of particular importance to
an understanding of the case study context was the war between clans of
the Upper Kaugel and clans of the Lower Kaugel which lasted from

---

[24]Cf. Strathern (1979a:6–10), for Ongka's recollection of the increasing worth of
introduced tools, especially the steel ax, vis-à-vis traditional emblems of wealth and
prestige like shells, pigs, and wives.

November of 1989 until April of 1990 and resulted in the loss of nearly forty lives and the cancellation of KTPPS classes. As a result, the two areas were made into separate political entities with a new Lower Kaugel government office dedicated at Alkena in 1995.

Kaugel history

Prior to the appearance of Europeans, Kaugel people were preliterate, without a written history. Kaugel people, however, had their own ways of marking historic occasions. Traditionally, the only "history" that mattered to them was contained in their origin myths and their legends—the places and people, flora and fauna around them, and the remembered past that they and especially their elders possessed. These could be called upon to settle (or, in some cases, exacerbate) internal and external disputes over land tenure issues, death by poisoning, warfare, treachery, or with respect to outstanding debts of pigs or shells incurred by themselves or other clan members (Strathern 1971; Merlan and Rumsey 1991; Meggit 1965:238–239 in Enga). However, since Europeans brought their kind of written history, along with the steel implements and kina shells, people of the Tambul Basin are now learning to deal with a conception of events matched against years, months, and days.

Rambai Keruwa's recollection of his people's first contact with Europeans (see KTPPS director, chapter 4) and the foreign culture that they brought with them coincides with the establishment of an Australian patrol post at Tambul in the early 1950s and the subsequent arrival of Evangelical Bible Mission (EBM) and Lutheran missionaries. However, there are accounts of a previous incursion by white men as early as the 1930s. Leahy (1991) writes of his visits to the Kaugel River Valley (called "Gowil" in his transliteration) and the northern and eastern slopes of Mount Giluwe ("Keluwere") in the period between April and June of 1934. Such a remarkable event must have become common knowledge in the area and supports the accounts I had heard in 1984 from Aika Diwi, a clan elder in his 70s, regarding an exploratory journey he had made as a young man with Aika Enga, the local *kamako* 'clan leader', to the Wahgi Valley to see the *kondoli yema* 'redskin men', i.e., Caucasians. Leahy recalled the difficulty of getting food for his line of carriers "principally because the people appeared to be so overcome and stunned by our visit that they just did not bring it" (p. 181).

This brief encounter (Leahy's party stayed perhaps three nights total in the language area) would not be repeated for another fifteen years. The Second World War, in which the Territories of Papua and New Guinea played a significant part, manifested itself to residents of the Tambul

Basin only in the occasional flyover of combat and reconnaissance aircraft, causing terror, bad dreams, and apocalyptic rumors now recalled
with embarrassed amusement to the younger generation.

   For the Kaugel people, and other Highland societies, the timing of European contact grows in significance when placed into the larger context of Papua New Guinea history. PNG's islands and coastal regions had their first
contact with European civilization already in the early sixteenth century, although a major influx of Europeans did not occur until the mid-nineteenth
century. Nevertheless, the island and coastal regions had contact nearly one
hundred years before the Highlands. As a result, Highlanders have felt themselves to be at a disadvantage compared to coastal peoples, accounting in
part for their public reluctance to see the Australian administration leave at
independence (see "Political Context" below).

   First contact with Europeans has been variously described by expatriate
observers (interpreting events from stories they have heard) as a Martian-
like visitation and as a cataclysmic and disruptive event to local cultures
that had enjoyed a stable, harmonious state for centuries, isolated from
the fragmenting and often destructive effects of Western civilization. Observing the pervasiveness of Western clothing, motor vehicles, and elec-
tronic communications, or glimpsing the befeathered and painted warrior
performing in a traditional *singsing* 'a dance with singing' wearing sun
glasses, a wristwatch, a pair of drover boots and holding a bottle of coke,
we may perceive a society staggering through some incalculable cultural
dislocation.

   Other more informed sources suggest that the Highlanders themselves
have an alternative vision/version of "first contact":

> [M.] Strathern argues that the European advent was, like an arti-
> fact, taken by New Guineans as a kind of image or perhaps
> performance, which could be grasped for itself, for the effect it had.
> Europeans may have thought their advent unique, but New Guin-
> eans already lived in a world in which images did not exist until
> composed (in performance, etc.). Hence, the "surprising" advent,
> she suggests, was one surprise among others. Further, the New
> Guineans may have been most surprised because of a sense that
> they created the effect, authored the European advent (as reflected,
> perhaps, in the fact that Europeans were widely seen as 'ancestors',
> not completely foreign beings). Hence, the European advent pro-
> voked self-knowledge, it made New Guineans think about what they
> might be—one may say, what they have been all along—with their
> new-found awareness of other possibilities. This provides some in-
> teresting insight into the ways in which Highlanders were able to
> deal with the European advent without experiencing a sense of radi-
> cal discontinuity. (Merlan and Rumsey 1991:189)

Connolly and Anderson (1987) relate an Australian patrol officer's remembrance of "first contact" in a way that supports the view above:

> Further to the west Taylor remembers that "two children recognised me as their dead father, recently killed. Each took me by the hand and brought their uncles to look into my eyes. And the uncles said, 'Yes! Here is your land, here are your wives and children, here are your pigs and dogs, here is everything! Now all we ask is that you stay'." (p. 91)

This phenomenon might also account for the relative ease with which a few dozen patrol officers, each with a handful of coastal police armed with rifles, were able to "pacify" the Highlands region in a relatively short period of time.

Political Context

Papua New Guinea

After the end of the war with Japan and under the auspices of the United Nations, the Australian government set up a joint administration of the two Territories under their mandate: the Territory of New Guinea (originally German New Guinea) and the Territory of Papua (originally British New Guinea), calling the combined entity the Territory of Papua and New Guinea (Banks 1995).[25]

The patrol officers who established the initial government posts throughout the Highlands regions also established Local Government Councils (LGCs). These provided local leaders with their first experiences in Western-style democratic government. The LGCs worked relatively well from the standpoint of traditional polity which, saving its strong male bias, was "egalitarian," given to the principle of each male person with a stake in the business at hand having a right to be heard.

In 1962, the United Nations sent its first "mission" to the Territory of Papua and New Guinea to inspect Administration plans and preparations for independence. The UN mission's subsequent report, written at the time of major and impatient independence movements in Africa and southeast Asia, severely criticized the Australian administration for its slowness in preparing the territory for self-rule and strongly recommended that an early date be set for independence (Connolly and Anderson 1987).

---

[25]For a more complete political history of Papua New Guinea, see Waiko (1993).

In 1964, the national House of Assembly was established. Members were elected from electoral divisions established in each District (i.e., Province) of the country. The House of Assembly assumed responsibility for all of the Territory's internal affairs in 1973, and on September 16, 1975, the Independent State of Papua New Guinea was inaugurated.

The introduction of provincial governments shortly after independence resulted in the decentralization of political and socioeconomic power from the national government in Port Moresby to the provinces. This initiative was necessitated by threats from people in North Solomons Province to secede if they were not granted an acceptable degree of autonomy (the issue being control over the land and the revenue generated by the huge Panguna [Bougainville] Copper Mine). To appease the North Solomons landowners and help ensure that revenues from the mine would continue, provincial government status was granted to North Solomons and, over a period of several years, to the other provinces. However, decentralization had its problems:

> At the provincial government level, the counter-secessionist strategy of decentralization proved to be very expensive, often inefficient, duplicative, and vulnerable to serious corruption—evidenced in the suspension of a number of provincial governments by the national government in the 1980s. (Fergie 1995:5)

In 1995, with passage of the Organic Law on Provincial Governments and Local Level Governments, the entire provincial political system was scrapped and replaced by a system that increased dramatically the roles of Members of Parliament (at the national level) and Local Government Councils (at the local level) in the provision of funds and services for local development (see below).

The Highlands

Following the UN mission in 1962, Australian representatives on the UN Trusteeship Council assured the Council that "the highlanders did not actually want independence" at least not until some time in the distant future (Connolly and Anderson 1987:292). On their subsequent return visit, the UN mission heard Highland leader after Highland leader proclaim their people's reluctance for the Australians to depart, feeling that Highlanders still had much to learn and gain from them.

> "I am very happy with the Australian government," announced Chimbu leader Kondon Agaundo, "and with all the laws they brought to New Guinea.... Just one thing you have said makes me unhappy. I have heard you want to give us self-government. I ask

you not to give it. When I feel strong enough I will ask for it, but I do not want you to force it on me....Before we can have self-government we need six things: pilots and aircraft factories; an arms factory; an ammunition factory; a mint to make money; factories to make glass and iron for houses; meat and clothing factories. All the work in these factories must be done by Papuans and New Guineans. When my people make these things I will know I am ready for self-government." (pp. 292–293)

Early independence (i.e., by mid-1970s) stirred Highlanders' fears that the educational and political advantage that island and coastal people enjoyed because of their extended contact with Europeans would be used to exclude Highlanders from ownership of businesses and from wage employment (p. 295). Even so, five years after independence, Highland politicians had formed their own political party and were making inroads into business and other development-related enterprises.

The Tambul Basin

The Giluwe (Tambul area) Local Government Council (GLGC) came into being during the mid-1960s and until the introduction of provincial government following independence, played a key role in local development. The GLGC was made up of councilors elected by voting members of the council areas, determined by population and traditional clan boundaries. Its role was to deal with the political aspects of local economy (e.g., road construction and maintenance, agriculture), social needs (including law and order and the courts), interclan conflicts, and the like. Prior to self-government in 1973, GLGC decisions and activities were always subject to the authority of the Australian subdistrict administrator (known as the *kiap* 'patrol officer'). Following independence, with decentralization and the establishment of provincial governments, local government councils ceased to perform much more than advisory functions until 1995 when they were reestablished as central to the provision of local funds and services.

Social Context

Papua New Guinea

Providing a brief overview of Papua New Guinea's social context with its over eight hundred language and culture groups is very challenging

(McNamara 1985). As with most Third World nations, the categories of social institutions generally referred to in brief synopses are those borrowed from Western models. I will briefly present those that actually appear in the presentation of the KTPPS program and findings.

Courts

The PNG justice system, from the top down, includes a Supreme Court, Regional and District Courts, and a wide ranging system of Village Courts, referred in the Kaugel area simply as *viles* 'village'. Village courts are mentioned throughout the Kaugel data, and court cases, generally heard publicly on a local *pena* 'ceremonial dancing ground' are frequently attended by children, some as young as those in the preschool.

Religion

Roughly 90 percent of the population claim membership in the Christian Church (about 60 percent Protestant, 30 percent Roman Catholic), with most of the remainder practicing various forms of traditional animism. Animist beliefs persist among some Christians and other nonindigenous religious groups (e.g., Jehovah's Witnesses, Mormons, Baha'i). As is demonstrated in the Kaugel case study (chapter 5), the impact of Christianity on the people of the Tambul Basin can hardly be overestimated. Parents' attitudes and actions are often comprehensible only through a knowledge of the particular denomination with which they are affiliated.

Economy

Papua New Guinea's modern economy is based on the export of its natural resources, including gold, copper, oil, natural gas, timber, copra, coffee, and tea. Less than half the employable population is engaged in economic activities that are part of the modern economic sector. More than half the population still practice some form of subsistence horticulture or hunting and gathering activities as their main source of sustenance (S. Malone 1997).

The degree to which PNG depends on mining exports for foreign exchange reserves is exemplified by the ongoing problems the government has faced since the closure of the Bougainville Copper Mine at Panguna in North Solomons Province in 1989 (cf. Ahai 1990). In 1993, the national currency, the kina, was floated and subsequently devalued by 30 percent. In 1995, amid much debate in the national press (for example, Lafanama 1995, August 9; Nongorr 1995, August 24; Warakari 1995, October 7), a Structural

Adjustment Program (SAP) was initiated as a prerequisite to obtaining needed loans from the World Bank and International Monetary Fund. The effect these events had on the KTPPS project, and others like it, is significant. The primary complaint from the KTPPS teachers regarding their part in the program centered on their income or, more precisely, their lack of it (see chapter 5). Simply stated, between the beginning of the KTPPS program in 1986 and the time of this case study in 1995, the value of the kina dropped by 30 percent, the cost of the materials needed to sustain the preschools increased significantly, and the amount of money available from funding sources diminished as budgets of supporting government departments (i.e., NDOE) were decreased in response to reduced revenue.

Health

General hospitals in PNG are primarily relegated to major urban centers, with Christian missions providing hospital care in some of the more remote areas. Smaller hospitals, known officially as Rural Health Centers and colloquially as *haus sik* 'house for the sick', operate in district government centers like Tambul. Formerly, a large system of aid posts, staffed by trained medical workers, provided first aid and basic medicines (antimalarials, antibiotics, bandages, splints, aspirin, and cough medicine) in the outlying rural areas. Since 1989, these have fallen into disuse because of budget decreases and staff retrenchments due to lack of revenue from the Bougainville mine (closed down by antigovernment guerrillas; see above) and austerity measures imposed by outside lending institutions on the PNG government. Health care is a major concern throughout the country and poor health care is a common complaint among Kaugel people.

The Kaugel context

Merlan and Rumsey (1991) provide an excellent ethnographic account of the Ku Waru people in the Western Nebilyer, a low mountain range removed from the Kaugel Valley. The Ku Waru and the people of the Tambul Valley share many linguistic and cultural characteristics.[26] Below are some of the key sociocultural traits Merlan and Rumsey list in describing the Ku Waru that also describe the Kaugel people at the center of this case study.

---

[26]The Ku Waru (a subdialect of a language called Mbo Ung in the *Ethnologue,* used alternatively with Bo Ung, Mboung (Grimes 2000) are related directly to people in the Tambul Basin. The Korika clan that shares oversight of the KTPPS program at Purare with the Kengelka clan is an extension of the Kusika clan that plays a key role in the events of Merlan and Rumsey's (1991) ethnography.

Action, not passive reception

Merlan and Rumsey describe the inclination of the Ku Waru people and their neighbors to value active rather than passive responses to daily decision making.

> People are usually not content to simply let events unfold or happen. More prevalent is a style according to which people seek to actively grasp events, make plans, make things happen. (1991:238–239)

The high valuation of active vis-à-vis passive stances when confronted by problems or conflicts can easily be observed in the life of the Ku Waru community. Merlan and Rumsey's "ethnography of the event" reports how a women's club marched out between two warring factions, carrying a PNG flag and various gifts of food, and negotiated an end to the armed hostilities between the male members of their clans. Similarly, the cessation of the Upper Kaugel-Lower Kaugel conflict referred to above resulted, in part, from Christian church leaders setting up a cross on each side of the fight ground, forbidding combatants to go beyond them, then camping out in the no-man's-land, day and night, until the two sides agreed to terms of truce (Rambai Keruwa, personal communication, July 1995).

The value of action in the face of problems or conflicts proves to be a key ingredient of the administration of the KTPPS program described in chapter 4, both in a positive and a negative sense. For people "in-between" the old and the new, new situations and new possibilities create uncertainty about the likely effects of their actions. Nevertheless, to act is generally preferred to resignation or, as Apé remarked in respect to a suggested course of community action, *Nogut yumi sanap na pasim han na lukluk tasol* 'It's not good for us to just stand there, fold our arms, and watch' (personal communication, December 1995).

Skin and soap

One of the most frequent comments heard in the KTPPS interviews, especially with the teachers, was *mi no gat mani inap long baim sop* 'I don't have enough money to buy soap'. The Tok Pisin term *sop* 'soap' has taken on a great deal more meaning than a simple reference to bar or liquid cleansing agents or laundry detergents. The condition of a person's skin is an indicator of his or her psychological and physical health (cf. M. Strathern 1991). *Sop* keeps the skin healthy and beautiful. Not to be able to buy "soap"—by analogy, the things that provide psychological and physical benefit and health—is to be seriously demeaned (cf. Merlan and Rumsey 1991:132, 148).

Tradition and government lo

The government, with its schools, roads, health centers, and police, in tandem with the introduced cash economy, impact the lives of the Kaugel people in many ways. Attitudes toward the government in the Tambul Basin strongly resemble those described by Merlan and Rumsey in the Nebilyer, in which the indigenous practice of compensation for casualties in war or accidents is essentially congruent with the more recent *lo* 'law' of the government.

The leader of the Ku Waru women's group whose intervention led to a cessation of tribal fighting argued that the requirements of "business" should take precedence over warfare. The same sentiment expressed by the leader of the Ku Waru women's group is echoed by Aika clansmen with regard to their traditional enmity with the Kanimbe clan. An Aika clan leader, who had been relating stories from the *ou koronga lupa* 'the long ago times' said, in effect, that, "The old men get upset with us young men because we prefer to do business ventures with the Kanimbes instead of fighting them" (name withheld, personal communication, March, 1989). This growing perception has implications for traditional politics in that it signals a new direction: what Merlan and Rumsey call "the possibility of universal parity" that

> resides in the linkage between *gavman* and *bisnis*, a powerful suggestion since many aspects of both resonate with practices (roll-calling, time-keeping, turn-taking) and values (orderliness and the very discovery and exploration of new values) that people wish to embrace. (1991:213)

Sociolinguistic Context

Papua New Guinea

A nation with over eight hundred languages will necessarily develop patterns of communication that involve bilingualism and multilingualism. Two national lingua francas—Tok Pisin from the northern and eastern provinces with the largest number of speakers and Hiri Motu from the area around Port Moresby with few speakers outside the Papuan provinces—are spoken by a large percentage of the population. In addition, several large church bodies have used regional languages as lingua francas (e.g., Kâte and Yabem in the Lutheran Church; Dobu in the United Church). With the recently piloted national mother-tongue elementary program, local languages are being used in the first three years of formal education but English is the language of

instruction for grades 3 and above. The number of Tok Pisin speakers contin-
ues to increase as many children, especially those whose parents have moved
to urban areas or plantations, learn to speak it as their first language. In most
cases of moribund mother tongues in PNG, Tok Pisin is the replacement language. An overview of the sociolinguistic status of the case study area necessitates a consideration of the impact of Tok Pisin and English on the Kaugel
speech community.

The Kaugel context

The linguistic context of the KTPPS program cannot be discussed mean-
ingfully isolated from its social dimensions. McConvell's model of social
arenas (in Romaine 1995:167), which he used to discuss language use by
the Gurindji, an Australian aboriginal group, has been adapted below to
present a simplified version of the sociolinguistic complexities that are a
common part of daily life for Umbu-Ungu speakers.

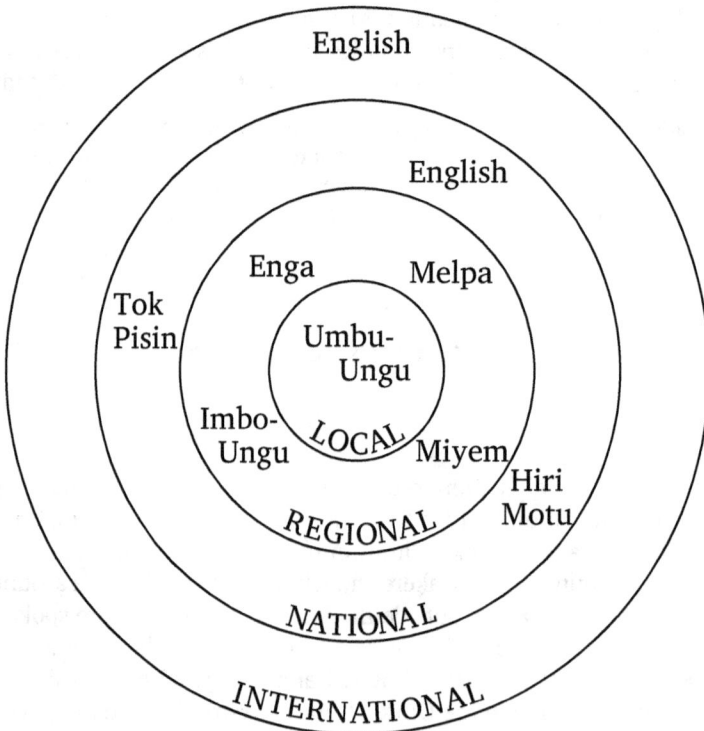

Figure 3.2. Kaugel social arenas for language choice.

What McConvell's model conveys for the Gurindji bilingual and multi-lingual speakers applies similarly to Kaugel polyglots, namely, that as they move between and among social arenas, they always have at their disposal at least two codes to choose from, depending upon the linguistic capacities of their fellow speakers. Thus, the multilingual Tambul children who attend Baisu Community School (within the Regional circle above) while their parents work in the Wahgi Valley coffee and tea plantations, are able to converse with fellow students from other language areas using their mother tongue, Melpa, Enga, or Tok Pisin as the occasion requires or permits.

The Baisu Community School represents a multilingual setting different and more complex than the one in the Tambul Basin. Speakers of many languages other than Kaugel, Melpa, and Enga also attend the school so children frequently use Tok Pisin, especially in mixed groups. Combined with Kaugel enclaves in the urban centers of Port Moresby, Lae, and Mount Hagen (which were not visited due to time and transport constraints), the Baisu situation represents a classic language shift environment.

Educational Context

Papua New Guinea

Formal education 1970–1994

The structure of the formal education system, established with the Education Ordinance of 1970, was largely unchanged until 1994.[27] Figure 3.3 gives the basic configuration of the three levels: primary, secondary, tertiary.

---

[27]The Education Ordinance of 1983 changed the name of the first level from primary schools to community schools, with an attendant change in curriculum giving more control of noncore subjects (subjects other than English, math, and science) to the provincial and local levels with the intention of providing a more practical and relevant course of studies. However, the revised curriculum included instruction methods, materials, and language for which the teachers were not adequately trained (McNamara 1985:3758).

Primary level community schools						Secondary level				Tertiary level universities		
Grade 1	Grade 2	Grade 3	Grade 4	Grade 5	Grade 6	Provincial high schools				Entry year	Degree, diploma, and certificate courses	
						Grade 7	Grade 8	Grade 9	Grade 10	National high schools		
						College of external studies				Grade 11	Grade 12	
						Grade 7	Grade 8	Grade 9	Grade 10	Teachers College	Port Moresby In-Service College	
						Vocational centers Year 1 Year 2				Year 1	Year 2	In-service courses

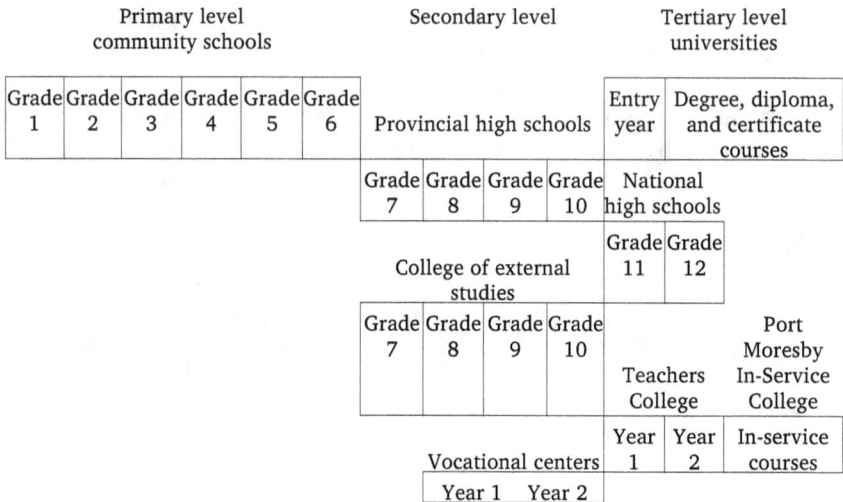

Figure 3.3. PNG education structure, 1970–1994.

The structure of formal education from 1970 until 1994 in figure 3.3 illustrates a system that prioritized economic development at the expense of relevant learning experiences for the rural majority of students:

> Paradoxically, the drive for economic independence through major "development" projects deemed necessary to finance an adequate budget...may reduce Papua New Guinea's ability to shape its own development and educational path. The choice is between independence of culture, life style, and educational programmes, and the very real attractions (for those who can afford it) of absorption into a cosmopolitan culture. (McNamara 1985:3758–3759)

Philosophy of education for PNG

As a response to what was generally considered an increasingly irrelevant and alienating education system, a ministerial committee was appointed to develop a philosophical statement that would guide the development of more Papua New Guinea-oriented schools. The committee, chaired by Sir Paulias Matane, produced the *Philosophy of Education for Papua New Guinea* (Department of Education) in 1986. Based on the concept of "integral human development" as promoted in the PNG Constitution, the report criticized the education system as a whole for overemphasizing the economic and political aspects of national life at the expense of the social and spiritual. One of its key recommendations was that the children's mother tongue or community language would be used for the first three to six years of education. The *Philosophy* was endorsed by the National Executive Council (i.e., Cabinet) in 1987, except for the recommendation regarding local language medium of instruction.

Education sector review

The Education Sector Review, undertaken in 1991, proposed a major restructuring of the educational system, including the addition of an elementary level in which children would be taught in a language they know, preferably their mother tongue. This innovation, previously considered impractical by PNG education administrators, gained credibility because of the large number of vernacular preschool programs that had operated successfully for a decade with little or no support from the national government. Due to the success of *tok ples* education, the NDOE established a Language and Literacy Section within the Curriculum Development Division in 1989 to help prepare a national vernacular education program and to support mother-tongue education projects already in existence.

Education Amendment Act (education reform)

The Education Amendment Act of 1995, following the recommendations of the Education Sector Review, aimed to improve access and retention in the formal system, and to improve cost effectiveness (see figure 3.4). It called for the creation of pre-primary "elementary" classes in local communities, using local buildings with local teachers and locally prepared materials (supplemented by NDOE-produced materials). Comprised of three grades—elementary prep, elementary 1, and elementary 2—the elementary level is to provide three years of mother-tongue instruction in a half-day curriculum that includes mother-tongue literacy, maths, indigenous health and science, and cultural studies (Guidelines for Establishing Elementary Schools, Secretary's circular no. 62/94, October 28, 1994). Primary schools, relieved of grades 1 and 2, are to retain grades 3 through 6 and add grades 7 and 8, a process known as "top-up" and one which, theoretically, requires no capital outlay since the facilities vacated by grades 1 and 2 can be used to accommodate grades 7 and 8. High school facilities formerly used by grades 7 and 8 are thus to be available for doubling the intake of grade 9 and 10 students, or for "topping-up" with grades 11 and 12 (Department of Education 1991a).

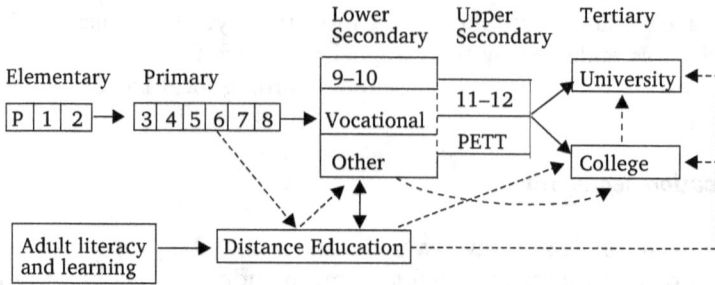

Figure 3.4. Papua New Guinea's restructured education system.

Notes:

P = Preparatory class with initial literacy and general education in the vernacular

Vocational = Two years of lower secondary education with a vocational skills bias

Other = A wide range of "permitted" institutions which offer two or more years of secondary education, usually with a strong vocational bias determined by the needs and opportunities of the areas which they serve

11–12 = Upper secondary or matriculation. Increasingly, upper secondary education will develop particular curriculum biases e.g., academic, agriculture, technical, commercial, etc. Figure 3.4 provides for grades 11 and 12 in separate institutions as at present, or added on to existing provincial high schools.

PETT = Pre-Employment Technical Training courses, which are for two years post grade 10, and located in technical colleges

College = covers the more than sixty nonuniversity "tertiary" institutions which currently take mainly grade 10 leavers but who are intending to raise their entry level to grade 12 as the pool of grade 12 leavers increases.

Distance education = College of Distance Education and the Extension Studies Department of the University of Papua New Guinea

(Department of Education. 1991a Education Sector Review, 1: Executive Summary and Principal Recommendations, Papua New Guinea, p. 4)

Implementation of Education Reform faces major challenges. These include training teachers for the new elementary level, retraining teachers for grades 3 and 4, 7 and 8, and grades 11 and 12, preparing all the necessary curriculum and instructional materials, and finding the funds to pay what some estimate will be at least 14,000 teachers for the elementary level (Government of Papua New Guinea, Australian Agency for International Development, Asian Development Bank 1995).

In their evaluation of elementary pilot projects in Milne Bay Province, Wari and Roakeina (1994) reported a significant lack of community awareness regarding the purposes and process of Education Reform. The result was that communities selected for the pilot projects were not prepared for them and consequently failed to provide the necessary classroom space. In the general population and even among the pilot project managers, there was confusion as to the goals and purposes of the

projects. Wari and Roakeina's final recommendation has particular significance for the Kaugel Tok Ples Pri Skul program and for similar programs
throughout the country:

> The Department of Education [should] develop an appropriate Ele-
> mentary School policy for endorsement by the National Executive
> Council which specifically states that provinces wishing to imple-
> ment education reforms recognise the establishment of elementary
> education as the first step for education reform. (Item 14, p. 18)

In the Western Highlands Province, five schools were chosen for "top-up"
(adding grade 7 to an existing community school previously housing grades
1–6), but no elementary schools were begun. Grade 7 was simply added to
the existing community school, requiring the construction of additional
classroom space, a requirement that the Education Reform was designed to
eliminate (P. Mayes, Assistant Secretary of Education, WHP, personal communication, November 10, 1995). Apparently, the Western Highlands Province was having the same difficulty noted in Milne Bay in understanding the
intents and purposes of Education Reform.

In 1995, the Kaugel language area included one provincial high school
(in the Lower Kaugel District), ten community schools in the Upper and
Lower Kaugel, seven church agency schools, and three government primary schools (figure 3.5).

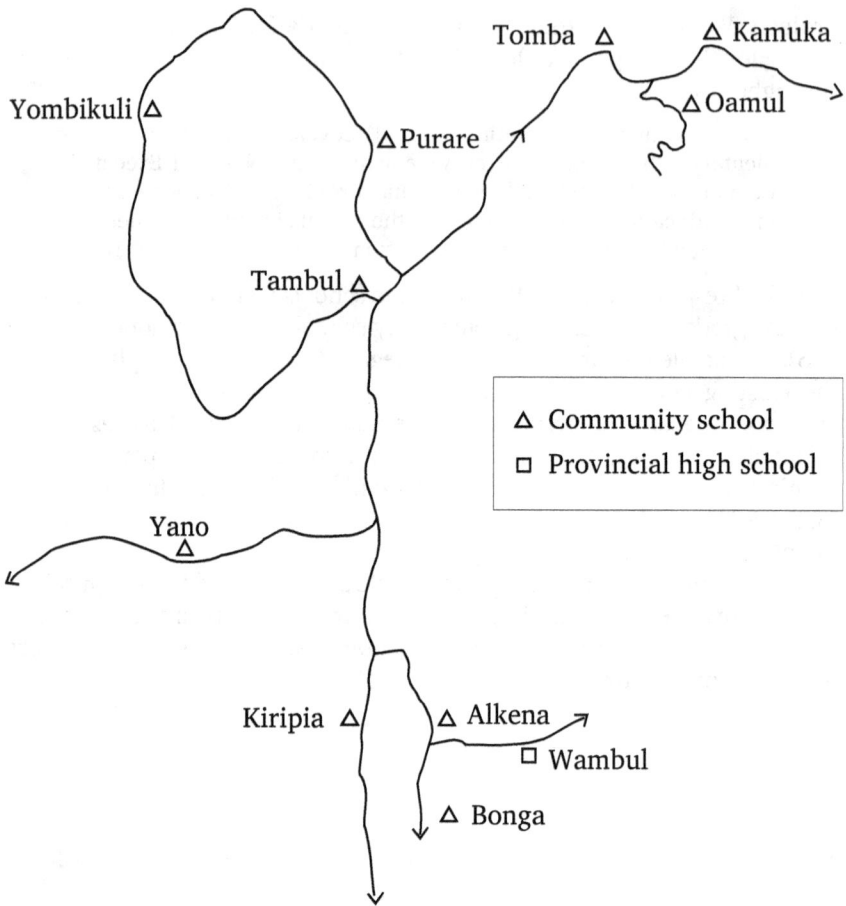

Figure 3.5. Kaugel schools: Formal education system.

Traditional education in the Kaugel area

With the plethora of Western-type educational institutions in the area, the poignant question raised in the *Philosophy of Education* comes to mind:

> Traditional education was integrated with the community and taught children to see the world through the eyes of the community. Through whose eyes do our children see the world now? (quoted in McLaughlin 1994:63)

Basing his comments on an in-depth search of the relevant literature, McLaughlin's article contrasting traditional and Western ways of knowing, is particularly relevant to a study of the Kaugel TPPS program. He finds that traditional knowledge tends to be the product of transmission (knowledge passed on from the knower to the novice), inspiration (knowledge gained through struggle and hard work), or revelation (knowledge received in dreams and visions or through initiation). Western knowledge tends to be a product of inquiry (questioning, problematizing experience), reflectivity (individual reflection, introspection), and creativity (finding the new, the novel, valuing change). The main difference between traditional and Western learning, in McLaughlin's account, is the tendency for Western education to focus on the potential and well-being of the individual, while most traditional education emphasized the acquisition of knowledge that promotes group welfare and the fulfillment of community aspirations. The tension between the goals of the two systems is reflected or, better, made manifest in the struggle of Kaugel parents who want their children to succeed in the formal education system but do not want them to lose their traditional ties to family and clan. See chapter 5 for a discussion of this topic.

Table 3.1 is a summary of the key elements in McLaughlin's (1994) version of "traditional" education in the lefthand column, with examples of Kaugel agreements and variations in the right.

Table 3.1 McLaughlin's elements of traditional education
applied to the Kaugel context

McLaughlin's elements	Kaugel notes
Traditional informal education	
Learning by observation and imitation	Four small boys dig a trench on the bank of the ditch beside the road, pouring water into it from a used can. Fifty meters up the road a group of men are digging the drainage trenches for a new taro garden.
Learning by personal trial and error	Peni's toddler of 1–2 years waddles around the yard of his grandparents' house wielding a carving knife with a ten inch blade; the adults seem more indifferent than unaware. The child neither falls, nor cuts himself, nor anyone else.

Learning in real life activities	Few adult activities are forbidden the children, including drinking beer, smoking, and chewing betel nut. As men are working a vehicle, the older boys (10–12 years old) are squatting beside them watching their every move.
Absence of the institutionalized office of teacher	"Teaching" of the verbal kind is done ad hoc and only related to real activities in which the child is involved. Kaugel parents encourage children to include a range of ages in a group so that the older children can teach the younger.

Teaching strategies

Motivation	Watching Apé's 13-year-old son climb to the top of a twenty meter gum tree, I remark that it looks dangerous. Apé replies that it is dangerous but since the family and community needs someone to be able to climb (or to cross a log bridge) they have to let the children take risks so they won't be afraid when they're called on to help the group.
Guidance	Four small boys by the new taro garden are called over to share food that has been cooked for the workers, learning in the process of distribution who gets served first and who gets more or less while being tacitly approved for their interest in the cultural event that is taking place.
Reward	My landlord relates how, as a young boy, he went to the forest with his uncles and carried back what for him was a large piece of firewood. When his father saw him, he called out to everyone around to come a see the "huge" pieces of firewood Suku had carried back for the family. Suku laughed as he recalled the incident realizing now, as an adult, what his father was doing, remarking that after that incident, he never failed to return home from the forest with a piece of firewood.

Myths and tales	Oral literature provides children and adults with the sense of who they and their clan are (or should be) and, in the process, teaching useful lessons. Many of these stories made their way into the Kaugel Reading Series (chapter 5) without being solicited.
Repetition	Repetition of and in stories, songs, and genealogies is a common discourse feature.
Traditional formal education	
Curriculum	Rambai's account of *sandallu,* the male youth initiation ritual, is an example of traditional formal education by ritual from which a "curriculum" could be deduced if better and more thorough information and interpretation were available.
Significance	The knowledge gained in *sandallu* was a prerequisite for leadership in the clan, an implication Rambai seemed to understand with his repeated theme of being chosen: Out of all the Aikas, why me?
Process	The esoteric nature of the revealed knowledge and magical words did not require a cognitive understanding of their meaning. Rambai learned them so well that he assured me that, had I the time, he could sing all the songs he learned during those several weeks of initiation over thirty years ago.
Teachers	For the *sandallu* ritual, some of the teachers were not Kaugel men but came from Enga. They were recognized as having a better or more complete knowledge of the power and scope of the chants they taught. They focused on inducing dreams, a sure medium for revelation and the impromptu composition of the song that encapsulated the meaning of the dream (see chapter 4).

McLaughlin identifies three learning styles—observation and imitation, personal trial and error, real life activities—that provide learners with learning in the full context of its use. This, as demonstrated in the vignette below, is in contrast to the kind of decontextualized learning usually required of children in community school contexts. And although the role of teacher was not institutionalized in traditional society, the following anecdote indicates how adult members of the clan assumed the role of "mentor":

> An old man invites 3 or 4 boys into the men's house in the after-noon after...a full day of playing and telling stories when he knew they would be hungry. They come in and sit around the fire with him, thinking, "Oh, now he's going to give us something to eat." As the old man talks with the boys, telling them interesting, exciting or humorous stories, he pulls four sweet potatoes out of the ashes in the fire pit. "Yes," the boys think, "He's going to give us some *kaukau*." As the old man continues his stories, he breaks each *kaukau* into smaller, bite-size pieces. The boys are *really* hungry by now and are waiting impatiently for the distribution. The old man continues storying, then one-by-one pops the pieces of *kaukau* into his mouth, eating and telling the stories simultaneously. Meanwhile, as the boys wait for their share, the old man downs all but the last three pieces. These he tosses to the...boys saying, "Wandering around, exploring, having fun, telling stories, playing... they're all right but you also have to work. If you don't work you'll always be hungry!" Now the old man's genial demeanor changes. He becomes rough, gruff, angry: "So, what are you sitting here for...? Go out and find some work!" He shoos the boys out. (Rambai Keruwa, personal communication, September 19, 1995)

Laughing, Rambai relates that, at that point, the boys are well-disposed toward murdering the old man or at least burning down his house. They will spend a lot of time berating the old man's stupidity, but they will not ever forget the lesson, and eventually they will appreciate the wisdom the old man shared with them.

Community schools

Three community schools operate in the focus area for this case study: Tambul Community School, a government-agency school (at least two classes each of grade 1 through grade 6 and a nonteaching principal), Yombikul Community School, a PNG Bible Church-agency school (one class of each of the six grades; the principal teaching grade 6), and Purare Community School, also a PNGBC-agency school in its first year (grade 1 teacher acts as principal). The Tambul school buildings are permanent, with corrugated iron roofs and plywood walls, except for grades 1A and 1B which have iron roofs but walls made of a woven cane matting. The following is an account of a visit to one of the community schools, taken from my field notes. The account is included for comparison with the traditional education discussed above, and with the KTPPS classroom discussed in chapter 6.

> [The grade 6 classroom contains fifteen wooden double desks which the teacher has arranged in five rows of three desks each. Two students are assigned to each desk. Twenty-eight of the thirty students are in attendance as the national grade 6 examination is less than a month away.]
>
> The grade 6 teacher directs students to the set of sentences written on a small chalkboard on the west wall, under the heading in colored chalk: HEALTH/SCIENCE. The first sentence is done as an example by the teacher and the students.
>
> "(1) paul told me that hes feeling sick"
>
> Student 1 adds full stop at end of sentence.
>
> Student 2 adds a comma after "that."
>
> Teacher says, "That's not right," and erases the comma without explanation.
>
> Teacher then crosses out the small "p" and writes "P" above it.
>
> Teacher finally adds an apostrophe, without explanation. (Field notes 3.2)

This particular episode is an example of language education in which mechanical, technical aspects of written forms are substituted for meaningful context. However, since the purpose of this activity was to provide practice on a language exercise similar to the kind that occur on the grade 6 exams, the lack of meaningful context might, in itself, have been helpful to the students since that is precisely the nature of the grade 6 exam activities. However, the lack of explanation in the above example seems to highlight an observation made by Apé Kolowa, my Kaugel research colleague: the community school teachers do not teach but instead assume the children are teaching themselves the meaning of the various punctuation marks. The teachers, then, restrict themselves to "testing" the extent of the students' self-instruction.

During the time of my observation of the grade 6 classroom, English was used exclusively in all interactions between teacher and students. Only one non-English sentence was used by the teacher during this period, and it came in response to a loud conversation in Umbu-Ungu coming from the adjoining principal's office: a Kaugel teacher recounting a humorous trip to Mount Hagen, the joking and laughing increasing in volume proportionately with the hilarity of the event. The grade 6 teacher finally called out in Tok Pisin, Hey, *yupela tok isi!* 'Hey, you all quiet down!' The office conversation turned out to be the only case of informal valuation of the local language observed at the community school. For whatever reasons the community school teachers go along with the "English only" policy in the classroom. This one conversation I heard in Umbu-Ungu, clearly audible to classes on both sides of the office, at least demonstrated its usefulness for interpersonal communication.

The only item I observed in the classroom that related to the local culture was a handmade poster showing a mountain and an open book with the caption: [name withheld] Community School *Ambolangoma skul leyangi* '[name withheld] Community School: Learn, children!'

As the class was being dismissed for morning break, I noticed the expressive arts curriculum poster hanging on the back of the classroom door. Since expressive arts is the primary (perhaps only) component of the grade 6 curriculum that is likely to refer to local culture, I am curious how much of the program the students have experienced. As some of the students are milling around nearby, I asked one young man which activities they had done that year. "None of them," he replied (Field notes 3.6).

Observations in a grade 2 classroom revealed decontextualized English language instruction patterns similar to the grade 6 classroom, but this time missing even the smattering of meaningful context the exercises are meant to provide.

The following sentence patterns were printed on the chalkboard: "How many pencils are there in my left hand?" "There are many." One boy reads the question. A second boy reads the answer: "Der are many." His language is grammatically but not semantically correct. The boy who asked the question has no pencils in either hand. (Field notes 3.9)

In regard to the teacher's language use, however, this classroom was less restrictive. The grade 2 teacher used Tok Pisin extensively during her math lesson, borrowing on occasion from both English and Umbu-Ungu.

Eighty percent of the community school staff members are from the Umbu-Ungu language area. However, when the local grade 1 teacher fell ill and had to go on medical leave, the teacher that took over his class was the one from the location furthest from Tambul, whose knowledge of local language and culture appeared minimal. The following are excerpts from my observations in his class:

> **Print environment: the ABCs.** The teacher has hung sheets of duplicating paper along the lower edge of the large chalkboard in front of the classroom. Each sheet has a large capital letter accompanied by a picture and one-word caption.

A	apple	I	insects	S	snake
B	ball	K	kite	T	truck
C	cup	L	leaf	U	umbrella
D	door	M	marble	V	violin
E	elephant	N	nest	W	wheel
F	family	O	orange	X	Ø
G	goat	P	plate	Y	yacht
H	horse	Q	queen	Z	zip
		R	rabbit		

The culture of the children, many of whom had not attended a *tok ples pri skul,* was largely absent in the classroom. Of the items pictured on the English alphabet list, apple, elephant, kite, queen, rabbit, violin, and yacht were completely alien to the children's experience.

> The teacher writes "village" on the chalkboard, pronounces the word as *willij* with the children repeating the word and pronunciation. He asks for another word for "village." A child answers, *ples* 'place' in Tok Pisin. The teacher writes classroom, house, grass on the chalkboard. A girl suggests adding *"beds"* [birds] to the list. The teacher then addresses a boy, "Manuel, come and draw us a piksa. Draw in da willij." Under his breath the boy says, *Mipela mekim pinis…* [We've already done this…]. I take this to mean that the children have previously done this lesson. [This is not unlikely. I have noticed that most community school teachers, when they are being observed, like to do review lessons because they are more confident that the children will do well.] Finally, the teacher tells the children to draw a village, pointing to a picture on the wall of a large Central Province village. [Central Province is the area around Port Moresby, not even in the same part of the country as Tambul. Also, Kaugel children and their families live in hamlets, not villages, their closest neighbor generally a garden or so away from them]. (Field notes 3.6)

These brief looks at the different community school classrooms provide an idea of the kind of curriculum the Kaugel children experience once they enter the formal system. When I asked the teachers directly about local culture and how they try to affirm it, the head teacher replied:

> When there is a *singsing,* we will let the children go and take part and using traditional paints and you know, whatever is and add it onto singsing.

> When there is a big feast, the children are let go to join in [with] their parents to have pig feast.

And if there is a funeral, the children are let go or sometimes teachers do take part with the children, children and teachers together they go if somebody important die in a community.

If things like, Monday we had some things here, *[reference to the public accusations of responsibility for death of a grade 6 teacher]* they are important, so children are [allowed to] take part in it and find out their own of what is happening in the community.

Or other government activities like Independence days or things like this we let the children go. (Head teacher, [name withheld] community school, October 4, 1995, T29A.11)

All of these are passive activities from the school's standpoint. If there are no cultural events for the children to attend, there is little likelihood of local culture being an active element of the children's classroom experience.

A private Christian primary school

In addition to the community schools, a private Christian primary school, with grades K through 6, provides yet another educational and cultural experience of "otherness" to the Kaugel children attending it.

The largest of the school's two rooms provides individual work spaces [desks] with sides that rise up about three feet above the desk top so that the student seated there cannot see anyone to his/her left or right—in fact, can see no one unless s/he moves around in the chair or stands up. On the cubicle next to where I stood observing is a small Coke can holding a small U.S.A. flag, a razor blade, plastic triangle, and pencils. On the "walls" of the work space are calendar photos of a North American autumn and a progress sheet filled with stick-on stars. On top of the desk are a ruler and six individual workbooks: Bible Readings, Math, Science, English, Social Studies, Word Building. A note book is provided for each workbook (published in consumable form but preserved for use from year-to-year).

The classroom is spacious, orderly, quiet. Students work steadily at their lessons. Although students do interact and talk quietly to each other at times, none of the interaction is of an educational nature. No student work was displayed, and no group activities were observed. The setting itself—with the North American photos prominent, a few American flags, the uniform dress of the students, the quiet, highly individualized learning activities, along with the exclusive use of English—seems conscious of its anti-local culture impact, and that this is a good thing. The cubicles themselves seem to strike at the heart of group and cooperative learning customs of traditional culture. The large Papua New Guinea flag—and small ones on the desks—act as important reminders to the visitor that he has not, mysteriously, stepped into the "little school on the prairie." (Field notes 1.62, September 28, 1995)

Rambai Keruwa, the KTPPS director, and his wife Nali send their 12-year-old son to the private Christian school. I asked Rambai why he had taken his son out of the community school to send him to this school, what he liked and disliked about it, and anything else he cared to tell me. Following is his response (written to me after my departure from the field):

1. Reasons for taking Rendi out from community school and send him to [private Christian school] program:
   a. Nali [Rambai's wife] and I were so concerned about all our children to be given a lot of opportunity on the Christian matters while they are in their early years at school.
   b. We discussed that one hour of religious instruction given in the community schools once a week was not enough.
   c. We seemed to see that the [private Christian school] program offers daily Bible teaching and lessons with Bible portions and scriptures as part of their curriculum.
   d. The good time in the life of growing children to have the word of God planted as a seed in their life was during their early ages.
2. What I like about the [private Christian school] program:
   a. Program offers more learning materials for the individual child than the community school does.
   b. Each student receives better supervision in their lessons.
   c. Each learner performs lessons at his own ability speed and that determines their grade level.
   d. Encourages individual child to master more than any one grade in a year if he/she performs lessons well.
   e. Classroom management and school discipline is well maintained.
3. What I dislike about [private Christian school]:
   a. Not enough time is allowed for students to interact orally among themselves.
   b. The children's acceptance in community or national high schools is not established.
   c. Program does not seem to provide an adequate system to upgrade and qualify the training of [private Christian school] teachers.

d. Some subjects, lessons taught in the program are not relevant. That is most of the social study lessons need to be revised and adopt locally relevant materials.
e. Curriculum and lessons are not basically prepared for local kids.
f. School fees are much higher than the cost of community school education.

(Rambai Keruwa, personal communication, October 26, 1996)

Nali herself wrote, expressing concerns that Rendi was not learning well at the community school, that the local community school teachers are not always well-trained, and that the community schools lacked sufficient religious instruction. An additional consideration included the fact that their youngest daughter Sendi, a KTPPS student during my field work period, was to enroll in the private Christian school and her brother would be able to look after her. Nali also included her feelings about the KTPPS program which each of their three younger children, Nensi, Rendi, and Sendi, have attended:

Tokples Pri-skul nem i gutpela long lainim ol pikinini pasin bilong kisim save long rit na rait long tok ples wantaim pasin long ples [na] [l]ong kisim gutpela save long pasin long ples. Ol 3-pela pikinini i kisim save long sampela pasin long ples i no olgeta pasin.	The Tok Ples Pri Skul program is good for teaching the children how to read and write in the mother tongue, along with local customs and [the children] learn well about local customs. [Our] three [younger] children learned a lot about some of the local customs, but not about all of them.

(Nali Keruwa, personal communication, October 26, 1996)

Rambai's and Nali's explanations of their educational decision for their child illustrate the often conflicting goals and desires of Kaugel parents for their children. While holding a conviction that their children need to develop understanding and respect for indigenous language and culture, they nevertheless enrol the children in an educational program that, in many ways, seeks to replace indigenous language and culture with imported cultural values and traits many of which are more appropriate to Kansas than to the Kaugel Valley. Rambai seems to understand the contradiction (see his items 3a, 3d, 3e above).

The temptation to stereotype the religious motivation that features prominently as a root cause for tension in educational approaches needs to be resisted (parents' attitudes toward Kaugel language and culture are discussed in chapter 5).

These three local educational institutions the KTPPS, the community school, and the private Christian school, only one of which emphasizes the use of local language and in which local culture is the basis for learning activities (see chapter 6) represent the complexity of the educational context for residents of the Tambul area. The differences among the choices contribute to the tension felt by Kaugel parents who want a good academic education for their children that also includes an emphasis on the social, cultural, and spiritual values important to their community and families. Of the three institutions described in this section, no single choice will meet all of these parents' goals.

4

The KTPPS Program

A concern with the point of view of the actor necessitates a consideration of the actual situation in which action gets constructed as well as the past experience of the individual and the history of the group, which locate both the actor and the situation he or she confronts in the flux of time and past event. (Lal 1995:425)

The Kaugel Tok Ples Pri Skul (KTPPS) program grew out of the intersection, across cultures, of several lives at a particular place and a specific point in time. The depiction of that intersection is aided and complicated by the fact that one of the lives is mine. Being part of "the flux of time and past events" blesses and burdens me with memories—no less partial and colored because they happen to be relevant to the KTPPS context—that at times confirm and at times question the memories of other participants. I have, therefore, to the best of my ability, refrained from "correcting" others' recollections and present them as they were spoken or written to me or to others. I present below the participants who played key roles in the planning, forming, and implementing of the KTPPS program, hoping that I have allowed them, across languages, to speak for themselves: the SIL literacy team (my wife Susan and me), the KTPPS director (Rambai Keruwa), and members of the Aika-Korika-Kengelka Literacy Committee and the Kaugel NonFormal Education Association.

The Participants

The SIL literacy team

In August of 1982, an Aika clansman who had left his home in the Tambul Basin to work as a butcher in the Eastern Highlands Province town of Kainantu, learned that SIL, based a short distance away at Ukarumpa, had just assigned expatriate members to work as a literacy team in the Umbu-Ungu language area. He traveled to Ukarumpa, to invite us—my wife Susan and I were the team—to settle in his clan area in the Tambul Basin. His older brother subsequently traveled from Tambul to Ukarumpa to confirm the offer and to take us out to the clan area to look for a suitable place to build a house. I include this as one more instance of the high social value that highlanders in general, and Kaugel people in particular, place on active human participation in the shaping of events, both for personal and community benefit.

In Papua New Guinea (PNG), SIL is a primarily expatriate organization with about 450 members engaged in linguistics, literacy, community development, and various support tasks, with the underlying motivational goal of assisting in the translation of the Christian scriptures into the languages of PNG's eight hundred ethnolinguistic groups.

Prior to our accepting an assignment in 1982 as literacy specialists for the Kaugel people, my wife and I had lived in the Highlands for seven years, working with a Christian mission organization in a neighboring province. As a result of that experience and of the emphasis in our SIL pre-field training on developing community-based literacy programs, we arrived in the Tambul Basin committed to beginning the literacy project only after local leaders had demonstrated an interest in establishing and guiding it. We discovered later that as we looked for local people to lead the program, the local leaders were also looking at us. That scrutiny covered the first eighteen months of our time in the area during which we concentrated on language and culture learning and on helping to alleviate the consequences of killing frosts during mid-1982 (described in chapter 3). It was not until January of 1984 that Aika Rambai[2] met with us and indicated his desire to provide leadership for a mother-tongue literacy program. As we learned several years later, at the time of our arrival in the Tambul area, we were perceived locally as potential human and material resources that, it was hoped, would help promote goals and plans that the community had already identified and/or put in motion.

---

[2] Rambai is known in the Kaugel social arena as Aika Rambai and as Rambai Keruwa in the provincial, regional, national, and international arenas. He is thus distinguished from Yano Rambai (Rambai of the Yano clan) who is known in the other social arenas as Rambai Poponawa.

KTPPS program formation (1984–1987)

The following time line (based on S. Malone 1988:17–45) provides an overview of the kind of activities that Rambai, other Kaugel participants, and my wife and I engaged in during the KTPPS program's formative period from January 1984 through mid-1987.

Table 4.1. KTPPS program formation, 1984–1987

Dates	Events/comments
January–June 1984	Rambai meets with Dennis and Susan Malone to discuss possibilities of working together to promote literacy in the Umbu-Ungu language.
	Rambai and Dennis conduct a sociolinguistic survey of the Umbu-Ungu, Miyemu, and Imbo-Ungu dialects, meeting with church leaders, community school principals, and provincial government education personnel in the Western and Southern Highland Provinces.
	A "pre-fab" dormitory building, 16' × 40' is purchased for K750 from the Kaugel hydro-electric project near Kaupena in the SHP. The building is re-erected at Purare to serve as a literacy center.
July–December 1984	Rambai and Dennis participate in the National Literacy Course held by SIL at Ukarumpa to train Papua New Guineans in village literacy programs.
	Rambai, Dennis, and Susan attend a Literacy Program Planning Workshop at Ukarumpa.
January 1985	The first writers' workshop for the Umbu-Ungu dialect is conducted. Four books of stories are produced (25 copies each) and used to test orthography and written style.

	Rambai takes responsibility for writing reports to provincial education officers and church leaders.
February–March 1985	Rambai, Dennis, and Susan continue to meet, talk, and plan the strategies for the mother-tongue literacy program.
April–May 1985	The team begins plans for a vernacular preschool, based on models from the North Solomons Province VTPS program, the Barai (Oro Province) program, and a pilot-project headed by SIL linguist-educator, Mary Stringer in Enga Province.
	Rambai, Dennis, and Susan conduct an orthography conference in the Imbo-Ungu dialect at Ialibu in Southern Highlands Province.
June–October 1985	A literacy committee is established to oversee the local program. It includes three local government councilors, the son of an Aika "big-man" and a local business woman/community leader. The committee chooses the first teacher to be trained for the preschool.
	A second Umbu-Ungu orthography conference decides to represent word-medial pre-nasalized stops (/b/, /d/, /g/, /j/) as |mb|, |nd|, |ng|, |nj| to conform visually to English and Tok Pisin spelling.
November–December 1985	Plans progress for a bakery/bookstore at Tambul as an income-generating project for the literacy work.
	John Mane, a local man, begins work in the program as artist and "literature coordinator."

	Rambai, although apparently ambivalent toward his leadership role in the literacy project, continues to accept more responsibility for decision making for the program.
January–June 1986	John Mane takes charge of all literature production. Several writers are producing stories which a gifted high school student edits, then gives to John to illustrate. John then cuts the wax stencils and prints them using a manual rotary duplicating machine. The plan is to create a 4-level "graded" reading series. Thirty booklets are quickly completed.
	The KTPPS pilot project begins in February with 33 students. Mana Tapuye, trained to teach during the half-year experimental class last year, is the main instructor with help from Rambai and Dennis. The literacy committee has suggested a second teacher to work as an apprentice with Mana so that the program can expand to Tambul next year. They choose Timothy Anju, a young Kengelka man.
	The Kaugel NonFormal Education Association (KNFEA) is formed in March, with representatives from area churches and District government departments, the Giluwe Local Government Council, and several community members. This is an advisory board to the expanding project, with special oversight of the income-generating projects. [The local committee continues to oversee the Purare TPPS.]

	The Kaugel Bakery and Bookstore is built at Tambul funded primarily by a $5,000 gift from the US. By June, the monthly profits from the bakery, staffed by three local people, cover most of the expenses of the literacy program.
July–December 1986	The first KTPPS pilot class graduates in December, able to read stories from the first two levels of the developing Kaugel Reading Series.
	Rambai and Susan attend a UNESCO-sponsored literacy workshop in Indonesia as representatives for Papua New Guinea.
January–May 1987	The Giluwe Local Government Council agrees to let the KNFEA occupy three unused offices on their grounds beside the Council chambers. Two rooms have been created in the Council chambers for a sewing and weaving project and for a KTPPS class which Mana teaches while Anju teaches the Purare KTPPS class.
	The John Mane-led literature production results in 130 story-booklets divided into four levels.
	A third KTPPS class begins in February on the grounds of the Yombikul Community School.
June 1987	Dennis and Susan leave PNG for an eighteen-month study leave.

Upon our return to PNG in 1989, my wife and I were "loaned" by SIL to the National Department of Education to assist with the implementation of a national vernacular education program. From January of 1989 to the end of 1991, we were able to spend only brief periods of time with Rambai and the other members of the Kaugel community involved in the KTPPS program. Thus, for all intents and purposes, Rambai has been directing KNFEA activities on his own since July of 1987.

The KTPPS director

Rambai Keruwa's account of his role in the formative years of the KTPPS program reveals an early ambivalence toward the leadership responsibilities he had assumed. The way in which he dealt with those tensions are prefigured, to a certain extent, in the earlier years of his life and also reflect the high value Kaugel society places on active responses to challenges and opportunities, noted in the previous chapter.

Rambai's father had two wives. One wife had four sons while Rambai's mother had three daughters and Rambai, her only son. Thus, he had a heavier load of traditional boys' responsibilities (e.g., getting and chopping firewood). At twelve years of age, Rambai and his age mates were presented with a novel opportunity around 1962: to attend a school at Tambul operated by the expatriate missionaries of the Evangelical Bible Mission in which students could learn to read and write in their mother tongue and also learn English. Rambai's parents, especially his mother, objected to his desire to attend the mission school:

> At that time she didn't want to miss me. And if I had to go, then...she wasn't to have somebody to look after her. And she didn't want me to go. But I didn't listen to her. I ran away. [laughs] and I took side with the boys and walked to Tambul. (Rambai Keruwa, interview, July 29, 1995, T1B)

Rambai's insubordination at this point in his life is not uncommon, especially with respect to his mother's preference for him to stay with her. Rambai had left his mother's house at about age seven or eight to join his brothers, father, paternal uncles, and older male cousins in the Kikuwa *yulke* 'men's house' (*haus man* in Tok Pisin). In many Highland cultures, this change of sleeping quarters had the express purpose of weaning boys away from their maternal attachments and female influence (cf. Meggitt 1965; Merlan and Rumsey 1991). Thus, it is not uncommon to observe boys, from toddlers to teens, in open defiance of female authority.

Rambai remembers that the classes in the EBM school were conducted in Umbu-Ungu and featured Umbu-Ungu literacy. In the afternoons, the children were taught English, as was the government policy for approved schools of that time. However, it was the experience of learning to read first in his own language that, at least in part, would later persuade Rambai that a mother-tongue pre-primary education project would benefit his community when the opportunity to experiment with one arose in 1985.

It was from this EBM school that Karoma came to fetch Rambai for the sandallu youth initiation, as described in the excerpt at the beginning of chapter 1.

The *sandallu* experience features prominently in Rambai's account of his formative years. Lacey (1985) describes the Enga youth initiations *sangai* and *sandallu,* descriptions that closely resemble Rambai's narrative of his personal experience. Although an ethnographic presentation of *sandallu* is beyond the scope of this case study, I present the following discussion of Lacey's account of these rites, and suggest how his insights shed light on Rambai's subsequent history.

First, the end product of *sandallu* was the transformation of this group of young, unmarried male initiates "into mature men, brave warriors, productive husbands, efficient cultivators, and effective negotiators in exchange transactions. They also carried into the public arena knowledge essential for the survival and prosperity of their people" (1985:91).

According to Lacey, a chief vehicle for transmitting the values and ethos of the community is the oral history of the culture. Within the oral literature is a widespread genre that he calls "journey and transformation." Dreams were an essential medium of knowledge transmission during the initiation and were linked to

> elaborate and beautiful poems of praise [commemorating] how significant named plants were won at great costs by heroic ancestors two or three generations previously. The heroes, having heard of feasts and dances or witnessed the effects of famed plants upon their possessors, set out on long and difficult journeys for their territories of origin, along homeland valleys, through high forests, across streams, and over ridges. Their travels often took them through enemy territories where, their lives at risk, they would often move at night guided only by light from bamboo torches. Finally, when negotiations were successfully completed and a great price had been extracted for these sacred plants and their chants *(nemongo),* the heroes would journey homeward carrying the powerful new possessions to a safe hiding place deep in the forest, near their own house of seclusion. There the plants were guarded, cultivated, and given to initiates; the new owners and their clan membership grew in strength, wisdom, bravery, and wealth. (1985:91–93)

Rambai relates how he was made Karoma's understudy in looking after the sacred plants that his *lapali* 'clan fathers' had brought to the *sandallu* and had given into the care of the Kikuwa *haus man.* His understudy role was aborted due to his subsequent schooling, but he still considers the experience as meaningful to his role within the Aika and larger Kaugel community.

For Rambai, the myths and legends and oral history that portrayed journeys of heroic clansmen were realized personally not long after the *sandallu.* The EBM school at Tambul closed after the second year and Rambai, one of four boys chosen to continue their English education at an EBM boarding school in the Southern Highlands trekked nearly thirty-two kilometers by foot from Tambul to Kaupena (see figure 3.1). Later he would do grade 6 at the Swiss Mission School at Minj in the eastern end of the Western Highlands Province. After doing well on his grade 6 exam, Rambai went to high school (grades 7–10) at the Asia-Pacific Christian Mission center at Awaba in the Western Province. In 1970, he entered a two-year teacher education program at Goroka Teachers College in the Eastern Highlands Province. (See figure 1.1 for the location of Minj, Goroka, and Awaba in relation to Tambul.)

Rambai's subsequent teaching career began with an initial year at Minj,[29] followed by two years at Tambul during which time he married Nali. After Tambul, they went to Piambil for two years, then to the demonstration school at Dauli Teachers College, then to headmaster positions, first at a school near Mendi, then at Pangia, all in the Southern Highlands.

The theme of "journey and transformation" that Lacey connects to a wide and varied number of Papua New Guinea oral histories, including the *sandallu* related rituals, sheds light on the possible motivations that energized a Kaugel teenager to journey to places stranger and far more distant than those sung of in the *sandallu* chants of praise for past cultural heroes. Whether he did so to bring back "sacred plants" (knowledge or *mana*) to his people to ensure their growth, vigor, material and spiritual well-being, for personal reasons, or for some combination of both, was not revealed to me. But it seems reasonable to suggest that a song attributed by Lacey (1985:96) to an Enga student is applicable also to Rambai's experience:

When I have taken possession of them,
Of the great books of the lowlands,
I'll stride happily back
To Wabag, that land of mine,
Where the quiet stars go by,
It's my heritage, the land of my proud fathers.
There I'll make my home,
And there I'll settle.
There I'll settle,
Where the stars will pass over me,
With books firm in my hand.

---

[29]This was a case of Rambai's willingness to journey to distant places resulting in an almost literal return with the "sacred plants." A series of severe frosts that year had wiped out almost all of the sweet potato gardens at elevations above 6,000–7,000 feet above sea level. Minj is in the Wahgi Valley around 5,000 feet above sea level and Rambai was thus able to gather bags full of sweet potato vines to bring back to Tambul for his family to plant new gardens (Rambai Keruwa, interview, July 26, 1995, Tape 2A).

Working with the National Government

Following a change in government in 1980, Rambai was seconded by the Department of Education to the Department of Minerals and Energy. He moved his family to Port Moresby where he took up the job of office manager for its new Minister, Wiwa Korowi.[30] As part of his responsibilities, Rambai accompanied the Minister on visits around the country and overseas to Manila and Jakarta. When the Minister lost his seat in the 1982 elections, Rambai decided to return to the National Teaching Service.

In order to return to his own people after his national government experience, Rambai willingly took a lower position at Tambul Community School (as assistant headmaster and grade 2 teacher) than his training and administrative experience had earned him. He was serving in that position when my wife and I took up residence in the Tambul Basin in late 1982.

Rambai's experience at Tambul Community School during the 1983 school year seems to have predisposed him to be looking for alternative modes of education for the Kaugel children as well as for the adults.

Although Rambai was aware that the new expatriates—my wife, children, and I—had arrived and were setting up house in his clan area, it was not until he was told of our background that he began thinking seriously about our purpose.

Although the nature of cross-cultural enterprises—such as the early stages of the KTPPS program—does not allow the culture-crossing participants to anticipate each other's thoughts with any degree of confidence, Rambai's account of his frame of mind during those first three years accords closely with S. Malone's intuitions (cf. S Malone 1988:35). As Rambai recalled:

> First I thought, oh, maybe after two years I'll go back and be able to teach.... I didn't know...when we...made some study travel, places like Enga and [the] Provincial Education Office and all these.... I said, oh, these are all my trial things. I didn't have any serious thoughts on...this is what we are going to do [for] the next part of my life, so I need to take this serious. I was not in that kind of thinking. I thought...Susan and Dennis are going to do it, I'm just...going to be there to observe them and find out what *they're* going to do...and how they're going to get that information and relate it to here.

---

[30]Wiwa Korowi, now Sir Wiwa Korowi, Governor-General of PNG, was one of Rambai's classmates at the EBM school at Kaupena, and subsequently at Awaba High School and at Goroka Teachers College. His very close relationship with Imbo-Ungu classmates like Wiwa and Peter Pepul (see "Funding" below) earned him a position of extraordinary influence and experience at this stage in his life.

And...oh man, after 1987...when you left and the job was on my shoulders, I sometimes thought, oh, those trips were doing much good for me, and I should have...taken them seriously and made special notes, and all those things. (Rambai Keruwa, interview, July 26, 1995, Tape 2A)

Rambai's account of the process by which he came to "own" the KTPPS program also reveals his thoughts about the cross-cultural intersection of our lives that led to the initiation of the program and how that led him to make a mid-life change in direction in his career.

I resigned altogether [from the National Teaching Service]. My reason to do this one was that [the] two-year period [1984–1985] had given me...enough time to assess my future and my job opportunities and all these. I said, well, if...we have started here, we're almost [in the] middle of the program now. We have started lots of things. We have opened up a few places, classes, *tok ples* schools, and we have done a lot of materials and we have done a lot of awareness here around the valley. I thought, if I just drop it and go back to my old job, then my question was, who [would be] the next person to do [the work]. Also I asked myself, if I [tell] the Malones to get another person to help them, then, how much time do they have to do it? It takes two years to train [a new person]. [laughs] All this kind of thinking, and that's all right, sorry, *maski* [never mind], I'll just leave it. [So] I went and resigned from the Teaching Service.... (Rambai Keruwa, interview, July 29, 1995, Tape 4A)

I learned later that Rambai's decision was not made lightly. The possibilities of other concerns taking precedence over Rambai's commitment to the literacy work were very real, although my wife and I were unaware of them at the time. This is another of the vicissitudes of cross-cultural partnership that make a minimum level of trust among the participants an absolute prerequisite:

Yeah, well...our decision [to drop out of the National Teaching Service] did not stop any questions arising relating to [it]. But...those two years had given us enough time to get ourselves established in the village, like making our own house and gardening and be able to associate with problems in the village and, so we said okay, we don't know what happens next....

And then, to ourselves, we said, okay—this we did not discuss with you—but we said okay, we have two years [1986-1987] to decide [and when] that [is] about gone, probably, we'll try to look for something else. And that was kind of...hidden talking, but we did not bring it up ourselves to you.

And then, we had a house, our children were able to go to school. So we said, okay, maybe we will try to think of next three years and then everything probably we [will] try to change...we will reconsider....

But afterward, we saw [that] our job with people here was of more concern than our own family affairs. And although we foresaw [the]...problem of sending our kids to school and meeting their fees and to have them in good clothes to wear to school, this we had to...

But then we had in mind our...program as it seemed [to be] going to expand, and it needed us and...we have to make some kind of sacrifice and...stay here...as it's our people, it's [our] place. And, in fact, that program became ours now.... So, well, we said, okay...let's forget it, we'll wait, depend on the Lord with prayer and we'll work on it. I think it has been...that way and we, we're glad we did it...so far. (Rambai Keruwa, interview, July 29, 1995, Tape 4A)

By 1987 the KTPPS program had been established with Rambai as its recognized leader, however tentative his own perception of that leadership may have been. Rambai's "in-betweeness" had become indispensable to the continued success of the program as he negotiated the intersections of relationships between my wife and me as expatriates and the human and material resources to which we were links, and between the KTPPS program and the Kaugel community. Rambai himself notes that this kind of linking, of partnership, is quite conscious in the minds of many of his contemporaries.

And...a lot of people are having this kind of thinking...[that] anybody, whether whiteskin or blackskin or whoever, from another area of the country or whoever comes from other countries, *they* have something to offer, they have something to give us....

And we say we should sit down and analyze these things...what he or she has in mind to offer, these...we should take...and then we should sort them out at our level. This is...the best that I can use...that is too hard for me or...it needs more intake from outsiders so that we can best use [it] at the level that we can be able to make them use[ful]....

And they love [this kind of collaboration]...the people like it. And...that's why I think, somehow...we are fortunate. In fact, I...myself, I feel this way. (Rambai Keruwa, interview, July 29, 1995, Tape 4A)

Participatory decision making and the community

The relationship between Rambai and my wife and me as the expatriate literacy "advisers" to the KTPPS program, although critical to a clear understanding of the dynamics of the planning phase, cannot account for all the dynamics of the implementation and expansion of the KTPPS program. Significant community participation in decision-making was required from the beginning.

The first Aika and Korika-Kengelka area KTPPS class was managed initially by a local literacy committee formed in 1984. The committee was made up of the three Local Government Councilors from Aika and Korika-Kengelka clans, a local businesswoman, and three traditional community leaders, along with Rambai and my wife and me. The committee made decisions with regard to the site on which the literacy building would be erected, choice of teachers, enrollment of children, school fees, income-generating projects, and community awareness. After the formation of the Kaugel Non-Formal Education Association (KNFEA) in 1986, the first committee continued to function as the supervisory group for the Purare preschool, a small clinic, and an income-generating trade store—specializing in seeds, fertilizer, and garden tools—that had been established to support the local program.

The KNFEA served as a supervisory board for the larger program and its planned expansion throughout the Kaugel area. The membership of the KNFEA included one representative from each of the local church bodies (PNG Bible Church, Lutheran, Catholic, and Seventh Day Adventists), the Department of Health (through the Tambul Rural Health Center), the Department of Primary Industries (DPI), the Giluwe Local Government Council (GLGC), Department of Education (District School Inspector), Office of Provincial Affairs (Assistant District Manager), and a community-member-at-large (Rambai Keruwa, Kaugel Literacy Up-Date 2, April 1986).

With respect to the KTPPS program, the KNFEA acted as a sounding board for implementation problems. It also supervised the building and operation of the Tambul Bakery, the program's income-generation project, and acted as a liaison between the preschool communities and the government agencies that the KNFEA members represented (Health, Primary Industry, primary schools, District administration). In addition, the KTPPS director and teachers, members of the local Aika and Korika-Kengelka committee, and the KNFEA promoted the KTPPS program by sharing information in informal community meeting places, such as post-service gatherings on the grass outside churches on Sunday mornings, at community school workdays when large groups of parents are usually present, and in incidental meetings with leaders from around the Tambul Basin and Kaugel Valley.

By 1993, the KNFEA membership had been expanded and reconstituted to reflect better the community work that it supervised. The April 1993 meeting listed five pastors among its fourteen members. And in 1995, nine years after it had been formed, the KNFEA continued to function in its advisory role for the KTPPS.

The Program

Administration

Rambai, as director of the KNFEA, is responsible for planning the expansion and maintenance of the KTPPS program (in consultation with the KNFEA), training and supervising KTPPS teachers, maintaining community relations, raising funds (including supervising income-generating projects), securing the supplies and materials, and evaluating program components. The only responsibility formally delegated to another person is supervision of teachers in the Upper Kaugel, a task assigned to Daniel Lawa, former teacher at the Laiakam TPPS.

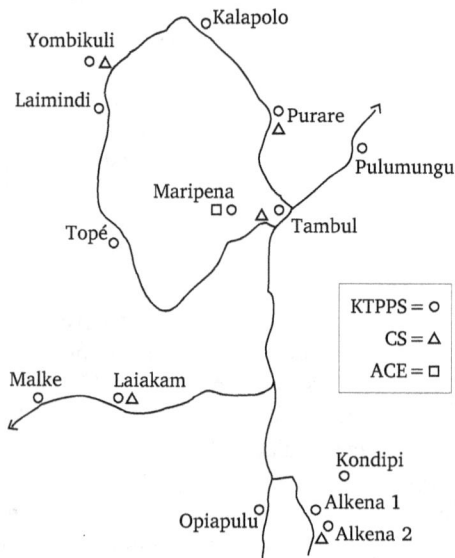

Figure 4.1. Kaugel area with KTPPS classes in relation to other schools.

Planning

An underlying motivation for this case study is the desire to learn how the program had been sustained over the previous ten years, and how and why it had grown from three classes in 1991 to fourteen in 1995. Rambai attributed the growing community interest in the program to its perceived success in preparing children for entry into grade 1 of the (English medium) formal school system.

> The children out of those three [preschools]—Purare, Yombikul, Laiakam—when they had gone to our community schools they were able to read—some, at least—in *tok ples*....That kind of helped. The parents of the other kids, they got jealous of this: "Oh, these children are able to read before they go to the community school." And they said, "What can we do about this?" I'm sure they had talked about this in their own circles and they had decided to open *their* children's preschool.... (Rambai Keruwa, interview, July 29, 1995, T4.18)

The result was constant pressure on Rambai and the KNFEA from communities around the Umbu-Ungu speaking area to start new classes. Rambai developed a set of three criteria which he presented to prospective preschool communities: (1) build a suitable classroom, (2) collect the KTPPS annual school fee, and (3) choose a suitable teacher to be trained (Rambai Keruwa, personal communication, T4.19). The school fee criterion served as Rambai's and the KNFEA's hedge against overextending themselves, as Kaugel people rarely contribute their limited cash resources to programs that have not yet proven themselves locally. Therefore, the KNFEA could use the lack of school fee collection to put off an anxious community leader lobbying for immediate action but who had not yet motivated people to support the project. When other circumstances or new funding put the KNFEA into a stronger position, the prepayment of school fees criterion was simply put aside—a practice that proved ill-advised when one funding source suddenly ceased and the parents had not developed a sense of financial responsibility for the *pri skul* program (see the discussion on the impact of the Village Services subsidies on the KTPPS, below).

Documented information about the KTPPS planning process was difficult to locate. Two sources were the regular (two or three times a year) "Kaugel Updates," written by Rambai and distributed to interested parties such as the WHP Education Office, SIL literacy office, churches, and individuals, and the minutes from KNFEA meetings. Rambai's personal letters to my wife and me were another source. From them can be constructed the following chronology of plans for KTPPS expansion and their outcomes.

Table 4.2. Plans and outcomes for KTPPS expansion

Year	Plan	Outcome
1987	Three Kaugel preschools are established: the pilot project at Purare and two new schools at Yombikul and Tambul.	The Purare and Yombikul schools operated successfully until the aftermath of the national elections in 1988 in which the government offices at Tambul were burned down. The Tambul PS closed in June (before the trouble) due to lack of attendance and teacher absenteeism. The tension in the area following the election violence caused low attendance at both Purare and Yombikul preschools.
1988	Purare and Yombikul preschools continue with a new preschool opening at Malke (the Yano people, the largest Kaugel clan).	The Purare and Yombikul preschools ran well, but the Malke preschool did not open because the community had not fulfilled the start-up criteria.
1989	Apparently, the plan for 1988 continued, the only change being the decision to locate the Yano preschool at Laiakam.	A large tribal war that began in November involving most of the clans from the Upper Kaugel administrative subdistrict against the clans of the Lower Kaugel subdistrict resulted in low attendance at Purare and Yombikul. As can be deduced from reports, the Laiakam preschool started up with Daniel Lawa, apparently after a truce was established in the tribal war.
1990	After further training at a national literacy trainers workshop in Enga Province, Daniel Lawa and Timothy Anzu, two experienced teachers, will help train a teacher for the preschool at Malke.	Due to the continuing tribal war, the Malke preschool did not start, and the enrollments at Yombikul and Purare were further reduced.

Year		
1991	Continue to run the Purare, Yombikul and Laiakam preschools and add Malke preschool.	All four preschools [Yombikul, Purare, Laiakam, Malke] started, each with enrollments around thirty students. "We are proud to report that for the first time for the Kaugel literacy program, all [4] of its Tok Ples Preparatory classes finished up with very good attendance all through the year."
1992	Continue the four preschools from 1991 and add four new ones: Pulumung (Kanimbe clan) and Yawere (Yapo and Yana clans) as well as Kondipi (in Lower Kaugel) and at Tambul (this time a Tok Pisin class).	All eight schools operated successfully throughout the year and special closing ceremonies were held at each one.
1993	After the KNFEA suggests adding 8 new schools (to the 8 already existing), Rambai convinces them to reduce the number to thirteen preschools [total] with fourteen teachers, one teacher, Daniel Lawa, assisting Rambai full-time with supervision. New classes to begin at Pakapena (Yano clan), Opiapul, and Kalapolo, and two at Alkena in the Lower Kaugel. All necessary materials ready by March.	Three village congregations who had lent church buildings for preschool use rescinded their offers. Two of these preschools were replaced with "bush" material buildings and classes resumed, each with new teachers who had been trained by Daniel Lawa. Eight of the fourteen preschools qualified for teacher salary subsidy from the new Village Services Department grant: [Laiakam], Malke, Tambul, Yombikul, Purare, Kalapolo, Pulumungu, and Kondipi. The others—Alkena, Opiapul,
		Yawere, Tope, Laimindi, Kulumindi—will need to meet certain criteria first.
1994	Continue with the fourteen preschools.	School closing ceremonies were held for fourteen preschools and 332 children.

This rapid expansion did not occur without its problems, mostly in the area of finances. The bakery—the primary income-generating project for the KNFEA programs—was known from the beginning to be a source of limited funds only. The gross income from the sale of bread rolls, tea, and coffee was used to pay two or three bakery workers approximately US$40 per month each and to purchase baking ingredients, tea, coffee, sugar, firewood, and bottled gas, with the remainder used to subsidize preschool teachers' salaries. School fees were to provide additional income for teacher salaries. When the bakery was required to support only three pre-school classes, the system worked well. However, when the program began expanding in 1992, the bakery could no longer, of itself, provide full subsidies (US$40) for all the teachers every month. (Rambai's efforts to secure additional funding are described below; see table 4.4.)

Table 4.3 lists the KTPPS classes and their respective enrollments at the time field research for this study was begun in July, 1995.

Table 4.3. KTPPS Enrollment and teaching staff, 1995

No.	School*	Teacher#	Male	Female	Total
1	Purare	Sai Kop	9	16	25
2	Kalapolo	Kiap Kiwa	11	9	20
3	Yombikul	Palame Aina	5	18	23
4	Tope	Albert Yelupa	11	9	20
5	Malke	Bob Golipu	15	7	22
6	Yano	Winisi Kapi	13	12	25
7	Yano	Daniel Lawa	3	14	17
8	Opiapul	Pelle Suri	17	7	24
9	Pulumungu	Ten Pena	11	15	26
10	Kondipi	Philip Oke	11	9	20
11	Alkena	Peter Paraka	23	13	36
12	Alkena	Tosep Wama	16	20	36
13	Maripena	Tenis Kiap	11	9	20
14	Tambul	Steven Kot	8	12	20
Total			164	170	334

*Twelve of the schools use Umbu-Ungu, two schools (Maripena and Tambul) use Tok Pisin.[31]

#Twelve of the teachers are male, two (Pelle Suri and Tenis Kiap) are female.

The figures in table 4.3 reflect the number of children enrolled in the program at the beginning of 1995, not the number that completed the year's course. For example, between August and December (my field work period), Purare preschool attendance ranged from a high of fifteen to a low of four, with an average daily attendance of ten for the nine days I observed the class. The balanced number of male and female students enrolled in the program has been maintained and contrasts with the early practice in Highland communities of sending primarily boys to school.[32]

The schools at Kalapolo and Opiapul had closed already when I arrived, the former because of the cessation of Village Services Department teacher subsidies (see below) and the latter due to interclan tensions arising from the death of a grade 6 teacher at Laiakam. The school at Yombikul had closed for the year when all age-eligible pre-primary children were moved instead into a newly formed grade 1 class of Yombikul Community School.

After my wife and I left for study leave in 1987, Rambai planned and implemented the KTPPS operations and expansion after the indigenous custom. He met with the KNFEA members, formally and informally, and with pertinent members of the community, as needed, to discuss the material and human resources needed for beginning a new preschool at a new location. He did not compose a formal, written plan, but kept those who needed and wanted to know informed through his updates, reports, and personal communication.

In 1992, four new preschools were added to the four operating in 1991, and in 1993, five more were added (reduced from the original eight suggested by the KNFEA). A discussion of the government initiative that triggered this change in strategy is necessary for a clear understanding of an administrative decision that resulted in much ill-feeling among the KTPPS teachers, and which threatened the survival of the KTPPS program itself. If nothing else, it is a cautionary tale for bureaucrats hatching large-scale plans with little accountability for their effects on the daily lives of people at the local level.

---

[31]Both of the Tok Pisin classes are located on "stations"—Tambul, the District government center, and Maripena, the PNG Bible Church district headquarters and regional Bible School—where many staff and students are from outside the Umbu-Ungu-speaking area. Children at these schools speak primarily Tok Pisin. That Rambai and the KNFEA felt the need to include two schools in which Umbu-Ungu was *not* the medium of instruction suggests that their perception of the purpose of the school is to prepare children for entry into formal English education at least as much as to prevent language and culture shift. This question is further discussed in chapter 5.

[32]In my previous experience as headmaster at a primary school in neighboring Enga Province in 1968 and 1969, a class of thirty grade 5 students, for example, included only five girls.

In 1992, the government-created the National Department of Village Services and Provincial Affairs, with a purpose to:

1. Empower our communities and rekindle their talents through the direct provision of resources, training, and information.

2. Harness the crucial role of our elders to work with and guide our young.

3. Ensure co-operation and partnership between government and community in the delivery of services.

4. Give the people a voice and a sense of responsibility and ensure participation by all in the process of development.

5. Support extensive local economic development and productivity through access to credit, training, and information. (Department of Provincial Affairs and Village Services 1995a:3)

According to policy documents, the Village Services Division saw itself taking a major role in establishing and supporting the community-based elementary-level classes that were to be initiated under the planned Education Amendment Act (approved by Cabinet in 1993, see chapter 3). According to the Department,

One way of providing this [educational] service is making it the responsibility of the Department of Education and hoping it will bear the cost. However, it will probably be more effective to allow this aspect of education to remain informal and develop to meet the differing needs across the nation.

Village Services has taken the important initiative of training, paying allowance, and providing materials for Tokples Literacy Education. This must remain a top priority and funds must be allocated to facilitate the program. (Department of Provincial Affairs and Village Services 1995b:28)

The training described in the excerpt above did not happen. The Division provided some materials for community production of reading materials (wax stencils, paper, ink, silkscreen duplicators) and most significantly, did provide literacy programs with K400 a year per teacher to subsidize salaries.

The earliest indication of Rambai's knowledge of the Village Services' plan to subsidize teachers' salaries is early in 1993 (Rambai Keruwa, personal communication, February 24, 1993). At that point, with KNFEA approval, he had submitted the names of seven teachers and was planning to start five new classes. The rationale for that initiative was that the KNFEA's income from the Tambul Bakery and school fees, together with the government subsidies, would be adequate for covering the expenses, including paying teacher salaries, in the expanded program. That the Village Services subsidy scheme did not fulfill the expectations that it raised among grassroots programs nationwide is a gross understatement. After a year and three months, Village Services stopped the subsidies, leaving the mother-tongue programs to fend for themselves. The ramifications of the failed Village Services subsidies for the KTPPS included communities even less inclined than before to provide financial support in the way of school fees, teachers left with little or no pay, erosion of the teachers' commitment to their work, and additional pressure on Rambai to obtain outside funding.

Funding

The KTPPS program has been sustained through diverse funding sources. Table 4.4 presents an overview of actual and potential sources, Rambai's attempts to access them, and the outcomes of those attempts.

Table 4.4. Funding sources, attempts, and outcomes, 1986–1995

Origin	Source	Attempt	Outcome
Local	Bakery	Construct bakery with funds contributed by overseas donors affiliated with SIL literacy team.	Bakery has operated continuously since it opened in April 1986. Income from sale of bread rolls and beverages that is left after operating expenses subsidizes KTPPS teachers.
	School fees	Assess a K3 school fee for all preschools (every year since 1987). The fee was increased to K5 in 1995.	Payment of school fees is erratic, at best, and an on-going source of frustration for KTPPS director and teachers (no doubt, parents and children, too).*

	Giluwe Local Government Council (GLGC)	Use council offices and chambers, request help with specific projects, encouraged to apply for portion of 1994 Village Service Division block grant to LGCs.	In 1987, GLGC donated three unused offices and portions of the council chambers for KNFEA use (offer rescinded in 1995). GLGC provided K400 in 1991 for bakery maintenance. The application for funds from the Village Services grant to GLGC, initially okayed for K6,000 was canceled due to misinformation from a local politician.
Provincial	WHP Education Division	Apply for classroom materials.	WHP NonFormal Education Office and Provincial Literacy Coordinator provided chalkboards, chalk, notebooks, pencils, pens, when available.
	Rotary Club	Encouraged to apply for assistance to erect a Literacy Center at Tambul beside the bakery.	Application was submitted, but no response was received, despite verbal assurances by RC president.
National	Literacy and Awareness Secretariat	Apply for provincial grant for training and materials production every year beginning in 1990.	LAS provided annual grants varying from K750 to K2,000, to be used only for literacy materials and training.

	Village Services Department	Apply for teacher subsidies for 7 KTPPS teachers.	Village Services Division provided monthly teacher salary subsidies for all of 1993 and first term of 1994. Subsidies suddenly ceased when Village Services dropped the scheme.
International	SIL-administered grants	Apply to SIL for grants to print the Kaugel Reading Series (KRS).	In 1987, SIL allocated funds from CIDA and AIDA grants (which pay 70 percent of cost) for producing the books.
	New Zealand High Commission	Apply for grant to fund wool weaving project in 1991.	No response to the application, despite repeated follow-up.
	SIL literacy team	Receive monthly "salary."	The amount of funds needed for personal living expenses was agreed upon between the Malones and Rambai and transferred from Malones' account to Rambai's each month from 1984 to 1996. (As of 1997, these funds go directly to Rambai from his supporters in US).
	SIL Literacy Revolving Fund	Apply for funds to reprint KRS.	Funding for reprints was provided in 1990 and 1993.

Overseas churches	Inform US supporters directly (through correspondence, and indirectly through Malones) of the program's specific needs.	U.S. churches and individuals were providing funds for special KTPPS projects (e.g., US$700 in 1992 to connect bakery to electric power) and to purchase schools supplies.

*A KTPPS teacher, observes how the school fees cause student attrition: The children like school and come, but their parents do not pay the school fee. The teacher tells the children to ask their parents to give the teacher the school fee. The parents say no or ignore the child. After two or three cycles of this, the child becomes too embarrassed or ashamed to return to class and stays away (Sai Kop, interview, Aug 10, 1995, T14A.6).

The problem of collecting school fees from parents was voiced repeatedly by Rambai and the KTPPS teachers. A government "free education" scheme that had caused problems in 1988 was reinstituted in 1994, with the same impact on the KTPPS program's ability to collect school fees.

> Each year...we've been able to collect some part of the school fees from the parents. Last year [1994], there wasn't anything. Nothing at all.... The reason...being [the] government now...is telling people this is free school now.... Free. There's no fee, nationwide.... And they [the parents] said, why should we pay for our *tok ples skul* when other...institutions are going to school free? So that was a big hit. (Rambai Keruwa, interview, July 29, 1995, T5.13)

In the end, despite the efforts made by the director and members of the KNFEA committee to create a sense of community responsibility for the preschools, many parents continued to view the effort as related somehow to the government and were unwilling or unable to provide the financial and other support the program needed. Rambai was left to try to find the resources to keep the program going. His accounts of his numerous attempts to secure much needed finances, especially after the sudden collapse of the Village Services subsidies in 1994, can be appreciated in light of his sense of a personal calling to serve his people that first materialized during his childhood *sandallu* initiation.

Village Services grant to GLGC

In 1994, the Giluwe Local Government Council, along with LGCs around the nation, received a large grant of money (about US$375,000) from the

Village Services Department to be distributed around the Tambul District for worthy projects, one of which was deemed to be the KTPPS program.

Rambai prepared a proposal which he went over, point by point, with the council president. The evaluation procedure required the president to take the proposal to the Council Finance Committee for approval.

> A couple days later he said, we considered your project worthwhile and the committee decided to allocate...nine thousand kina. We thought that was a good figure [but] after talking for awhile we...came to six thousand kina. And I said, Oh, that's still a big [amount of] money. We never had anything like this...! (Rambai Keruwa, interview, July 29, 1995, T5.7)

After accepting an invitation to address the entire GLGC in session and receiving widespread verbal support for his proposal, Rambai felt confident that the loss of the Village Services subsidies would be ameliorated by the K6,000 which would enable him to provide "back pay" to the long-suffering KTPPS teachers (Rambai Keruwa, personal communication, T5.7).

However, at the final vote on allocations, the Finance Committee met again, this time with the member of Parliament for Tambul-Nebilyer, an influential voice in the area. According to Rambai,

> I heard he got up and said, "No, [the] Kaugel NonFormal Education Association [allocation] should be pulled out and put into other projects because we [i.e., members of Parliament] directly made money available for...nonformal activities at the provincial level through [the] Provincial Education Office." And they quickly got together—that committee—they quickly got together and pulled that six thousand kina [out] which they [had] put for us and put it into other projects. (Rambai Keruwa, interview, July 29, 1995, T5.9)

Participating in SIL's Vernacular Elementary Education Survey at the time (SIL, 1994), Rambai was unable to attend that particular meeting. Had he been there, he could have corrected the member's misunderstanding regarding the funding. Needless to say, on his return to Tambul, the news came as a depressing jolt.

> When I came back after my provincial trip on [the] literacy survey, I came back and then the president said, "This is what happened.... They told us you [are] supposed to get some money out there [i.e., NonFormal Education Office], and what we allocated has been pulled out and put to other projects." And I was *disappointed....* (Rambai Keruwa, interview, July 29, 1995, T5.9)

An abject exhalation accompanied that final word—disappointed—as if he had just relived a blow to the solar plexus of his soul. His subsequent trip to the provincial NonFormal Education (NFE) Office revealed what

Rambai already suspected: no funds had been allocated by Parliament to mother-tongue literacy projects through the NFE officer. Thus, in the space of eight months, the KNFEA "lost" K2,240 in teachers' subsidies from Village Services and the K6,000 grant from the GLGC.

The proposals to the Mount Hagen Rotary Club and the New Zealand High Commission are stories in themselves. Each required considerable time and effort and travel. Again, neither proved productive.

The KTPPS program has been sustained since 1987 by a patchwork of available resources, few of which could be considered secure over the long term. Although the unsettled nature of funding was an obvious source of discontent among the teachers, most of them have continued on the job, although perhaps not with the same enthusiasm as they had when on regular salaries (see chapter 6). Still, it is clear that something other than a steady source of income is responsible for the sustainability of the KTPPS.

Training and supervision

Local training

Early training of KTPPS teachers took an apprenticeship approach in which trainees learned by observing and imitating:

> You remember those three classes...?[33] We did not actually have a teacher training, because there were not many to [train]. And...for example, the Kalapolo school here [in 1993], just a few kilometers from Purare, when I wanted to have a teacher trained I just asked him to...walk down and observe, sit down with Sai, and see how he teaches, and then [he] would go back and teach. (Rambai Keruwa, interview, July 29, 1995, T4.20)

As the program expanded, however, not all the teachers were within walking distance of an existing preschool, and a more formal training plan was needed. Once a decision was made regarding the number and placement of new preschools to add to the program each year, Rambai enlisted experienced teachers to help him train the new ones. Along with demonstrations of how the mother-tongue literacy materials are used, the veteran teachers shared examples from their experiences.

---

[33]Rambai refers here to the 1986 Purare pilot project class and the Yombikul and Tambul classes, both established in 1987. During the experimental half-year class in 1985, Mana Tapuye observed Rambai teaching the children and took his turn as he felt comfortable. During the pilot year, Mana did the bulk of the teaching with Rambai supervising and Timothy Anzu observing and helping as needed. In 1987, both Mana (Tambul) and Anzu (Purare) helped train Palame before he started the preschool at Yombikul.

Rambai credits this procedure of enlisting experienced teachers to train new teachers informally, in a kind of pedagogical apprenticeship, for making possible the rapid spread of the KTPPS program throughout the Kaugel Valley from 1992 onward.

Provincial and national training

National and provincial mother-tongue education training courses began in earnest during the 1990 International Literacy Year and continued afterward. In Western Highlands Province, training was usually held during the school holidays (December and January) in or around Mount Hagen.

Since most "new" teachers had already had from six to eight months of teaching experience, they came to the training courses with a clear idea of what the classroom was like. "Whereas William [Aua, the Western Highlands Provincial NFE officer] would actually get completely new people...ours were somebody who already knew something about *tok ples* schools" (Rambai Keruwa, interview, July 29, 1995, T4.21). In addition, Rambai would usually bring one of the veteran KTPPS teachers as a staff assistant in order to get formal teacher training experience.

In 1994, Rambai learned of a series of training courses (the Supervisors' Tokples Education Program or STEP) being run under the auspices of SIL. The program was established to train experienced mother-tongue educators to administer local "systems" of village-level pre-primary or adult mother-tongue education programs. Each STEP course consisted of five one-month training modules interspersed with four to six months of supervised village assignments (SIL 1993). Rambai indicated that when he learned about the course, he immediately saw the possibility of using it to extend the KTPPS into the Lower Kaugel area which is too distant for him or any other Upper Kaugel supervisor to administer. Through a local PNG Bible Church pastor, Rambai identified two young men from Lower Kaugel communities who possessed the educational requirements (grade 10-level English equivalence) to attend the course. He himself accepted a position on the STEP course staff and served as trainer/mentor for the Kaugel participants. This opportunity came with a price as it contributed to the demands upon Rambai's time and energies and to the KTPPS teachers' complaints that they are inadequately supervised and supported (see chapter 6).

KTPPS teachers

Typical of most KTPPS teachers, Doa [not his real name] lives in a thatched-roof house from which he makes the morning walk to his KTPPS classroom. The classroom keys are in the pocket of his well-worn imitation-leather jacket that wards off the early morning chill. His four-year-old son may walk with him or, by other spousal plans, may accompany his mother to one of the family gardens in the forest a thousand feet or so above the Basin. Relations between husband and wife are probably strained these days in 1995 because the devaluation of the national currency, rising inflation, and the financial problems within the KTPPS have conspired to reduce substantially their economic resources.

The thought that sums up Doa's feelings—which was repeated variously by other KTPPS teachers—is this: *Aku olio we* **sop** *liamili ulu ilinga aema* **tumas komplen** *mele telemolo. Akulinga mindi olio pali umbuni ili ambololemolo* 'It's just because of our desire to get physical necessities [lit., soap] that we complain a lot. That is the sole source of our troubles' (T14A).

> Thus, Doa arrives at the...classroom, unlocks the door, looks at the photocopied sheets from the KTPPS teacher's guide on which are sketched the lessons for the week, finds the books from the Kaugel Reading Series that are suggested for the day (usually because they relate to the weekly cultural theme). While he searches the stacks of reading books, piled on a narrow counter along the north wall, his son searches the chalk tray at the front of the room for the nubs that his father allows him to use to decorate his face. Finding the two books suggested for the day, [Doa] returns to the teacher's notes to remind himself of the day's keyword and the activities that will be used with it. Then he goes outside, picks up a stone, and "rings" the school bell—a long ago discarded 30 lb. gas cylinder, narrow, shaped like a bomb. In the Basin, sound travels well. Anywhere from four to fifteen children will be lining up at the doorway in a matter of minutes. (Field notes 1.29)

Doa, a grade 6 school-leaver, husband and father, was selected to be teacher in 1991 by the leaders of the local church, attesting to his reputation for honesty and responsibility in the community. His preparation consisted of a two-week literacy and awareness training workshop sponsored by the Western Highlands Provincial government and a subsequent course at Tambul for KTPPS teachers supervised by Rambai Keruwa. Doa's classroom—in terms of curriculum and instruction—features in the discussion of problems and potential for the KTPPS in chapter 6.

In the sketch above, Doa represents a group of fourteen KTPPS teachers who range in age from their mid-twenties to late forties, with anywhere from a grade 6 to a grade 10 education in the formal English-language education system. Since their specific training for the KTPPS program is minimal by most teacher education standards, their longer experience as students influences their understanding of their role in the classroom, having observed teachers at work from six to ten years (observation of adult models being one of the traditional Kaugel learning styles; cf. chapter 3, "Traditional Education").

Teacher attitudes toward KTPPS director

Although Rambai's central role in establishing the program is acknowledged within the community and also at provincial level, I learned that his role as administrator was not without its critics, especially among the teachers themselves. Their complaints fall into two general groupings: relating to pay and relating to supervision.

Teacher pay (or rather, lack of it) was an issue in every teacher interview, whether individual or group, whether Rambai was present or not. Teachers' reactions to not receiving the set pay (K20 per fortnight) were expressed as anger, frustration, malaise in the classroom, family strife, and anxiety. Several of the teachers speculated that the source of the problem of low pay could be traced to Rambai's decision to expand the KTPPS program, thus diluting the bakery resources. That the real culprit is the Village Services' failed subsidy scheme, that had encouraged Rambai and other *tok ples pri skul* directors around the country to expand their programs by promising to subsidize teacher salaries at K400 a year, seems clear enough. It offers little solace to the teachers, however. Neither does pointing a finger at the Giluwe Local Government Council for rescinding their promise of K6,000. The teachers reply that if Rambai had been in the Tambul area doing his job instead of off on the SIL survey he could have been at the GLGC meeting and prevented the mistake.

Thus, Rambai's extensive travel and time away from the language area was a repeated complaint of the teachers. Both from the standpoint of their pay and that of their supervision, the teachers resent Rambai's traveling out of the area. Rambai's outside responsibilities are considerable, a tacit recognition of his high reputation as a literacy educator in the province and nation. As Highlands representative to the National Literacy and Awareness Council, he spends a week in Port Moresby twice a year for council meetings, and another two weeks traveling to the five Highland provincial capitals to get updates from literacy officers for his report to the NLAC. As Highlands representative to the Bible Translation Association (BTA) board, Rambai spends another week or two in meetings and consultations at Ukarumpa in the Eastern Highlands. Assisting SIL in the Vernacular Elementary Education (VEE) survey and with the preparation of a large proposal by SIL to an international donor, had taken another month. Finally, he was further absent for 2–3 months each year helping with the SIL Supervisors' Tokples Education Program (STEP). When absent from the area, Rambai has relied on other community leaders to look after the bakery receipts and distribution of pay to teachers.

The point here is that to a certain extent, Rambai is overextended and absent for too many days of the year to be a truly effective administrator. What the teachers apparently have not understood is the degree to which Rambai's travels have allowed him to develop the networks, contacts, and knowledge that keeps him in touch with funding opportunities and have provided the program with income to supplement the dwindling bakery receipts.

The teachers' complaints appear to be justified and, for a few of them, their teaching reflects an attitude of indifference. But they continue to teach. Rambai expresses hope that the education reform will resolve many of these problems by incorporating the *tok ples pri skuls* into the elementary level of the formal system (i.e., the government will pay the teachers).

In the meantime, fences needed to be mended. At the end of the school term, when community schools have their public festive closings for the year, Rambai hosted a special KTPPS teachers' get-together, inviting them to bring their spouses and providing the food and a special end-of-the-year monetary gift for each teacher in addition to their fortnightly pay. At the gathering, he commended the teachers for their perseverance and expressed his firm conviction that their suffering on behalf of the children will be for the long-range good of the community and the children. I had the strong feeling that the teachers would be back in their classrooms in 1996.

Buildings and classroom facilities

The range of venues for KTPPS programs is surprisingly wide. No "typical" facility was found. Classrooms constructed of primarily "bush" materials (i.e., materials traditionally available) can be found at some KTPPS sites (as at Pulumungu and Laiakam) while more permanent Western-style classrooms (usually already existing) were observed at others. Classrooms at Maripena and Alkena, for example, have concrete-slab floors with some type of weatherboard exterior walls and corrugated iron roofs.

The classroom at Purare (the first of the TPPS classrooms) is a relocated pre-fabricated dormitory that was originally used as a workers' dormitory during construction of the Kaugel Hydroelectric Project in the Southern Highlands Province. Sitting atop a gum tree-covered knoll beside the Basin Road at Purare, the building is painted white with its plywood doors and windows (actually shutters) painted red. To ward off the chill of the Basin's frequent cold wet mornings, a wood-burning, used-petrol-drum stove had been installed, its stove-pipe chimney protruding about four feet above the corrugated iron roof. On frosty mornings, with a plume of smoke, flattened out behind the chimney by the cold, heavy air, the building resembles a "little engine that could," inert, waiting....

All of the classrooms, including the most rustic "bush" buildings, include a large chalkboard, chalk, some large size paper (often used computer paper) used for copying the children's experience stories for display around the classroom, and, occasionally, various cultural artifacts that the children have brought or made. All the classrooms also have a set of the Kaugel Reading Series. Thus, if no other materials are available, the KTPPS has stories for reading and chalkboards and chalk for writing. As will be seen in the discussion of literacy materials below, these basics have contributed significantly to the program's sustainability.

Materials and instructional media

The Kaugel reading series

The primacy attached to the development of native-authored literature is well documented by S. Malone (1988, especially pp. 33, 34–35, and 37). Table 4.1 at the beginning of this chapter sketches the development of what became a series of seventeen 40- to 50-page books with a total of ninety-six stories (see appendix B for facsimiles from each of the four levels and a complete list of story titles and authors).

The original stories were written by Kaugel writers (see "Writers, editors"), literate in English or Tok Pisin, who were quickly able to transfer their reading and writing skills back into their own language. Their stories were minimally constrained, the only limitations being the number and length of sentences per page. The lowest level stories were to be based on an indigenous theme, with four or five pages and one sentence and one picture per page; second level books had four to six pages with one or two sentences per page; third level had five to eight pages with two to three sentences per page; and the fourth level stories could have seven or more pages with four or more sentences per page. The stories were selected or rejected through a review process; those that were accepted were assigned to their appropriate level and edited by a gifted grade 10 student at the local high school,[34] using an editing check-list to ensure local relevance and natural language. The edited stories were then given to the KTPPS literature development coordinator, John Mane, who put the stories onto wax stencils, illustrated them, duplicated them (fifty copies per story)—using a hand-operated rotary

---

[34]Luke Siminji, the editor, received the second highest score in the Western Highlands Province on his grade 6 exam. He subsequently graduated from the School of Law at the University of Papua New Guinea in 1994.

duplicating machine—then collated and stapled them. By the time the KTPPS pilot class began at Purare village in 1986, approximately 130 of these story-booklets had been produced.

With the prospects of expanding the program after 1986, funds were sought for the development of a more durable version of the booklets. The 130 or so stories were further evaluated and revised with a final selection of ninety-six stories divided among seventeen books.

A grant from the Canadian International Development Agency (CIDA) and the Alberta Agency for International Development (AAID) was used to print 250 copies each of the seventeen books in 1987 at the SIL printing department at Ukarumpa. Four books with a total of thirty stories comprise the first (red) level; five books with a total of twenty-seven stories are in the second (blue) level; five books with twenty-five stories are in the third (yellow) level; and three books with fourteen stories are in the fourth (green) level. According the KTPPS *Buk Bilong Tisa* 'Teacher's Book', only stories from the first seven books are actually designated for reading lessons (for the children to read themselves). However, teachers are told that all the stories in the series are for them to read *to* the children, selected according to a story's relevance to the weekly cultural theme (see "Curriculum and Instruction" below). The KNFEA reprinted the first two levels (red and blue) in 1990 and again in 1993, with assistance from SIL's Literacy Revolving Fund.

Writers, editors

The first writers workshop, held in January, 1985, helped identify the most gifted and productive writers in the community at that time. By the end of 1986, four writers had produced the bulk of the reading series:

Table 4.5. Authorship of the Kaugel Reading Series

Writer	Level 1	Level 2	Level 3	Level 4	Total
Children*	4	0	1	0	5
Mana Tapuye, teacher	8	4	8	9	29
Mutenke Kristen, church worker	12	6	5	0	23
John Mane, production coordinator	5	7	0	0	12
Rambai Keruwa, director	1	7	4	3	15
Jack Algo, high school student	0	1	0	0	1
Tendepo Meke, community member	0	1	0	0	1
John Nia, medical student	0	1	2	0	3
George P. Miki, community school teacher	0	0	2	0	2
Garu Puli, NT co-translator	0	0	1	1	2
Luke S. Diwi, high school student	0	0	1	1	2
Timothy Anzu, teacher	0	0	1	0	1
Total	30	27	25	14	96

* Refers to children's experience stories, written by teachers and incorporated into the reading series

Curriculum and instruction

The KTPPS curriculum is developed around a set of cultural themes, generated originally at a writers workshop, with a different theme for each week of the school year (e.g., *kongi* 'pig', *langi koelemolo* 'we steam-cook food', *maketena pulimulu* 'we go to market', etc.). The weekly cultural theme is used as the topic for the language experience activity, the shared reading, and the story writing that are part of the "Story Time" track.

The KTPPS curriculum, as observed during visits to the Purare, Pulumungu, and Maripena schools, focused almost exclusively on the children's literacy acquisition. The "multi-strategy method," developed by Mary Stringer (Stringer and Faraclas 1987), includes two tracks of four lessons each, each track approximately one hour long, separated by a recess. As reconstructed from the lessons I observed during my data collection (which is not necessarily the curriculum according to the *Teacher's*

Guide),[35] the daily lessons can be divided into eight segments, as shown in table 4.6.

Table 4.6. Kaugel literacy lessons, general daily pattern

Story time [before recess]	Word time [after recess]
Children's experience story. (15–20 minutes) This is based on the cultural theme for the week (e.g., marsupial, house, lizards, etc.). The class as a whole has a brief experience (e.g., goes out to look at a nearby house or pig or pandanus tree). This leads to a discussion and a story, generated by the children and written on the chalkboard by the teacher. The story is then read to the children as a group and with some individually.	Keyword lesson. (15 minutes) A keyword (e.g., *lapa* 'father') that highlights the syllable and sound in focus (but which may be only coincidentally related to the weekly theme) is broken down to its component syllables then built back up into the word: lapa la pa la a a la la pa lapa
Listening story. (10–15 minutes) The teacher reads a story from the Kaugel Reading Series (KRS) to the children, showing them the illustrations as he reads. Also includes silent reading time.	**Listening to words.** (15 minutes) The children engage in various activities that demonstrate the correspondence between symbol and sound.
Reading story. (15 minutes) The teacher reads a story from one of the first six KRS books. The children read along with the teacher (similar to a Big Book).	**Big box.** (15 minutes) This is a grid of learned syllables that are pronounced and then used to build into words the children can read.

---

[35]The KTPPS teacher's guides *(Pasin bilong tisa)* were in such short supply at the time of data collection that I was unable to obtain a copy. In fact, the teachers I observed were all using photocopies of the teacher's guide pages that the KTPPS Director had made for them. During the last two weeks of my field work time, I worked with Rambai Keruwa and Apé Kolowa to produce a new teacher's book.

Writing a story. (15 minutes) The children use their chalkboards or, less frequently, a sheet of paper, to draw a picture on the weekly topic and write a caption/story to go with it.

Writing words. (15 minutes) The children practice letter formation, spelling, and writing words and sentences that the teacher dictates to them.

The instructional method is, in practice, a teacher-centered approach, although the "story time" is designed to be used as a language experience, learner-centered pedagogy. In lessons observed at one school, the teacher even provided the children with the specifics of their drawing in the creative writing component: "Draw a picture or write about a man. Don't build [i.e., draw] a house, draw them cutting the wood, draw a picture of some boys, draw a tree, write it" (August 1, 1995; T9.15).

The two tracks—story time and word time—can be characterized as whole-to-part and part-to-whole, respectively. According to Stringer and Faraclas (1987), the two tracks should be taught by different teachers, each trained only in their respective track, to avoid "causing confusion in the minds of the teachers and the students" (p. 12). Although the purpose of this case study is not to evaluate the educational merits of the KTPPS instructional program, observations of one of the classrooms indicated a significant degree of confusion on the teacher's part regarding the purpose of some of the Word Time (part-to-whole) activities—confusion expressed by the teacher himself (T14.8–9).

The teaching aid used most by the instructors in the four KTPPS locations I visited is the large chalkboard and chalk. Teachers used the chalkboard for writing the children's experience stories, writing the keyword exercises, drawing syllable boxes, drawing illustrations for keywords, and writing the children's names as a way of dismissing them from the classroom for recess or at the end of the day. The teacher at one of the Tok Pisin classrooms used syllable cards during a Word Time activity with her students while one of the KTPPS teachers, who had several sets, did not use them at all.

The KTPPS program grew out of the collaboration of several sets of lives: an SIL literacy team committed to assisting in the establishment of a community-based mother-tongue literacy effort; a local community leader who took seriously his understanding that he had been given responsibility for community welfare from his youth; and a community prepared to take active steps to meet the challenges and opportunities of a changing and uncertain social, political, economic, and cultural environment.

The KTPPS program grew slowly during the first four years of its existence while a stable, supporting infrastructure was developed, primarily through the efforts of its director, Rambai Keruwa, and the Kaugel NonFormal Education Association that acts as an advisory board to the program. After 1991, the program grew from three KTPPS sites to fourteen, at one point enrolling in excess of five hundred children.

However, the tension between the two goals of the KTPPS program—preparing children for a successful entry into the formal system while also supporting language and culture maintenance—exists in another form: between the community's desire to control its own mother-tongue education program and the need to seek additional resources from outside the project area. Attempts by Rambai to secure outside funds have been many and diverse with a wide range of results, from steady and supportive assistance from the National Literacy and Awareness Secretariat (NLAS) to the almost disastrous, aborted assistance of the Department of Village Services.

As a community education innovation, the KTPPS program emphasizes mother-tongue literacy acquisition. The curriculum is centered on cultural themes, and the instructional method is evenly divided between whole-to-part and part-to-whole activities. A key element in the whole-to-part portion of the program has been the Kaugel Reading Series, a seventeen-book series, with five to six stories in each book. All the stories are authored and illustrated by local people, male and female. Classrooms of the KTPPS vary in size, permanence, and materials. All teachers are furnished with at least a large chalkboard, small chalk boards that children can hold in their laps, chalk, and the Kaugel Reading Series.

The essential components for a "successful" mother-tongue literacy program are in place (i.e., sustained, with a strong community-based infrastructure, adequate materials, and staff). The fact that the program has been maintained for a decade, in spite of numerous problems, attests to the commitment of its teachers and administrator. The fact that parents continue to send their children to classes indicates that they perceive the KTPPS as meeting a need of some kind. Chapter 5 seeks to identify what those needs are as it analyzes the attitudes and actions of people in the Tambul Basin who seek to negotiate between their concerns for their children's formal English education and their desire for the children to be integrated into the Umbu-Ungu community.

5

Language and Culture in the KTPPS Community: Sociological Findings

Mipela i rait man-namel man-long wokim   We're the right people—the
tingting bilong ol pikinini long bihain na   in-between people—to shape the chil-
mipela ken luksave wanem narapela   dren's thoughts for the future and we
tewel wankain ol bin i stap pastaim ol   can judge whether their new kind of
papa i stap long em.   soul will be like their ancestors had.
(Apé Kolowa, interview, December 13, 1995, T63.13)

During the drive in his four-wheel-drive double-cab pick-up from Ukarumpa to Tambul at the beginning of my fieldwork, Rambai told me, "You'll notice lots of changes in the place." He was referring to the Aika and Korika-Kengelka clan area where my wife and I had lived and helped him establish the Kaugel Tok Ples Pri Skul Program between 1982 and 1987 and to which I was now returning to carry out my research. In this chapter I begin with an album of the sights and sensations I observed in my "reacquaintance" walk on the road around the Tambul Basin. This walk provides a frame of reference for the three topics to be discussed in this chapter: language, culture, and identity as viewed by the partici-pants, the bane and blessing of English-language schooling in the Kaugel community, and bilingualism as a community goal and practice. Each one of these topics relates to the intersection of Kaugel culture with that of the West and each has had a significant impact on the implementation and maintenance of the KTPPS program.

The Basin Road itself is a product of that intersection, cut out of local garden ground to create an artery for local trucks to connect the local

residents and their cabbage, broccoli, carrots, zucchini, and white potatoes (all introduced crops) with the road that leads to a large open-air
market sixty-five kilometers away in Mount Hagen, and beyond.

Following the road's horseshoe shape from Kikuwa at the Aika clan's
southeastern end, around the Basin to Maripena at the southwestern end,
the following features stand out from the otherwise uniform array of
tawny thatched-roof houses, the neatly formed mounds of sweet potato
gardens, and the numerous vegetable and white potato gardens, all of
which blend into the many shades of green of the flora on the Basin floor
and the surrounding hills. The following descriptions are a composite of
many field notes.

- Rambai Keruwa's "modern house" has a corrugated iron roof and a
  separate, more traditional thatched-roofed cook-house in which, if you
  are invited to enter, you will discover the neat, stone-bordered fireplace
  and a wall covered with a large green chalkboard on which Rambai's
  and Nali's children write and draw pictures.

- Tepatoli's thatched-roof house, a mixture of traditional and European
  materials, with a more European than Kaugel design, features a
  verandah on the north side, six square windows with aluminum-framed
  glass louvers, a large central meeting room with sawmill-plank flooring,
  and an end room with a floor made from split pandanus tree planks.

- The PNG Bible Church at Kikuwa has a corrugated iron roof and
  painted walls, and a solar panel set on the north slope of the gabled
  roof. For a few years the solar panel powered a 12-volt car battery
  which, in turn, lit a set of 20-watt fluorescent lights inside the sanctuary
  for evening prayer meetings and the adult literacy class. For whatever
  reason, the solar panel is no longer in use. To the south of the church a
  large, neat thatched-roof house with woven-blind walls serves as the
  parsonage for Pastor Uwa, an Imbo-Ungu speaker from the Southern
  Highlands Province.

- Pamenda's house stands just north of the Kikuwa church grounds. The
  two-storey iron-roofed frame house sits back from the road, guarded by
  a wire-mesh fence. Another, similar two-storey home, owned by Yano
  Rambai, Rambai's childhood friend and schoolmate, can be seen at the
  Maripena end of the horseshoe road.

- Tradestores line the Basin Road, one in each small settlement. Typical is
  Win Yapo's one-room store with a large window opened to the public
  from which the local resident can buy canned mackerel or sardines,
  canned corned beef, kilo bags of white rice, sugar, coffee or tea, soft
  drinks in bottles or cans, cigarettes, and beer. A sign painted in white
  letters on a plain piece of plywood nailed just below the rafters on the
  front of the store reads: *Tok save: Salim bokis bilong daiman long hia.
  prais: K80.00* 'Attention: We sell coffins here. Price: 80 kina [about
  US$60.00]'.

- Gum and pine trees, imported from Australia with the arrival of government services in the early 1950s, are ubiquitous reminders of European contact. At Sakaleme they provide a kind of cultural analogy. A line of indigenous pandanus trees have been planted to the west about fifty meters back from the road. Behind them tower a stand of the nonindigenous pines. One estimate by a local man was that they were planted in the 1970s. They now dwarf the pandanus trees by perhaps as much as 40–50 feet. The race between old and new, indigenous and nonindigenous is being played out in the botanical world as well as the human one.

- Also at Sakaleme are two small "grave houses" that serve as markers for the burial sites of two distinguished male members of the clan. Both are about 4' x 3' x 3' with gabled, corrugated iron roofs. One erected for a young medical worker is painted white with bright red crosses on the front and red horizontal stripes around the bottom and middle of the walls. The other grave is painted alternately with wide horizontal stripes of red and blue. Stakes, like those used at ceremonial pig exchanges, mark the corners of both grave areas. Between them lie large stones painted alternately white and red. The half-dozen used truck tires fixed neatly into the ground around the second grave commemorate the fact that the deceased was a victim of a road accident.

- At Pombol, beside Councilor Dopenu's trade store, is a perpetually running faucet, attached to the end of an L-shaped galvanized pipe which is secured in the ground by a square of concrete into which the constantly cascading stream has already formed a trough for run-off. Connected by almost a kilometer of pipes to a clean water source in the hills to the east of Pombol, the *wara saplai* 'water supply', as it is known locally, is a source of pride as well, confirming several portrayals of the Aika clan as a community of avant-garde innovators. Many similar water supply systems were installed around the Basin. Most, if not all, of those outside the Aika clan area are no longer working.

- Akilio's gardens and pig projects lie along the Basin road beyond the Aika clan at Kalapolo, in Korika-Kengelka clan territory. His piggery, made of a mixture of traditional and imported materials, stretches half the length of a soccer field. Typical pig sties in the Basin may run up to 8 stalls; Akilio's number in the dozens.

- Continuing on the road, just beyond Kalapolo is Itaki's *haus piksa* 'video theater' and card club. Down an embankment and across a small clearing, the large thatched-roof well-constructed "bush" building is about 40' × 24'. A trade store that comprises half of the front end has a window for buyers and sellers that opens out to the clearing. The other half is an empty area able to accommodate two large or three small groups of card players sitting in circles on the floor.

- On the other "leg" of the horseshoe shaped road, Yombikul Community School consists of four large permanent classrooms (iron roofs, plywood walls, louver-glass windows). At the 1995 end-of-the-school-year closing ceremony, Councilor Gonoli Keruwa (Rambai's brother), sitting beside me among the other guests of honor, leaned over to inform me that this year's was "the thirteenth grade 6 class to graduate in the school's fifteen year history (the first two years without a grade 6). He also said that five Yombikul graduates have gone to University and three have graduated, one as an aircraft engineer."
- The Tambul Basin road ends by traveling through the Department of Primary Industry's High Altitude Experimental Agricultural Station, with its large flock of sheep first donated in the early 1980s by the New Zealand government. It goes past the Tambul Community School's large campus with its double classes of each grade from grade 1 through grade 6. It then rejoins the main road that connects Tambul government station with Mount Hagen and Mendi, and with the Lower Kaugel communities that make up the western half of the Tambul-Nebilyer District.

This rapid pan of the physical setting of the Tambul Basin reveals little of the underlying language and cultural situation facing Kaugel parents and children or of the social changes that have taken place over the last four decades. Hopefully, it helps the reader to understand better the context in which the KTPPS is established and to situate the voices that will be "speaking" in the following pages.

Language, Culture, and Identity

One of the Department of Education's goals for "tok ples preparatory schools" was that the schools would "enable children to develop close ties to the local community" (Department of Education 1990:1; see also chapter 1). As discovered through interviews for this study, Kaugel parents have their own diverse and frequently opposing views about the purpose of the preschools, especially with respect to their children's linguistic and cultural identity.

Negative attitudes toward language and culture maintenance

In response to the interview question, "Some people say that their children should only learn English in school. What do you think?" Aika Siminji, father of six children, replied:

Nane nanga kangamboloma kepe ya   I think that if my children understand
Ingillisi Ungu piliku...wi kondolima kene   English and live like the whites, I
kapola molemelkanje papu nimbu pilio.   think that's good. That's what I think.
Aku nimbu plilo.
(Aika Siminji, interview, August 31, 1995, T22.2)

Siminji and his wife Akia have five sons and a daughter. Their daughter is married into another Basin clan and visits them frequently. Their eldest son is a lawyer, having graduated from the School of Law at the University of Papua New Guinea in 1994. Their second son is finishing an undergraduate degree in business management at the University of South Queensland in Australia. Their middle son dropped out of community school in grade 3 and has been living at home. The next youngest is currently in grade 1 at the Purare Community School, while their youngest has not yet attended preschool. The four older children did not attend KTPPS but the son now in grade 1 did. The family lives in a thatched roof home beside the Purare KTPPS classroom.

Later in the same interview, when reminded of the concern expressed by some community members that Kaugel children are forgetting their old customs and language, Siminji made the following response (S = Siminji; A = Apé):

S: Akuline okunduli munduku kelkolie   They're saying that because [the chil-
kinie wi kondenga lo komindili lingi   dren] are abandoning the old ways in
pulimele aku siku niku piliku nilimili.   favor of the good new ways.
A: Nakolo nuni pe kinie nambulka ningu   But now what do you think?
pililtu?
S: Pe nane aku nimbu pililuka.   I think the same way.
A: Ou ulu puluma munduku kelkolie....   Abandon all the traditional ways....
S: Ou ulu puluma keri, pe kinie ulu   The traditional ways are not good. The
***sukuli** tepa **Inglis** pilipe ulu teli akuli*   good way is to go to school and learn
komindi nimbu pilipulie nane akulika   English, and that's the way I support.
paka tolio konopu akuli pekemo.   That's my firm conviction.
(Aika Siminji, interview, August 31, 1995, T22.8)

Siminji used the phrase *kondenga **lo** komindili* 'the good new way', borrowing the Tok Pisin term ***lo*** 'law, custom, rule', rather than using the Umbu-Ungu term *umbu ulu* 'indigenous habit, custom, practice, action, way of life'. Merlan and Rumsey (1991) describe the neighboring Ku Waru people's view of *gavman lo* as something to attain to, not a practice necessarily opposed to indigenous custom per se but opposed to tribal warfare, sorcery, murder, those traditional practices that interfere with the course of *bisnis* 'business, trade' and material well-being. In that respect, *gavman lo* is "continuous" with the traditional concepts of what kind of actions promote community harmony and mutual prosperity and are not seen by the people to be in opposition or conflict with the past (p. 196).

Although Merlan and Rumsey's conclusion is consistent with much of the data in this case study (see, for example, Aika Kopatoli's views below), Siminji's view of "the new good way" and the concept of *gavmen lo* and *umbu ulu* appear to be mutually exclusive. During an interview with Rob and June Head, SIL linguists in the Kaugel project since 1969, June recalled a conversation with Siminji's eldest son, Luke, who at the time was attending grade 12 at Aiyura National High School in the Eastern Highlands:

> Luke told us one time that when he first went to the English school as a little boy, his family told him, all right, you're now going to learn the white man's ways; you're going to get the white man's education. You don't need to know any of your cultural things. You don't need to go to the bush or learn those stories or anything like that. And he said, "No, I want my cultural heritage." And at weekends he said he used to talk to his father and his uncles and say, "Tell me the old stories; take me to the bush and show me things and tell me things." But he had to *push* them to get them to do that. And it wasn't just him and his parents. He said it was a trend then that all the parents felt that the child had to virtually cut itself off from the old culture in order to be immersed in the new culture because this was the way that the money was going to come and so on, and they were going to get the material things they wanted. It wasn't really a—what do you call that—...material cult thing....
> (June Head, interview, December 3, 1995, T59.21)

The cargo cult mentality alluded to by June Head refers to a nativistic movement in which members of one or more communities claim to have had a revelation of the secret and mysterious access to the seemingly endless material goods to which Europeans have access (Lawrence 1964). One of the unfortunate consequences of most cargo cult movements is the participants' disengagement from their work and normal daily activities as they await the "imminent" arrival of goods and money. Such a mentality would be difficult to ascribe to Siminji and Akia, both of whom are widely known and respected for their indefatigable garden making and work ethic. Meggitt (1968) describes the difference between PNG's coastal areas (where cargo cults thrive) and the more pragmatic Highlands with respect to people's views of the source of wealth and prosperity:

Indeed, in a sense, many highland religions do not really offer a substitute for ordinary skills and hard work in attaining certain culturally valued ends. At best the rituals try to avert undesirable supernatural hindrance of men's actions, and their performers would, I think, generally echo Cervantes' maxim that "diligence is the mother of good fortune, and sloth, her adversary, never accomplished a good wish." (p. 306)

When asked to hypothesize on the kind of changes that would occur in the local community if all the children lost interest in Umbu-Ungu and spoke only English and Tok Pisin, Siminji leapt over the less drastic consequences, suggesting that

Makali ulu pulu kepe kongi topa koeli ulu pulu kepe akuma manie pulkanje kangambolama sukuli tekolie Ingillisi Ungu komindima pilikulie kangambolama molko konjangi kupulanumu akulika pililka... Ingillisi Ungu piliku Pisini Ungu piliku olando olando pangi konopu akuli paa ulu tondolo we nimbu nane konopu akuli panjilio.	If the customs like the pig exchange and the killing and cooking of pigs wane, then the children will go to school, learn to understand English well, and concentrate on living well...Deep down I'm convinced that if they understand English and Tok Pisin well they will go higher and higher [in the education system], because [those languages] are powerful.

(Aika Siminji, interview, August 31, 1995, T22.11)

This parent clearly does not believe that the local language and culture are his children's primary source of identity—the "positive ethnic identity" that Giles and Johnson consider a necessary component of active language maintenance (1987:72). Rather, he sees in English and Tok Pisin powerful alternatives to life with only local language and culture.

Siminji's response is particularly interesting because of his own behavior, including his use of language. Whatever complaint he may have with the traditional language and culture, he himself stays close to them. He is one of the few men in the Tambul area that consistently speaks Umbu-Ungu, even with expatriates who struggle with the language. When Apé asked Siminji hypothetically whether he would be willing to live in a town with his successful sons and not return to the village, Siminji replied,

Aku tenga kongono tepo anju pupu molopo telkanje, aku Akene kepe meltenga anjipe pulkanje aku molkanje manda naa telka nimbu pilikiru.	If I went to live and work in Hagen or if I went somewhere more distant, either way it wouldn't be satisfactory.

Molopolie altopo kelepo sukunduka   To live, I'd come back to the place my
ombolie nanga koliana kelepo we nanga   mother gave birth to me to stay and
meringi koliana kelepo sukunduka olka   be buried and that would be that....
kene aku sukundu nanga koliana ka
molka kene ono telemela akuna ka pora
nikimu....

Aku ulu anju anju molo nanga ya inie ga   Traveling around like that, no, I'd pre-
tepo nombolie nanga we inie molopolie   fer living here, making sweet potato
na ono tengi akuli manda nimbu pilikiru.   gardens, eating, and just living, then
                                              they can bury me here. I think that
                                              would be satisfactory.

(Aika Siminji, interview, August 31, 1995, T22.16–17)

Despite his convictions regarding the power of English for his children
and the great value he puts on their possessing it, in the end, Siminji identifies himself with the Umbu-Ungu language and culture implied in his
use of *nanga kolia* 'my place'. Even for someone with as strident a view as
his, some ambivalence exists.

Other parents echo Siminji's estimate of Umbu-Ungu as inadequate in
the domain of socioeconomic power. After complaining that his "fathers"
had taught him mainly worldly things and forcibly prevented him from
going to the English school, Nokindi voiced his approval of the KTPPS,
but then added,

Akulinga ya ilini we pawa mele sikimu   It is that [English schooling] that will
ilinga olione kinie Umbu-Ungu akuli   give [the child] the power and knowl-
kangambola kapola mane naa   edge we cannot teach him/her in
simululinga nane pilikiruli, nanga   Umbu-Ungu. So I think a child cannot
kangambolama akusipe mane kapola naa   learn properly that way.
silka nimbu pilikiru.

(Aika Nokinde, group interview November 14, 1995, T47.17)

Aika Jiwa, a Kaugel parent living in Mount Hagen, also expressed the
view that English is of greater value than Umbu-Ungu and of greater
worth in promoting children's economic, social, and political well-being.
The dialogue below took place at Jiwa's home in Mount Hagen.

D: OK, tasol, sapos ol mekim olsem long   OK, but what if [a hypothetical gov-
ol pikinini [na] ol bai kisim narapela tok   ernment] did that kind of thing to the
ples, em bai givim wanem hevi long [ol]?   children and they all learned another
                                              language, then what kind of problems
                                              might that bring?

J: **Well,** sapos ol laik skulim long Inglis   Well, if they wanted to learn in Eng-
na mekim em **still** gutpela...bilong ol yet.   lish and use it, that would still be
Em bai gutpela yet.   good...for them. That would be quite
   good.

D: ...sapos ol i kisim Inglis na ol i no   ...if they learn English and don't learn
kisim Umbu-Ungu em bai....   Umbu-Ungu, that will....

J: Em...i orait tu.   That's also all right.
(Aika Jiwa, interview, November 8, 1995, T42.17)

Jiwa's own children do not speak Umbu-Ungu to him (although he speaks it to them). The social arena, of course, has changed for this family as they have moved out of the Kaugel Valley where Umbu-Ungu is the dominant language to a town in which Tok Pisin and English serve as the main lingua francas. As Jiwa expresses his feelings, "Without talking English you cannot understand anything, [and] you're more or less like a dumb person going around" (Aika Jiwa, interview, November 8, 1995, T42.18).

Taking a slightly different approach, Aika Kopatoli, whose daughter Esta is a TPPS student, separates Umbu-Ungu language ("It's good; it will survive") from its culture, which he divides between customs that are best abandoned and those whose vitality is required for the continued well-being of the community. Kopatoli's extended discourse below is included for several reasons. First, he "spoke well," as indicated by the reaction of the nine other parents who were part of this particular group interview. Second, he is, like Rambai and Apé, a *namel man,* an "in-between person" who is able to compare the before and after of European contact. Third, he appears to be at home in his changing culture as evidenced by his participation in traditional activities such as flute playing (but using a flute made out of plastic tubing). Finally, Kopatoli is respected in the community and an elder in the Lutheran congregation at Pombol, itself founded on the intersection of indigenous and nonindigenous cultures. The following is his response to the question: "Some people say that the children are forgetting Umbu-Ungu and are abandoning the old ways. What do you think?"

*Aku paa kinie olio **tumbuna**ma teko moloringi, olio yandopa yandopa kanoko liku moloringi aku mele nimbu tekero. Akuli ne yambo mare ele toloma teko nosiku toko meme ondo siku louni toko kinie yambole tokomolole papu niku piliku ene aema kandamele teko yambo akuma topo nokoro niku kinie manga umbu talo oe panjikulu kinie.*

I want to tell you about what our ancestors did and about us who have descended from them. They were the people who made bows and spears for killing and spilling blood, and killing with axes. The people who killed thought they were doing something good so they celebrated [lit., did the stomping dance]. Thus, there was a mark [i.e., blood] placed between the two clans.

Korika-Kengelka kinie Aikatolo opa teringili. Aku kinie tekelo kinie aku siku pilikulu, yambole tokolo ma kolia ono tekolie we konopu kaiyu piliku enenga kongi toko koeko nongo ulu aku teringi. Teko akuli paa nanga ulu mulure tekero niku teko meko andoringi. Aku ululini altopa kelepa olando mando pupa kinie nirimu yambo kupuna mingi pora topa le neambu wendo omba, aku tepa kinie nirimu yambo mini kepe kangi kepe te wasianele umbu li naa liringi.

Before, Korika-Kengelka fought with Aika. When they did that and people were killed, they buried them, and happily cooked pork and ate; that was the custom.

This is what they thought reality was, so they carried [those customs] around. They did all these customs repeatedly, and brought in poisoning, [but] they did not do anything to care for body [lit., skin] and soul.

Mini kangitolo tepa keri molorumu kinie yamboma oli pakopo, kola tepo, olio molemolo none tepo kinie "ambo kanuli kolopa pora simu, ye kanu opana tongi" nimbu, kuru nimbu koerimululi tene omba boropa noi naa norumu. Olio oliolio nombo kinie "kuru kanu simu nomu" nimbu tepa konjirimu aku kinie aku sipu nimbu molorumululi.

When a person's body and soul were sick, the people smeared on wet clay and wept. We, the living, would say, "That woman has died," or, "That man was killed in a fight." We would sacrifice the pig to the ancestral spirit, but no one came to take the pork from the cooking pit and eat it. When the food was thoroughly cooked, we ourselves ate [the pork] and said that the spirit had eaten it. That's how we did it.

Aku aema ulu kerimane olio molopo aema naa konjirimulu. Ulu keri akuli kinie manie purumu.

Truly, we did not prosper doing those evil things. All these evil customs are now on the wane [lit., have gone down].

(Aika Kopatoli, group interview, November 14, 1995, T47.8)

The undercurrent of Kopatoli's argument is a new understanding of the significance of ancestral customs that promoted and celebrated the enmity and killing of members of clans whom people now would almost consider brothers and sisters. It highlights another aspect of the privileged perspective

of the *namel manmeri:* they have experiential knowledge of the change in attitude and atmosphere that made tribal fighting illegal and opened up a freedom of movement-without-fear, a golden age of peace and good will that
many older Kaugel people recall with a kind of nostalgia.

Later in this same interview, Aika Kopatoli complained about the effect
he has observed of English-language schooling on the children:

Ya kangambolama kewa unguna mindi leko, **Pisin** *ungunama* **Inglis** *akumanga* **skul** *tekemele akumane tekolie ya umbu uluma aema munduku kelingi ombele tekemele.*	The children here are just using Pisin. They are going school in Pisin and in English and, as a result, they tend to abandon indigenous customs and become unruly.
Aku kanokorolenga pe Umbu-Ungu akulinga kelko **Inglis**ina *molko,* **Pisin** *akuna molko teko kinie kelko ya olionga ulu akulinga tenis teko tengi aema uluma piliku sundukumili.*	What I've seen is that they spend their time talking Pisin and English, and when they try to do something indigenous they change it and are not able to do it properly.
Akuli nambulka, **sumbun**anga *ulu mundupa keleli akumanga mare naa nikiru. Enenga ponie teko nongi kepe, pe ulu olionga ungulinga ningi kepe aku marene aema piliku lou liku piliku sundukumili.*	That's for what? (I'm not talking about the ancestors' customs that we've rejected.) It's making their gardens and using Umbu-Ungu when they speak. They really foul it up.

(Aika Kopatoli, group interview, November 14, 1995, T47.17)

Kopatoli's assessment of a justified "cultural loss" sheds a different light
on the notion that minority group members' individual and corporate
identity is bound up with their language and/or culture. Kopatoli does not
view his culture as a monolithic whole, a take-it-or-leave-it proposition.
Rather, he sees it as a collection of activities, some of which he perceives
negatively, while others he considers precious. He clearly distinguishes
between the set of ancestral customs that he believes have justifiably been
rejected (at least by members of the Christian community) and those he
considers necessary for contented living in the Basin. His observations
correspond closely with Merlan and Rumsey's (1991) contention, mentioned earlier in this chapter, that the Ku Waru people consider the "new
order" to be a not-incompatible extension of the ancestral order:

> There are aspects of **bo ul** 'indigenous practice/custom' which peo-
> ple see as continuous with **gavman lo,** not opposed to it. One of
> these is in fact the practices of giving compensation, paying for
> woundings and killings.... Any such payment of reparation may be
> referred to by the phrase **lo te-** 'to make/do law'. The use of the Tok
> Pisin term emphasizes that people see this aspect of their

indigenous practice as continuous with **gavman lo,** not in conflict with the new order. (p. 196)

Kopatoli catalogs the useful role that government and church have played in bringing about a better way of living by proscribing destructive elements of traditional culture, enhancing the people's identity and cultural destiny, rather than replacing it.

Ulu keri akuli kinie mania purumu.	Now these evil customs have declined.
Gapaman *wendo omba ulu kerima topa*	The government appeared and killed
konjirimu: ele toloma konjirimu aku	the evil ways, the bow and arrow, the
kinie, kinie **skul** *wendo omba, omba*	spears. Now that schools have arisen,
gapaman *omba,* **skul** *wendo omba pe*	government has come, the Bible *(miti)*
miti, lotu *nambulka mele akuma wendo*	and worship services *(lotu)* and
okomo kinie olio yambo kinie konopu	what-all have come, we are thinking
kaiyu pilipu molopo konjipu tepo	and doing quite well....
molkomolo....	

(Aika Kopatoli, group interview, November 14, 1995, T47.8)

To summarize, the speakers in this section all share some negative views of their language or culture. Considerable variation is evident, however, in the underlying rationale for their views. Siminji, Nokinde, and Jiwa all see English as the language of power and the culture associated with it as dominant, views they do not hold for their mother tongue. Kopatoli, on the other hand, esteems Umbu-Ungu but not the associated cultural customs of the past that he considers destructive. Although he admires the government and church (the nonindigenous institutions) for the change in local life that they instituted, he deplores the influence of English and Tok Pisin on the young people's ability to learn and appreciate the indigenous attitudes and skills necessary for basic "good" living.

Taken together, the speakers above express the ambivalent attitude that Kaugel people regularly adopt toward the new and old. Even those predisposed to characterize English as the language of power vis-à-vis Umbu-Ungu show little intention of making the exchange personally.

Positive attitudes toward language and culture maintenance

According to Giles and Johnson (1987), Welsh minority community members' positive attitudes towards their mother tongue can be viewed either as contributing toward strong language maintenance or as a naive over-confidence vis-à-vis rampant language shift (cf. Hornberger 1988). Parents' attitudes toward their language affect their attitudes towards their children's education. Henze and Vanett (1993), reporting on a six-month exploratory study of a Yup'ik Eskimo bilingual education program, contend that "one way to grasp the complexity of cultural shift is to look at the language situation, since language is one of the more salient carriers of culture" (p. 119). The people below present their views of the language situation in the Kaugel area.

Olionga umbu ungu papu. Umbu-Ungu	Our local language is good.
papulinga olionga ya Purare koliana suku	Umbu-Ungu is good therefore inside
ya Umbu-Ungu , olionga ungulinga pepili.	this place Purare, let Umbu-Ungu be
Manda tengili. Kinie kondoli yambo	spoken here....They'll be able to do
koliamanga enenga ungu aku yunga	that. Now in the whiteman's home
unguna nilimili aku mele pe olionga	place the talk is in his language. In the
kangambolama pe molongi mulu ma pora	same way—provided heaven and earth
naa nimu lemo aku pe olionga ungunaka	have not finished—our children will
kapola kangambolama ningili.	be speaking our language.

(Aika Kopatoli, group interview, November 14, 1995, T47.1)

Kopatoli's argument is that it is only proper that Umbu-Ungu, as the traditional language of the Tambul Basin (and specifically Purare village), should be spoken there, as English is spoken in America. He makes a larger statement with regard to his view of Umbu-Ungu: as long as this place (the Tambul Basin and surrounding area) exists, Umbu-Ungu will be spoken by the children. A similar view is expressed by Lyaka, a Korika clan father.

Kinienga ya olionga Umbu-Ungu nikimu	Regarding that, he [the previous
Umbu-Ungu **skul** *kapola nikimu pe ungu*	speaker] said it's our language, and
mongo te lupa naa nimulu. Ungu mongo	it's good to have Umbu-Ungu schools
telumuka nikimulu. Olio ungu telumuka	because there's no other language that
nikimulu.	we will speak, only the one. We speak
	only one language.

(Korika Lyaka, group interview, November 14, 1995, T47.2)

Lyaka is in favor of the KTPPS program and sees the need for mother-tongue education. His purpose here is to summarize the previous two speakers' thoughts about Umbu-Ungu and emphasize his agreement with them. That the statements are hyperbolic is indicated in his following speech which is sprinkled with lexical borrowings from Tok Pisin and English (including several words with legitimate Umbu-Ungu equivalents). Although bilingualism and multilingualism are becoming common among Umbu-Ungu speakers, it appears that, among most local residents, Umbu-Ungu is still perceived as the present and future language of the place.

In fact, when presented with an interview item proposing an hypothetical government ban on Umbu-Ungu, parents and teachers expressed their own strong attachments to their language and described their fellow community members as sharing their feelings:

Akumu kinie ne olionga ungu,	Umbu-Ungu, that is our language, our
Umbu-Ungu, olionga ungu kanumo kinie	true language. If the government were
*akumu ne **gapamanone** molo nilka kepe*	to ban it, we would hide [somewhere]
marenga opi tepo molopo kepe umbu	and continue to use the language in
ungumu lelemolamo.	secret.

(Iri Dari, mother of KTPPS student, interview, November 19, 1995, T54B.10)

Akunje ne manda, marenga suku yambo	I suppose that would be okay, and
*kanopolie **Pisini** telka nakolo nananu*	when I would see people around in
konupulini Umbu-Unguli we nimbuka	[Tambul area] I'd use Pidgin but in
molkale, ambu anda kepe akuma kanopo	my heart and mind, I'd think in
kinie.	Umbu-Ungu, especially whenever I'd
	see the old people.

(Kuku Waliwa, mother of KTPPS student, interview, November 19, 1995, T54A.20)

Akunje manda naa munduku kelemela.	To abandon [Umbu-Ungu], that would
Aku yambo [laughter] aku siku	probably not work. [He laughs as if
nilimilanje yambo toko nomi karu leko	the idea is too outrageous to contem-
tolemelanje nimbu pilikiru.	plate.] I think that if [the government]
	said that they would have to slit the
	people's throats and kill them.

(Kanimbe Ten, KTPPS teacher, interview, November 6, 1995, T38A)

Following after Ten's emphatic affirmation of Umbu-Ungu, Dopenu, one of the Aika clan's two Local Government Councilors, used several graphic metaphors linking Umbu-Ungu to Kaugel identity.

Umbu ungu lengi kinie aku peya olio	We now understand how [our infant
pilipu pora sililinga, Pulu Yelini olio	children] speak Umbu-Ungu. God
umbu unguli mere anumunga olona suku	gives us Umbu-Ungu while we are yet
molamili sirimulini pe akuli olionga	in our mother's womb, so it's the lan-
ungulini anju yando kapola nimbu	guage of this place, so that's why we
molemolo, akuli manda....	are able to converse in the language
	and that's good.

Na nanu konopu monjiliole pe nanga   I love [Umbu-Ungu] because it's my
ungulika na nanu konopu monjipu nimbu   language, the one I love to speak. Our
mololio. Ungule, ne umbu ungulene olio   language holds our life. The language
*yambonga mololi ululi...**laipele**. **Laipele***   is the source of the life that pulsates in
lope telemo ulu pulu akuli ne unguli   us, do you realize that? This beautiful
pilikinui? Akuli ungu kaiyu wele olio   language is good and it lives in us.
kinie pelemo.

Pe kinie ungule ne kinie naa nimulu lemo   Now, if we do not speak this language
pe ne kololi ululi limbe kinie kere pipi   then death will fetch us and our
simbe. Unguli olionga ungu tondolole.   mouths will be shut. Our language is
  our strength.

(Aika Dopenu, interview, November 17, 1995, T53B.36–37)

Dopenu views the language, perhaps in a literal sense, as something God gives to Kaugel people in utero. Over the mountains to the west are valleys and basins similar to his own but children there grow up speaking the Enga language; that, too, is divinely ordained. Given such a premise, the rest follows logically. Dopenu, in a sense, reiterates Kanimbe Ten's suggestion that the only way, hypothetically, to end the use of Umbu-Ungu would be to "slit the people's throats." As long as their hearts beat, they will speak Umbu-Ungu. Not to speak the language of the place would be to die, culturally if not physically. Dopenu's comments below regarding his observations of the affects of English schooling on the community suggest that he is aware that not all of his neighbors share his enthusiasm for the mother tongue.

Dopenu also contends that *umbu ungu* 'indigenous speech' is inextricably linked to *umbu ulu* 'indigenous custom'. In response to the question, "What if the younger generation abandons Umbu-Ungu altogether?" Dopenu responded,

*Aku **Pisini**li kinie **Inglisi**li kinie mindi*   If [the young people] only understand
pilingi lemo aku ya olionga unguli   Tok Pisin or English, and if they aban-
munduku kelingi lemo pe umbunga   don Umbu-Ungu, they will also aban-
unguna sukundu ulu lelemoma pali   don all of the customs we have within
munduku kelengi. Akuli olionga umbunga   us. Our mother tongue is the one
unguna suku ulu pulu ausipe lelemolenga   which contains within it all of the cus-
*aku **tumbuna**nga molopa kinie ulu*   toms and practices of our ancestors.
terimuma pali omba omba umbu unguna   All the ancestral customs we have now
suku pelkanje olemolenga kinienga aku   have come to us in Umbu-Ungu. Thus,
unguli pali munduku kelingi lemo pe ne   if this language is lost then all these
uluma pali munduku kelingi kenie kewa   customs will be lost with it. If they
unguna lelemo unguli wendo limulu   [the younger generation] try to get

ningu tengi, **Pisini***na ulu lelemo*	out of the foreign languages the cus-
akuliwendo lipu temolo niku tengili pe	toms that are in them, they will be
akuli kapola naa temba.	unsuccessful.

(Aika Dopenu, interview, November 17, 1995, T53A.10)

Here Dopenu echoes Kopatoli's observations of local customs reputedly botched by the young people because of too much dependence on Tok Pisin or English. The alternative explanation—that the problem stems from an inadequate understanding of Umbu-Ungu, the result of the children's long hours and years of sitting in English-language schools—is taken up below by Dopenu and others (see "Bane and Blessing of English Schooling," this chapter).

Lal (1995), in her overview of symbolic interactionist perspectives on ethnicity and identity, points out that members of ethnolinguistic minority groups give expression to their group's uniqueness under certain conditions (e.g., in order to promote group solidarity) and emphasize their similarity with dominant groups under other conditions (e.g., to enhance group prestige). Quoting Blumer and Duster, Lal describes the same tension that I observed among Kaugel people:

> "The conflict for groups (and individuals inside these groups) at the base of the social, economic, and political structure, most simply put, is whether to celebrate and retain their 'likeness' [read 'uniqueness'] (which some may feel consigns them to the base), or whether to emulate and assimilate".... These two contradictory attitudes may be held by different members of the group at the same time and even by the individual at the same time. (1995:429)

Thus, in the ebb and flow of daily living that provides the individual and group with changing conditions and relationships, expressions of group and personal identity change, too. We should not be surprised, therefore, when members of the Kaugel community define themselves in a variety of ways with respect to their local language and culture. Such a constant reassessment of "who I am/who we are" is "itself a reflection of the optional voluntary character of ethnic identity in particular and the ability of the individual to respond to his or her environment in unpredictable ways" (Lal 1995:432).

Thus, Rambai Keruwa, director of the KTPPS program, eloquently defends the need to actively provide mother-tongue education for Kaugel children to ensure their attachments to the language and ways of their place, then enrolls his son in a private school in which the goals and curriculum are often hostile to local culture and language (see the discussion of a private Christian school in chapter 4). Below, Rambai repeats Dopenu's assertion regarding the important link between Kaugel language and culture:

Umbu Ungu mundupu	If we abandon Umbu-Ungu, then all
kelemolanje...akunje olionga ya ulke	the traditional customs we practice
kolia tekemolo ulu pulu tekemolo akuma	cannot be done properly. If we aban-
sumbi sipe naa lelka. Umbu Ungu	don Umbu-Ungu for some other lan-
mundupu kelepo ungu lupa te nikimulka	guage, we'll have difficulty
akumanga ulu pulu lupa te le...pelemo	understanding our traditional customs
ulu pulu akumu olio pilimulundu mindili	because the [new] language will be
silimula...ungu kapola naa telka.	inadequate.

(Rambai Keruwa, interview, July 24, 1995, T1A.2)

Thus, even for those community members persuaded that Umbu-Ungu represents an irreplaceable vital organ in the life of the community, the tension remains with respect to making choices for their children's formal education.

Bane and Blessing of English Schooling

For as much criticism as the formal education system has received—justifiably in most cases (Dept. of Education 1991; Ahai and Bopp 1993; Yeoman and Obi 1993)—the irony is that the Department of Education can barely keep up with demands from local communities for new schools. One of the primary goals—perhaps *the* primary goal—of education reform is to increase access to all levels of formal education. The Kaugel parents interviewed for this study consistently confirmed their desire for their children to have access to all levels of formal education.

Kuku, the mother of one of the Purare KTPPS students, approves of English schooling for her children, reasoning that the Bible is written in English, and she wants her children to be able to read it. "If they don't go to school they won't be able to read it, and I like the Bible, so I am happy they are going to school" (Kuku Raliwa, interview, November 19, 1995, T54A.1).

Aika Siminji's unqualified approval of English-medium formal education (described at the beginning of this chapter) is not shared by others in his clan. Councilor Dopenu, for example, raised a concern about the source of perceived disrespect shown to parents, especially compared to Dopenu's own generation's childhood. Dopenu's concern was subsequently expressed by others participating in this study:

Aku kinie ya i sipu olionga **pri** *andoli ulu pulu ya i sipe kakara nili ulu pulu te naa lerimu. Olio akuni* **banisina** *mindi molorumulu, oliolo.* **Pemilima pali banisima mindi molorumulu nakolo kinienga anupili lapalinga ungu lipu su sikimulu ulu ili , kinienga te ya* **lo** *orumu, kondoli yambo orumu,* **skul** *orumu akuni kinienga anopili lapalinga ungu ima kinie olio lipu su sikimulu.*

[There was] no disrespect for those in authority then. We were all fenced in together. We all lived together inside the fence. But now we're all arrogant, defiant toward what our parents tell us. Now the "law" has come [i.e., from outside], whites have come, schools have arisen, and now [therefore] a time of defiance toward what our parents tell us [has also arisen].

(Aika Dopenu, interview, November 17, 1995, T53B.23)

Dopenu goes on to say that the content of the English-language school produces pride and ambition in the children, but the custom of respecting parents [if taught at all] never penetrates the children's minds, so they misbehave:

Akuli kinienga olione kanopolie olionga kinie kangambola ambolkomolo, olionga unguli naa pilikimili akuni, olione kinie sukundu lipulie kangambola molko konjangi mele mare mane siku tengili kinienga kondoli yambone mere **skul**inaka kangambola sukundu likimu kanopo kinie, akunaka mane sipe kaiyu temba molongika nimbu aku sipe molio pilikimulu.*

This is what we're seeing now, that all the children in our charge, they no longer pay attention to what we say and do. Now all the children are gathered in by the school and all are learning about how to live well. Now whites who have brought the children into the schools will have to teach them so that they can live.

(Aika Dopenu, interview, November 17, 1995, T53B.24)

Dopenu then observes another phenomenon, also supported by others, that when the children go to school they are de facto taught to learn in a new way, through English (and, by inference, through literate skills and the decontextualized knowledge typical of Western schools). Those new ways frequently become manifest, to the *namel manmeri,* as antisocial.

Aku tekemelelenga, kinienga akuna kinie mere, **Inglis** *ungu mindi mane sikimili akuni olionga umbu ungulinga kinie mere mane simulu tekemolo akuli mere ongo olio tongi tekemele.*

However, when they learn things in school they learn in English, and when we try to teach them something in Umbu-Ungu they want only to hit us!

Nema enenga **laikim** *wa nokomele o kakara nikimili o pena angilikulie olio kinie kouni tongi tekemele pilikinini. Kopene tongi tekemele.*

Their own desire is to steal, to insult, to be arrogant and defiant and to throw stones at us. They want to hit [us] with clubs.

Kinie ka singi nimbu olio kamu pipili	Now we suspect they'll put us in jail,
kolkomolole. Ne skul teko pulu piliku	so we're in fear of them. We think
tekemele nimbu. Akusipu molkomolo	they are learning this kind of attitude
pilikuni.	in school.

(Aika Dopenu, interview, November 17, 1995, T53.25–26)

That the kind of violent behavior referred to by Dopenu actually occurs was brought home to me on the final day of my field work. I was in our former village house entertaining neighbors who had come to bid me farewell as I was to leave the next morning. It was a typical Sunday afternoon. Young men of the Aika and Korika-Kengelka clans were playing a game of touch rugby on the Purare Community School grounds across the road from the house. The following is the account of the episode from my field notes.

> Suddenly, the door opened and Suku staggered in the front door, his right eye and cheek swollen to the size of a baseball, and bleeding profusely. I grabbed a piece of clean cloth,…wet it and tried to soak up some of the blood. His right eye was now only a slit, like a seam in cowhide. I made the mistake of rinsing out the rag, resulting in the blood evidence literally going down the drain. [The bloody rag will be tangible evidence of Suku's injury when the inevitable court case comes up.]

> While this is going on, the room is alive with questions and speculation: Who hit him?.... Was he playing rugby? Yes, it was rugby!.... *Long ai, long ai stret!* "in the eye, straight in the eye!" Suku says to me, but I'm not sure to what he's referring....the eye is completely shut now. (Field notes 4.38, December 17, 1995)

As it turned out, Suku had been beaten by some Pombol men (two young men and one of their fathers) after he had complained to them (and allegedly slapped one of the boys) because the boys were playing rugby on the school ground and running into the sweet potato and taro gardens that border the play field on the north and south. I did not have time to confirm the exact details of the altercation other than that the assailants ran up to Pombol where one of them donned a motorcycle helmet to await the inevitable arrival of Suku's brother-cousins.[36]

> The import of this incident is the way it confirms the older generation's frequently voiced fear of the young men as capable of doing unexpectedly hurtful things. The complaints, "We don't say anything

---

[36]This is a nontechnical term frequently used both by male English-speaking Papua New Guineans and English-speaking expatriates to describe a man's "extended family" in the typical *haus man:* all of one's father's brothers' sons are "brothers," which in the Kaugel kinship system is a relationship much closer to the Western concept of brother than it is to cousin.

> to them"—when the young men exhibit bad behavior—"because they
> might hit us" seems warranted. (Field notes 4.38, December 17,
> 1995)

Between the poles of assimilation of English language and culture and of Kaugel language and culture maintenance, Kaugel parents spread out along a meridian of stress, with the tension greatest at the center, among the *namel manmeri*. On the one hand, they are convinced that English education is the primary—perhaps the only—road to wage employment and access to the resources and materials by which they and their children can gain control of their lives. On the other hand, the parents are experientially aware of the need for informal or formal education in the mother tongue if the children are to learn the essentials of good living according to their long and trusted tradition of social interactions and activities that build community solidarity.

The Kaugel community is traditionally an event-oriented society—as opposed to time- and product-oriented, which, in a grossly general way, defines most Western cultures. But, events require time, of which there is only a finite amount. The formal school system occupies Kaugel children for seven to eight hours daily, forty weeks of the year. Thus, in terms of the Kaugel parents' goals and aspirations for the well-being of themselves and their children, English schools constitute an enigma. Desirable because they alone provide children with the skills and attitudes that allow them to function in the "new" society of business and wage employment, the schools are also objectionable because, in effect, they remove the children from their parents' sphere of influence for long periods of time, during which the children receive nonindigenous—and to the parents—often incomprehensible, language and culture socialization (cf. Wong Fillmore 1991).

If there is an escape from this dilemma, it appears that it is in children's ability and opportunity to acquire an education that will allow them to travel between and among the language and culture domains that make up their world without yielding their ethnnolinguistic identity. For that they will need, in the parents' eyes, a balanced bilingualism.

Umbu-Ungu English Bilingualism as a Community Goal

As might be suspected from the mixed feelings expressed above, many Kaugel parents as well as teachers view bilingualism and multilingualism favorably. Their main concern, in addition to their children's English-language education, is that they as parents retain the ability to communicate with and socialize their children. Parents' desire for a practical bilingualism for their children appears in various forms in the interview data. Iri Dari, a mother from Kikuwa whose two daughters, Catherine and Naumi, attended the Tambul Community School and Purare KTPPS, respectively, had these views.

Q: Some people say that, if children do three years of Umbu-Ungu [in the new elementary level], they won't be able to learn English well. What do you think?

Akumu kumbi leko Umbu-Ungumu tengi akumu peanga. Tengemo, yunga tenga kewa ungu tenge, akumu yunga **tisa***mo molemola, akumu manda mane simbe. Mane simbe kenie kewa unguna manda pilingi nakolo Umbu-Ungumu pilingimu paa komindi.*

It's good if [the child] first learns in Umbu-Ungu. After that, then their teacher can teach them in the foreign language. Then they will learn to understand the foreign language well but the best is for them to understand Umbu-Ungu.

Q: If your children get bored of Umbu-Ungu, and just use Tok Pisin or English, what kind of changes will arise?

Akumu **Inglis Pisin***tolo peya pilingi kinie Umbu-Ungu topele....tongimu yando mindili tepa aku tembamonga Umbu-Ungu* **Boku Baibel** *kanonge akumu kumbi lepamo.*

When they hear Pisin or English then they'll have to translate the Bible into Umbu-Ungu, and that will be hard for them, so it's best for them to be able to read the Bible in Umbu-Ungu first.

(Iri Dari, interview, November 19, 1995, T54B.4)

Iri's view contrasts with Siminji's (earlier in this chapter) in that Iri expresses a value for Umbu-Ungu that cannot be replaced by acquisition of a second language. She herself is bilingual in Umbu-Ungu and Tok Pisin. She accepts her daughters' bilingualism as a matter of course, but insists on the primacy of their mother tongue.

Q: Will your children reject Umbu-Ungu or not?

Aku pe eltenga umbu unguna, eltenga ungu kamumu lembelemo. Kewa ungu lengili kepe pe Umbu-Ungu ya ulkendo ongo na kinie molkolie Umbu-Ungu lelemolo.

It's their indigenous language, it's their own language. [The pair] use Tok Pisin but when they come home and sit together with me, we speak Umbu-Ungu.

(Iri Dari, interview, November 19, 1995, T54B.8)

Another mother, Kuku Raliwa, had a similar reaction to an hypothetical question about the loss of Umbu-Ungu through acquisition of a foreign language.

| Q. What if [your son] Metyu succeeds in school and doesn't return home? | *Akuli yunga **skul** teremumu kandu yanga kelo kinie Purare terimu kandumele tepalienga yunga pilili tondolo pukumuna marenga pukumulamo nimbu pilipu, na Pulu Yeli walsipu we molka.* | If he continues what he learned at Purare then the other schooling will help him to succeed else-where and I will trust God and be content to live by myself. |
| Q: But what if you need money, and he doesn't return or you're sick, and he doesn't come to visit you? | *Aku andombalenga wakalenga aku sipu yu kondoleno waka lelkana konupu akupu akulima pililka nalo, kou **mone** we tolembale akuma na naa pililka, yunga melerenga lipemona andopamo nimbu pilipu andopili mundunjipu siye kolopo, nane pomo menjipu arenga topo molka.* | Knowing that that kind of education will take him a long way away, I would love to see him, but if I have no money I would give that no thought. I would pray that something bad has not happened to him. So I would support him by praying for him. |

(Kuku Raliwa, interview, November 19, 1995, T54A.10)

The two mothers here seem to be expressing ideal outlooks which may or may not bear up under actual events. The kind of parental abandon-ment of which Kuku speaks with regard to her young son would very likely be the source of much anxiety. I have heard many conversations in which the local reputation of clan members living in distant places hangs on their pattern of returning (or not returning) to the Kaugel homeland, their interest and support (monetarily) of community projects, and their sharing of material resources with their local family. That is not to deny the spiritual resources that either of the mothers may have at their dis-posal should the unthinkable occur; rather, I merely emphasize that the consequence of such a development in their children's lives would inevi-tably be the cause of much grief and anxiety. I include this discussion here because it adds yet another dimension to the tension inherent in success-ful education for children in the Tambul Basin: the process not merely permits travel outside of the language areas, but—given the limited num-ber of secondary and tertiary education institutions—*requires* it.

Aika Boké bemoans that very aspect of the products of English educa-tion and, in the process, echoes Dopenu's concern about the lack of es-teem by the younger generation for their parents.

Kinienga kangambola olione mekemoloma kinie kanokomolama kinie nanga **mako** *i na Bokene nikiru nanga* **makona** *mando mando kinie olio kanokomoloma akuna olando olando kinie olio kinie iri tongi kinie kewa ungu leko iri tokomele. Omba enenga kupula anumu andongindu kewanga sait akundu mindi pilikimili. Umbunga ulu pulu akulinga te naa pilimili.*

Akulinga kinienga molko kepe ne nambulka tengi, ulu pulu akumane pakiye yambore kolko kepe uluri tengi kepe kinie akuma liku ai naa sing nakolo. Pe kinie **Mosipi** *molomu lemo* **Lae** *molomu lemo* **Lae** *anju molomba ya i yambore kolkomo ningi lemo ya molombaleneka kanopa anjipe kongiri, langiri lemu lemo ya molko akumaneka koeko noko yando tengi kinie wili akuma yunu kewa ungu, kamele panjipe anju molopa kelengi. Ya ongo kinie uluri tengi nimbu olione kinie pepeya molopo kanokomolole kapola naa manda aku tenginje nimbu kanokomolo.*

Kinienga we kewanga **sait** *aku* **longa sait** *i kundu kinie pepeya suku puku molko pora sikimili. Olionga kangambola mekemolomane kamu anjipe mengi akuma paa* **lo saitina stret** *puku molko andi tenginje nimbu olione kinie we molopo mele kanokomolo akusipe mele kanokomolo nimbu, aku na Bokene nikiru.*

These days our children—the children we [parents], my age and under have begotten—we look at them and see that as they go up, up in school, using the foreign language, they are always defying us. When they wander around they only think about the foreign way of life. They don't care about any indigenous customs.

Thus, what will they do in the future when a person dies? They won't know how to pay respect to the mourners. And then, when they go to [Port] Moresby they'll stay in Moresby; if they live in Lae, they'll stay in Lae; and if they're told that someone here has died and is being prepared for burial [they won't come]. If the pigs and food are gathered here and we steam cook the food and eat, those out there will be talking their foreign language and staying where they are. Now all of us here observe this and know they will not come here and participate in one single activity. Now they have gone altogether over to the foreign side, the lo side. We are observing that our children's children will certainly all go over to the foreign side. I said, that's what we're observing, and I, Boké, am talking.

(Aika Boké, group interview, November 14, 1995, T47A.18–19)

Like Dopenu above, Boké observes the younger generation—he's in his late thirties—and sees a dim future in the lack of knowledge and interest the children express in indigenous ways. They speak the foreign language—English—and imitate foreign ways, but pay little attention to the ways and wisdom of their parents' and grandparents' generations. He envisions the same future posed to Kuku. Although grim, Boké's vision implies a concern that his children and their peers receive a more balanced education, one that will entice them to learn enough of community practices that they can participate intelligently when—if—they return home.

A more positive view is expressed by Korika Lyaka who considers the physical proximity of the Purare KTPPS and the Purare Community School to be a visible confirmation of the community's desire for a stable Umbu-Ungu/English bilingualism.

*Ya Gonoli, Rambai keme ungu mare niringi ne **skul** akumu lemba niringimu kinie nuni aku wendo likinumu, olionga koliamo tepa auli lemba, Umbu-Ungu, **Inglis** tere lepa pemba kinie **skul**solo teluna **lepel** lemba kinie olio kapola, Korika-Kengelka, Aika kangambola kapola tondolo lingi....*	Gonoli, Rambai, [the rest] planned for this [community] school to be here and now [with] the one you started, we can see [Purare] is turning into a big place. Umbu-Ungu and English have been joined together, and the two schools can become equally important now, and Korika-Kengelka and Aika children will be empowered....

(Korika Lyaka, group interview, November 14, 1995, T47.2)

Lyaka approves of the new education reform which is establishing a three-year pre-primary level in the local communities and using the local language as medium of instruction. In his response to the hypothetical assertion that three years of instruction in Umbu-Ungu instead of English will handicap the children's acquisition of English, Lyaka suggests that those who prefer the "submersion" theory of L2 acquisition do not understand how children learn. In his conversation he provides a modest Umbu-Ungu equivalent of Cummins' (1986) "interdependence theory."

*Aku ulu **pawa**mo Umbu-Unguna manda tengi, Inglisina naa tengi...naa manda pilingi aku konopumu lawa tekemo pilikimili.*	[The children] will be able to get understanding [lit., strength] doing Umbu-Ungu, not doing English...[because] they won't be able to understand it; [those people] have the wrong idea.
*Aku ulu akumu Umbu-Ungumu **Inglis** akusolo **sem** tepa. **Skul**isolo lipe tere lepalie teluna pekemo kinie, **skul** akusolo kapola tengili kinie kapola pupa enge pepa pawa lemba kinie **skul** akuma yu mele mele lipe tere leko oro toko pilingina.*	This practice in Umbu-Ungu is the same in English. If the two schools join together in one place that will be good, and they'll have stability and strength, and all the other schools will join together in the same way.

(Korika Lyaka, group interview, November 14, 1995, T47.2)

Lyaka's observation that the physical presence of the new Purare Community School beside the Purare KTPPS is analogous to the community's desire for Umbu-Ungu/English bilingualism supports a general attitude among the research participants that, although English is the most necessary language for academic success, without a corresponding education in Kaugel language and culture, the end product, as expressed by Boké, is unsatisfactory.

A look at some activities of a community intent on bilingualism, however, exposes another set of tensions, those involved in the dynamics of language spread ("an increase in the users and uses of a language or language variety" (Cooper 1989:33); cf. chapter 1) and language shift (when the second language (L2) begins to be used in some or all of the language domains formerly used exclusively by the L1).

The diverse and nearly polarized views regarding the need for or desirability of language and culture maintenance find their meeting ground on Sunday morning at the Kikuwa and Pombol Christian congregations which are attended by a large number of children, including many of the KTPPS students. One of the indicators of language shift in table 1.2 (see chapter 1) is the loss of religious services—originally the domain of the L1—to the dominant L2.

From a strictly linguistic point of view, a Sunday school session can easily pass for an exercise in conscious language shift, with the Sunday school leader as officer-in-charge. Equipped with an inexpensive six string acoustic guitar, he leads an enthusiastic group of about fifty children, ranging in age from two or three years to mid-teens, in a multilingual program. The catalog of language use during a particular session reveals that (1) of the nine songs sung during the session, only two used Umbu-Ungu lyrics, one used words from a closely related dialect, while eight of the nine had some Tok Pisin lyrics; (2) none of the songs were sung to indigenous melodies; (3) the leader used the English tag "Okay" eighteen times; and (4) other than songs and Bible readings (all done in Tok Pisin), Umbu-Ungu was the dominant language being used for all interpretations and explanations of songs, Bible verses, and Bible stories.

Three languages were being used during the singing: Umbu-Ungu, Tok Pisin, and English. On the surface, the children's loud, tuneful rendition of the song indicated that the language used was being understood. The assumption that the children function in all three languages would be misleading, however, as the children rarely use English outside the community school and Sunday school contexts.

A good deal of bilingualism is being modeled by the leader. If bilingualism is, indeed, a community goal and observation and imitation of models are two traditional learning styles, the Sunday school event could be considered a step in the right direction. However, this is obviously *not* the Umbu-Ungu/English bilingualism that the community desires. Table 5.1 shows the distribution of lexical items by language, tabulated from a 60-minute taped transcript of a Sunday school session.

Table 5.1. Distribution of lexical items by language, Sunday school, August 20, 1995

Language	Total number**	Percentage
Umbu-Ungu	3872	54.0
Tok Pisin	2595	36.2
English	193	2.7
Melpa	75	1.0
Wiru	47	0.7
Lexical borrowings*	388	5.4
Total	7170	100.0

* "Lexical borrowings" are English and Tok Pisin words/phrases used in otherwise Umbu-Ungu utterances.

**The figures in this column represent the number of lexical items contained in utterances and/or song lyrics in that language.

If anything, the bilingualism on display during this Sunday school session was Umbu-Ungu/Tok Pisin, not Umbu-Ungu/English. Although no statistically valid comparison can be made from a single Sunday school session to the community in general, the result here is consistent with a general finding reported by Brenzinger, Heine, and Sommer (1991:40) in their study of language shift and language death in Africa.

> European languages are very often labeled as being the primary danger to African languages and cultural heritage. A closer look at reality in most African nations today reveals, however, that it is African lingua francae and other African languages with national or regional status which spread to the detriment of vernaculars.

Tok Pisin, as the primary lingua franca in Papua New Guinea, represents a large and growing linguistic influence. The ample use of Tok Pisin in the Kikuwa PNG Bible Church congregation is recorded in my data (although not reported here), as the congregation is frequently used as a preaching station for students from the PNG Bible School at Tambul, many of whom are from outside the area and do not speak Umbu-Ungu. A more complete study of language use in the Kaugel language area and in the Tambul Basin in particular would be of value in assessing the current status of Umbu-Ungu vis-à-vis Tok Pisin.

Romaine (1995) points out that, although code-switching and lexical borrowing have gone on for hundreds of years in some stable bilingual communities, the practice is almost universally stigmatized. Whether through the linguistic influence of local leaders or (equally likely) through the influence of imported music heard on battery operated radios and cassette players, lexical borrowing and code-switching are common among children and young people in the Tambul Basin. In fact, the widespread and conspicuous use among Kaugel young people and children of Western melodic idioms might qualify the melodies as "loantunes," if ethnomusicologists use such terms. During my visit to the Kalapolo *haus pikisa,* I noted that the children were singing along with music videos in languages as far-off as Kuanua (East New Britain Province) and Kerema (Gulf Province). This multilingual musical selection serves as a metaphor for the complex sociolinguistic context in which Kaugel children are growing up: Melpa and Imbo-Ungu border Kaugel on the northeast and southeast, respectively. Both are from the same language family and the latter is readily intelligible to Umbu-Ungu speakers. Enga is just beyond the mountains at the back of the Basin. An interview with a KTPPS teacher from that area indicated a strong Umbu-Ungu/Enga bilingualism in the half-dozen clans in that area, noting that in more than a few homes Enga as well as Umbu-Ungu is spoken around the evening fires (Kiap Kiwa, personal communication, November 5, 1995, T36). English is the most difficult language for the children in terms of speaking and understanding as it is rarely, if ever, heard outside the classroom in natural language settings.[37] Thus, the goal of Umbu-Ungu/English bilingualism expressed by parents interviewed seems less likely to evolve, given the current situation, than bilingualism involving Umbu-Ungu and Tok Pisin.

Having considered the tensions present in the socialization and education of Kaugel children from the parents' point of view, in the next chapter I will look closely at how a particular KTPPS preschool is affecting language and culture maintenance in the Kaugel community.

---

[37]The exceptions to this are children whose parents, like Rambai and Apé, are fluent in English and teach their children in natural contexts at home.

6

Language, Culture, and Education in the KTPPS Classroom

Temane tolemolole ya kinie kangambolama we sukusingina mele molemele. Ulu pulu talonga sukusingina mele molemelelinga kanopolie temane tolemolo. Te kinie kewa ululinga molko pe ouinga olionga kolepali moloringi aku **tumbuna pasin** *nikimili akulinga kinie* **hap** *tekoka molko, kewa ululinga* **hap** *teko molemelelinga kanopo kinie, kinie ou teringi ulu akuli panjipu temane kange kepe temane kepe pilingindu konupu silimili kanuli.*

(KTPPS teacher, interview, October 12, 1995, Tape 14B)

When we tell stories these days, we say that our children are in-between. We observe that they are living in the middle of two ways of doing things, so we talk about that. One is the foreign way, the other the way our grandparents lived in the past—what we call the "ancestral way." [The children] live partly in one and partly in the other, so when they hear stories of the old ways, along with the legends, they are happy about that.

As noted in chapter 1, one of the Papua New Guinea government's dual goals for *tok ples pri skuls* was "to enable children to develop close ties to the local community" (Department of Education 1990:1). This goal, and the increase in the number of *tok ples pri skul* programs in the country, was partly a response to the language and culture shift that had already resulted from contact between indigenous language groups and regional lingua francas (especially Tok Pisin) and/or English. As noted in chapters 2 and 5, a frequently used sociolinguistic approach to language contact situations like PNG's is to examine language data for indicators of bilingualism, a necessary but not sufficient condition of language shift. In a

153

study of language use in schools, then, the language(s) actually used in classroom communication becomes as pertinent as the semantic content of the language(s) in determining whether or not the classroom is fostering the maintenance of the local language and culture.

Umbu-Ungu, the medium of instruction in most but not all[38] of the KTPPS classrooms, provides the communicative vehicle by which close ties to the community are supposedly developed. In this chapter, language data from a specific classroom is presented featuring interactions between the teacher and students, relating code-switching and lexical borrowing to the language maintenance goal for the *tok ples pri skul*. This includes a description of the use of lexical borrowing in the stories of the Kaugel Reading Series (KRS). Specific problems relating to language use in the curriculum and instructional method are discussed, including the effect of frustrations with lack of pay on the teacher's classroom performance. The success of local involvement with curriculum development and the need for more complete community participation in and control of curriculum development in the future is discussed. Finally, I look closely at the Kaugel Reading Series to discover why teachers repeatedly identified the stories as a key focus of interest for the children. I relate the story content of the Reading Series to Roger's (1992) notions of "concept distance" and "cultural otherness." One specific culturally close feature of the KRS as a whole is analyzed, with implications for producing locally-authored literacy materials for mother-tongue literacy acquisition programs in general.[39]

Language in the Classroom

The teacher-pupil dialogue that follows took place during a classroom "listening story" about a boy who stole sugar cane from an old man's garden. The KTPPS teacher had asked the children to speculate about what they think would happen to the boy. The following exchange "erupted" more than "took place." It was very animated, with several children replying simultaneously (C = children; T = teacher):

---

[38]Two of the fourteen KTPPS programs use Tok Pisin as the medium of instruction. One is at Tambul, a government station, and the other at Maripena, a regional Bible school—both multilingual situations.

[39]Due to the nature of the data presented in this chapter, I have been intentionally vague about names, dates, and locations to protect the identities of those who participated in the study.

C:	*Kot tenjilka...aku kot tenjilka!*	He would take him to court...He would take him to court for that!
T:	*Kot tenjipe pe nambi telka?*	If he took him to court *then* what would happen?
C:	*Selna pulka...selna pulka!*	He'd go to jail...he'd go to jail!
T:	*Selna pupa, pe? Selna pupa nambi telka?*	He would go to jail then? He would go to jail *then* what would happen?
C:	*Pelka...pelka.*	Stay there...stay there [lit., sleep].
T:	*Selna pelka, nambi terimu? Inie kinie nambi terimu?*	He'd stay in there [but] what happened [in the story]? In here [the story] what happened now?
C:	*Selna purumu...selna purumu...lipe memba purumu.... Selna purumu.*	He went to jail... he went to jail...he took him to jail...he went to jail.
T:	*Meli purumu...*	He took him there...
C:	*Hmmm.*	Yes.

(KTPPS classroom visit 1, July, 1995, T8A)

The lexical borrowing in this selection is initiated by the children; the teacher simply accepts the terms and repeats them in his replies. *kot* 'to take to court' and *sel* 'jail/prison', both refer to a judicial system that is a product of *gavman lo* 'government law', that is, both refer to social institutions introduced by the Australian colonial administration in the Tambul area in the 1950s, with various modifications over the years. The children, of course, have known no other system than the village courts that take place, ad hoc, on the local *pena* 'traditional ceremonial meeting ground'. Other than the teacher's earlier use of *pikisana* 'in the picture'—a term whose widespread usage has earned it the status of a loanword—and *orait* 'okay', a tag switch from Tok Pisin, these two terms comprise the only lexical borrowings during the lesson.

Ironically, in the lexical borrowing-rich Sunday school session in chapter 5, teacher and children consistently used an Umbu-Ungu equivalent of jail: *ka ulke* 'jail, prison' [lit., rope house]. The Umbu-Ungu verb phrase *ka si-* 'tether or tie up' (lit. to give rope) referred traditionally to tethering pigs to stakes or trees to prevent them from roaming into the sweet potato gardens. This indicates a missed opportunity on the part of the KTPPS teacher to insert an accepted L1 term for the children's borrowed one. Instead the teacher let the borrowing stand, tacitly approving its use. The children's use of the term indicated that it has been integrated, at least temporarily, into Umbu-Ungu morphology, taking the locative affix -*na* 'in, toward, on' at each occurrence.[40]

Certain lexical borrowings are now so fixed in the children's minds that only direct instruction will change them, if then. The following exchange took place during a "listening story."

T:	*Kango nambi sipenga imbi?*	How many boys' names [are there]?
C:	*Tripela, tripela!*	Three, three!
T:	***Tripela,*** *eh! Yupoko lem, sikeye?*	Three, eh! Three there, is that right?
C:	*Hmmm.*	Yes.

(KTPPS classroom visit 2, August, 1995, T9A)

Later, when the children were drawing pictures on their lapboards, the following exchange took place:

T:	*Kango yupoko unju te toko ulke takonge teringi...*	Three boys chopped down a tree to build a house...
C:	*Tripela.*	Three.
T:	*Kango yupoko...*	Three boys.

(KTPPS classroom visit 2, August, 1995, T9A)

In both exchanges the teacher uses the traditional Umbu-Ungu numeral for three, *yupoko*. However, since European contact and the introduction of a cash-based economy, counting has moved inexorably from the traditional base-four system to the Western base-ten system. All the children count using either Tok Pisin numerals (*wanpela, tupela, tripela, fopela,* etc.) or English (one, two, three, four, etc.—with phonological adaptation, e.g., three is pronounced *tere*). Outside the classroom I observed a grade 1 student counting his deck of cards in English (7/27/95. Field notes 2.2–4) and listened to a tape recording of two young children counting their "stolen" berries in English (with varying degrees of success) (8/29/95, T15).

Other occurrences of lexical borrowing by children are detailed in table 6.1. In chapter 2, I discussed the distinction between established loanwords and nonce borrowings (Poplack, Wheeler, and Westwood 1987). In this chapter I have also included occurrences of code-switching under the general

---

[40]*sel* 'jail' has also undergone phonological integration. However, I have not analyzed L2 borrowings phonologically and, therefore, the transcripts which I used were written phonemically, not phonetically. The exact phonological adaptations are not recorded.

heading of "lexical borrowing.[41] One way of distinguishing them is to analyze "the degree of integration of the borrowed items in the base language" (Romaine 1995:143).

> Haugen (1956) proposed that bilingual phenomena could be situated along a continuum of code-distinctiveness with switching representing maximal distinction, integration (or borrowing) representing maximum leveling of distinctions and interference referring to overlapping of two codes. While it is commonly recognized that not all languages can borrow, it has not been appreciated that not all languages can integrate borrowed material with equal ease without undermining their structural integrity. This is of particular interest when the languages in contact are typologically different and sentence planning strategies may be at odds with one another.... (Romaine 1995:143–144)

Many sociolinguists distinguish forms of lexical borrowing from types of code-switching (Haugen 1956; Poplack and Sankoff 1984; Poplack, Wheeler, and Westwood 1987; Myers-Scotton 1993). Since my focus is on the degree to which any of the phenomena of bilingualism is evidenced in the KTPPS classroom, I have used the term "lexical borrowing" as a general category in table 6.1, subsuming types of code-switching.

In figure 6.1, the idea of the integration (phonologically, syntactically, morphologically and semantically) of borrowed lexical materials into the L1 is contrasted with code-switching, defined as the use of two separate codes, each spoken as a monolingual speaker of each language would speak. INTERFERENCE represents occurrences of utterances in which the codes are "mixed" in a way that would not be spoken by monolingual speakers of either language. The definition of the term "interference" is still being debated among linguists, especially because of its negative connotations. The continuum is valuable for this study because it provides an indicator of the degree of bilingualism in evidence in the KTPPS classroom and the community. A larger proportion of code-switching indicates a higher degree of bilingualism; a larger proportion of integration indicates a much lower degree of bilingualism; and a larger proportion of lexical borrowings (the middle of the continuum) indicates a greater possibility that language shift is occurring.

---

[41]The distinctions between code-switching and lexical borrowing identified since Haugen proposed his continuum have been debated and elaborated considerably as bilingualism has increasingly become a topic of research. However, the relationship among the three categories has remained relatively stable. Haugen's continuum in figure 6.1 (adapted from Haugen 1956) is helpful in interpreting the presentation of data in tables 6.1 and 6.2.

L1< >L2   L1> <L2   L2 > L1
Code-   >   >   >   > Interference >   >   >   > Integration
switching

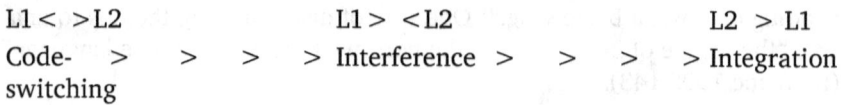

Figure 6.1. Continuum: Code-switching and integration in lexical
borrowings.

The data presented in table 6.1 relates to the use of lexical borrowing
and code-switching by children in a KTPPS classroom during a total of six
school days over a two-week period. The first column displays the specific
borrowing or code-switch with a gloss. The column headed "Type" presents a label that distinguishes borrowings as code-switching, nonce
borrowings, or loanwords (see chapter 2 for definitions). The "Nbr." column shows the total occurrences of the borrowings recorded. The curriculum component or extracurricular event in which the borrowings
occurred is listed under "Context." Any pertinent information is given in
the final "Notes" column.

Table 6.1. Lexical borrowings by KTPPS children

Type	Lexical borrowing	Nbr	Context	Notes
code-switch intersentential (TP)	*pora, pinis, pinis long en, pora* 'Finish, finish, it's finished, finish'		listening story	
code-switch intra-sentential	*ulke haus kol* 'house, modern bush house'	1	experience story	
nonce borrowing (E)	*kopiket* 'copycat', *kopi* 'copy' *Pas* 'Pass'		shared reading review of listening story	
nonce borrowing (TP)	*raskol* 'criminal'	2	listening story	
	busina 'to the bush/forest'	1	listening story	common U-U equivalent: *kondena* or *lamana*.
	lain 'line'	1	child-to-child	commonly used U-U equivalent: *talape*.[42]
	welman 'wild man'	1	shared reading	U-U term, *wenewene*.
loanword (E)	*gan* 'gun'	1	listening story	no accepted U-U equivalent.
	gol 'goal'	1	syllable game	no U-U equivalent.
	sikisti 'sixty; speedy, swiftly' as in *givim sikisti* 'go like sixty; fast'		review of listening story	U-U equivalent: *lkisipe te-* 'do quickly, swiftly'.

[42]There may be another interpretation of this—that of gender deference—because *talape* often refers to the line of *men* who represent the clan at traditional public ceremonies, and to the clan generally; I doubt, however, that that is the case here since children and teachers commonly use the term in school situations for forming lines for assembly, etc.

loanword (TP)		1	between lessons	*boku* is standard usage in the community.
boku 'book'				
haus kol 'modern bush house' [lit., cold house]		1	experience story	
pos 'post'		4	experience story	
stoa 'store'		1	assembly	no accepted U-U equivalent.
tripela 'three'		4	story writing	
tripela 'three'		4	listening story review	traditional term exists but is rarely used by children.
popela 'four'		1	syllable game	
paipela 'five'		1	syllable game	
hia 'here'		79	multiple settings	
bokis 'box'		3	syllable drill	
sok 'chalk'		1	writing letters properly	

The Tok Pisin term *hia* 'here', with seventy-nine occurrences, was the most problematic as far as analysis goes. Phonologically and semantically it is similar to the Umbu-Ungu locative *ya* 'here'. The children use the term when clamoring for the teacher's attention as s/he calls for volunteers, with the subsequent rapid-fire, *hia, hia, hia, ya, ya, ya*...(both meaning 'here, me') being distinguished from each other only by the slight initial aspiration audible from time to time. The large number of occurrences of the term, therefore, does not represent as important a usage as a clearly borrowed term would have.

The eight occurrences of *tripela* 'three' (most often pronounced *terepela*) confirm a general observation that the children rarely use traditional numerals other than *telu, talo* 'one, two', preferring the Tok Pisin *wanpela, tupela, tripela, fopela,* etc. or English, one, two, three, four, etc. This phenomenon is not surprising since the introduced base-ten counting system dominates the country's cash economy.

The children's use of the Tok Pisin term *bokis* 'box', is an echo of the school term for the grid put on the chalkboard by the teacher to teach syllables. In the community, the term generally refers to cardboard cartons and any other box-like container. The only possible Umbu-Ungu alternative, *mingi* 'container, vessel', is used primarily to denote rounded containers, like water gourds, sauce pans, bottles, et cetera. The term *pos* 'post' had been featured in the children's experience story for that day and was written on the chalkboard. The frequency of that word in the count was the result of its use as part of the lesson. Finally, the two occurrences of *raskol* 'criminal, gang member' were used by two different students, both in reference to ambiguous illustrations which they and the other children had been asked to interpret (see appendix B.3 for facsimile of this story). The artist intended to depict three young men horsing around playfully, with one of the fellows holding one of the other two by the foot. The first student interpreted the illustration as two *raskol* attacking the third fellow. The same student subsequently interpreted an *ama* 'hammer' in another illustration as a *gan* 'gun'. Although the teacher explained that the characters were carpenters, another student interpreted a third picture as a *raskol* on his way to the *bus* 'forest, wilderness'. Noteworthy also is that all of the characters in these stories are dressed in completely Western-style clothing with nonindigenous tools. Thus, to a certain degree, the artist and author conspired to create a new, *gavman lo*-type of context which, surprisingly, elicited only three lexical borrowings (*raskol, gan,* and *bus*) from the children.

To summarize, the KTPPS children I observed during the period of my field work demonstrated a frequency and range of lexical borrowings that is hardly alarming. Umbu-Ungu clearly enjoyed a privileged status in and out of the classroom. However, since Kaugel children's traditional learning style (as discussed in chapter 3) includes observation of adult models as a key vehicle for their acquisition of cultural values, the role of the classroom teacher needs to be considered. In KTPPS classrooms, the teachers provide a model for language use. Therefore, an analysis of the teacher's use of code-switching and lexical borrowing will provide a sense of the degree to which the KTPPS program provides an auxiliary context to the home for language maintenance. Table 6.2 details the types and occurrences of one teacher's use of code-switching and lexical borrowing.

Several points demonstrated in table 6.2 bear special mention. First, only two occurrences of code-switching were recorded, one of which was clearly related to my presence in the classroom. Since code-switching is the stronger indication of bilingualism, its virtual absence from the teacher's language modeling can be interpreted as an indication that this particular classroom represents a safe "domain" for L1 maintenance.

The second point is that the teacher's most frequently occurring lexical borrowings were all related to pedagogical "patter": *wan-tu-tri* 'one-two-three' (used thirty-seven times), *pikisa* 'picture' (used sixteen times), *sok* 'chalk' (used eight times), *blekbot* 'blackboard' (used five times), *stat* 'start, begin' (used four times), and *boku* 'book' (used three times). All but one of these terms represent objects or practices that have no corollaries in traditional culture. The only exception is *stat* 'start' which has a commonly used U-U equivalent, *pulu monji-* 'to begin, commence' as in *pulu monjamili* 'let's begin'.

Tag switches—*Okay* (used five times) and *orait* (used twelve times)—are the only other frequently used borrowings. Tag switches are commonly used by almost all Kaugel bilinguals. Umbu-Ungu tags—*manda* and *kapola* both of which convey the sense of 'good, all right, sufficient'—are readily available and also commonly used by the teacher in the classroom.

Of the remaining borrowings, five are simply "echo" repetitions—immediate, usually verbatim restatements of the children's own borrowings. When the teacher asks the children to predict what would happen to the boy who stole sugar cane in the example that begins this chapter, the children introduce the Tok Pisin terms *kot* and *sel,* which the teacher repeats for the purpose of eliciting a further response. He repeats the same process for the children's introduction of *raskol, stoa, tripela.*

Table 6.2. Lexical borrowings by KTPPS teacher recorded over six observation sessions

Type	Lexical borrowing	Nbr.	Context	Notes
codeswitch intersentential (U-U-TP)	*Pupulie ulka kanopolie kelepo omolo. Mipela bai go ausait liklik.* 'After we go and see the house we'll leave and come back. [To me] We're going outside for a little while…'	1	experience story	
codeswitch intrasentential (TP-E-U-U)	*Tenkyu, Lod Jisas, sukuli temolondo…* 'Thank you, Lord Jesus, we are about to do school…'	1	prayer	
tag switch (E)	*okay*	5	multiple settings	
tag switch (TP)	*orait* 'okay, all right'	12	multiple settings	
nonce borrowing (E)	*selna* 'in jail/to jail'	3	listening story	U-U equivalent, *ka ulke.*
	stret 'straight, flat, smooth, correct'	1	spelling lesson	U-U term equivalent.
	point 'point(s)'	2	syllable game	No commonly used U-U equivalent.
nonce borrowing (TP)	*wan wan* 'each'	3	experience story	
	bihainim 'to follow'	2	experience story	U-U equivalent *lombili le-.*
	traim 'to try'	1	experience story	
	stori 'story'	1	experience story	U-U equivalent, *temane.*
	blesim 'to bless'	2	prayer	U-U equivalent available, but *blesim* is frequently heard in church services.

raskol 'criminal'	1	listening story	
tambuim 'prohibit, forbid'	1	to a person outside the classroom	
bungim 'collect, join, gather together'	1	review of children's experience story	
laikina 'as you like'	1	story writing	
laikim 'to like, to want'	1	syllable lesson	
stat 'to begin, start'	4	experience story/ syllable game	
pes 'face'	1	keyword lesson	
Sande 'Sunday'	1	syllable activity	U-U equivalent is *koro awili* 'big rest [from work],' a loanshift, in Haugen's terminology.
redi 'ready, prepared'	2	spelling lesson	U-U equivalent is available.
sekim 'to shake, bounce'	1	announcements	
loanword (E)			
wan-tu-tri 'ready, set, go (as in "one-two-three")'	37	experience story	
integrated loanword (TP)			
bokuna 'in the book'	2	listening story	No U-U equivalent.
buk 'book'	1	between lessons	
kot 'to take to court'	4	listening story	
pikisa 'picture'	8	experience story	

integrated	*pikisana* 'in the picture'	5	listening story	
	pikisale 'this picture'	3	keyword lesson	
integrated	*bokunaka* 'in this book'	1	listening story	
	stoa 'store'	1	line-up outside to start school	
	blakbot 'chalkboard, lapboard'	4	story writing	No U-U equivalent.
integrated	*blakbotma* 'chalkboards, lapboards'	1	story writing	No U-U equivalent.
	sok 'chalk'	8	story writing	No U-U equivalent.
	tripela 'three'	2	shared reading	
	bokis 'box'	2	syllable lesson	No U-U equivalent.
integrated	*bokisna* 'in the box'	1	syllable lesson	No U-U equivalent.
integrated	*golnale* 'compete for goal(s), points'	1	syllable game	
	paip 'five'	2	syllable game	
	skul 'school'	2	prayer	

TP = Tok Pisin, E = English, U-U = Umbu-Ungu, T = teacher

A comparison of nonce borrowings with the more established and widely used loanwords shows them evenly divided in terms of items—eighteen nonce borrowings and seventeen loanwords—but unevenly distributed, with twenty-eight occurrences of the nonce borrowings and eighty-five of the loanwords. This also indicates that the teacher limits ad hoc lexical borrowings in the classroom, and is more likely to introduce those which are already widely used in the community. All of this supports the assertion above, that this KTPPS classroom provides a positive context for mother-tongue language maintenance in a multilingual setting.

The total number of lexical borrowings listed in tables 6.1 and 6.2, when compared to the total corpus of lexical items recorded over the six days, indicates that their use in the classroom is relatively infrequent (table 6.3). In fact, the ease with which code-switching and lexical borrowing can be identified in the recorded texts suggests limited usage.

Table 6.3. Code-switching/lexical borrowings in KTPPS classroom

Visit	TS	CS1	CS2	LB1	LB2	Total CS/LB	approx. % of text	[total words][43]
#1	8	1	2	70	11	92	3.4%	[2,721]
#2	5	0	0	98	11	114	3.6%	[3,152]
#3	4	0	1	55	9	69	1.5%	[4,526]
#4	0	0	0	16	0	16	0.7%	[2,334]
#5	0	0	1	0	2	3	0.2%	[1,182]
#6	0	0	0	42	0	42	3.1%	[1,352]
Total	17	1	4	281	33	336	2.4%	[15,298]

TS = tag switch
CS1 = code-switch intersentential
CS2 = code-switch intrasentential
LB1 = lexical borrowing isolated
LB2 = lexical borrowing integrated

The figures in table 6.3 are the composite of the code-switches and lexical borrowing in tables 6.1 and 6.2, along with the lexical borrowings from the KRS stories read by or to the children during recorded sessions. The totals include the problematic *hia* and *ya*. If that usage is discounted (included under the column LB1), the percentages will drop even further.

[43]The perecentage recorded in this column is approximate because the tape recording equipment in the classroom was insufficient to record all the language used by the teacher and students.

Comparing the over-all occurrence of lexical borrowing in the KTPPS classroom with those in the Sunday school class described in chapter 5, a dramatic contrast appears. Table 6.4 displays the number of lexical borrowings used by the Sunday school leader and children on a single occasion.

Table 6.4. Code-switching/lexical borrowings, Sunday school class

Date	Non U-U[44]	TS	CS1[45]	CS2	LB1	LB2	Total	approx. % of text [total]
8/20/95	2,910	24	(83)	(48)	292	72	3298	46% [7,170]

TS = tag switch
CS1 = code-switch intersentential
CS2 = code-switch intrasentential
LB1 = lexical borrowing isolated
LB2 = lexical borrowing integrated

The mixed linguistic signals communicated in the single Sunday school session represents a situation that, according to experiences in other parts of the world (chapter 1), is clearly promoting language shift. The songs that were sung by children and song leader included lyrics in Tok Pisin, English, Melpa, Wiru, Imbo-Ungu, and Umbu-Ungu. A long prayer was offered in Tok Pisin and all scripture reading and memory verse practice was in Tok Pisin. When compared to the Sunday school, the KTPPS classroom is seen even more clearly as a small but important refuge for the mother tongue.

An additional consideration emerging from this analysis of lexical borrowing is the presence of non-Umbu-Ungu terms in the Kaugel Reading Series. The large number of lexical borrowings on class visit 2 derived from the story for the day and the follow-up discussion. The story of three brothers—"Hammer," "Nails," and "Saw"—and their father, "Machine," engaged the children's interest immediately and held it throughout (see following section, this chapter). Is this story, with its inherent interest and delight and its attitudes favorable to language and culture shift typical of the stories in the KRS? If it is typical, one could be justifiably concerned that the KTPPS goal of enabling children to develop close ties to the local language and traditional ways is being compromised. Thus, a review of

---

[44]The non-Umbu-Ungu lexical items include: Tok Pisin, 2,595; Melpa, 75; Wiru, 47; English, 193.

[45]The numbers for CS1 and CS2 are not included in the total as they are simply a tally of the occurrences of intersentential and intrasentential code-switches, not a reference to the number of lexical items involved (the latter being included under the "Non-Umbu-Ungu" category).

the ninety-six stories of the KRS is warranted in order to determine to what extent the books do or do not support L1 maintenance over L2 acquisition.

Of the total ninety-six stories in the Kaugel Reading Series, twenty-four have occurrences of lexical borrowing. The total of one hundred twenty-seven borrowings,[46] however, are not evenly distributed among the twenty-four stories. Six stories account for ninety-three of the total borrowed items. As shown in table 6.5, the focus in each of these six stories is on an encounter with some aspect of the new culture, for which borrowed terms are normally required.[47]

Table 6.5 Lexical borrowing in Kaugel Reading Series stories
(representing 73% of total number)

Nbr.*	Title	Topic	Borrowings
6.4	"Ambola Teresenga Temane" (Teresa's story)	Ideal girl at school/ home	*Teresa* '[girl's name]',** *sukuli* 'school', *bello* 'bell', *tisa* 'teacher', *tisamo* 'the teacher'
9.3	"Mekene Temane te Olio Topa Simbe" (Mek is going to tell us a story)	Trip to the Hagen Show, 1973	1973, *Akena* 'Mt. Hagen', *So* 'Show', *Sona* 'into the Show', *ellepende* 'elephant', *karo* 'car', *rapa* 'rubber'
10.2	"Lopa Posi Temane" (The pussycat story)	Boy raises a cat to sell at market and buy things at the store	*posi* 'pussycat', *posimu* 'the pussycat', *makete* 'market', *maketena* 'to/in the market', *paono* 'pound/£', *pame* 'to buy', *mone* 'money', *sukuli* 'school', *sukulina* 'to/in school'

---

[46]I have not elaborated on the types of occurrences as their relevance to this case study is minimal. The distinction made above between isolated and integrated borrowings yielded a similar distribution to tables 6.1 and 6.2: of one hundred twenty-seven total borrowings, only seventeen were integrated grammatically into the L1.

[47]Although some linguists contend that the languages of even the most isolated ethnocultural groups have the potential to name or express any new objects, concepts, or processes that affect their lives, the actual practice, at least among Umbu-Ungu speakers, is to adopt ready-made terminology from the L2 culture. Thus, in Umbu-Ungu, *buru mingi* 'container that makes the *buru* sound like certain insects' for airplane has been replaced with the Tok Pisin term, *balus* (pronounced /ballose/ by most Umbu-Ungu speakers).

13.2	"Ulke Takolemele Melemanga Temane" (Story about things for building houses)	Carpenters— hammer, saw, nails and ma- chine—build modern houses fast!	Ama/ama 'hammer', So/so 'saw', Pirimu/pirimu 'nails',*** Masine/masine 'ma- chine', kapa 'iron'
13.4	"Ambo Ambu Tenga Langi Koyerimu Temane" (Story of the old woman who cooked food)	An old woman gets mixed up between two new words: mar- garine and soap	girisi 'grease/margarine/ butter', sop 'soap', sitowa 'store'
14.4	"Kango Talo Tauno Kolia Puringili Temane" (Story of the two boys who went to town")	Two boys go to town and have an adventure	Jane 'John', Janene 'John-actor', Pollo 'Paul', Pollone 'Paul-actor', tauno 'town', sitowa 'store' sitowana 'to/in the store', karo 'car', mone 'money', pame 'to buy'

*"Nbr." indicates the book and story number.

**Proper names taken from Western languages have been included as "bor-rowing" in spite of the common practice among Umbu-Ungu speakers to take names from other languages (e.g., many Lutherans have Kâte names because a Kâte evangelist accompanied the first expatriate missionary into the area)

***Pirimu is Umbu-Ungu, originally denoting long sharp thorns. Its meaning has expanded to include 'nails' as its primary definition; Haugen calls this form a loanshift (i.e., semantic borrowing); cf. Romaine (1995).

It is important to note that, in contrast to the borrowings recorded in the KTPPS classroom and Sunday school sessions, none of the lexical borrowings in the KRS were terms that have a commonly used equivalent in Umbu-Ungu. As shown later in this chapter, the ninety-six stories as a whole also present content and characters that the children perceive as "near" in a cultural as well as a psychological sense. Thus, the reading ma-terials combine with a medium of instruction that primarily—if not exclu-sively—affirms and supports the children's mother tongue.

The data on lexical borrowing and code-switching above are not meant as a criticism of any one KTPPS or Sunday school teacher or group of chil-dren. It would be pointless and unfair to stigmatize users of loanwords for displaying a bilingualism that elsewhere I argue is a legitimate and neces-sary community value (chapter 5). In fact, current theorists and researchers in the area of bilingualism are increasingly reluctant to cast any type of code-switching and lexical borrowing in a pejorative light.

Tables 6.1 and 6.2 display the kind and extent of lexical borrowing that is going on in the KTPPS classroom context. If bilingual speakers are in control of their borrowings, there may be situations and occasions in which selectivity is highly desirable. For example, as demonstrated here and in chapter 5, worship, usually considered an important domain for language maintenance (chapter 1), gives strong indications of promoting shift to a more dominant language (Tok Pisin). Those L1 domains that still remain may need to be actively and consciously protected in order to maintain the mother tongue. The home, of course, remains the pivotal element in successful L1 maintenance (Dorian 1981; Fishman 1991; Wong Fillmore 1991; Moll 1992). However, creating and protecting auxiliary domains that promote L1 can help to relieve some of the pressure from more dominant languages—*if* that is what a majority of the community desires. The KTPPS classroom is an excellent example of such an auxiliary domain. It gives strong indications that its mother-tongue curriculum and instruction can provide Kaugel children with a physical context in which L1 usage is privileged. Whether it can also provide a safe haven for Kaugel culture maintenance is the subject taken up next.

Culture and Traditional Values in the Classroom

The KTPPS teacher squats between the two lines of students—6- to 8-year-olds—his back to the chalkboard. He wears an old pair of beige flannel dress pants rolled up to the knee, a well-worn, dark blue short-sleeve knit shirt and a lightweight jacket. The morning mountain air is cool.

On his left, ten girls sit crossed-legged or kneeling. One girl who has been singing a *lotu* 'worship' song quietly to herself wears a skirt with a red cardigan that partially covers her t-shirt announcing AVIATOR and COMMANDO FIGHTERS (to those who read English) in large block letters which are partially obscured by the small, colorful netbag hanging around her neck. Beside her, another girl wears a print dress and sweat shirt zippered in front but partially open, with a netbag around her neck. In fact, looking down the line of girls, only one has no netbag.

On the teacher's right, three boys sit crossed-legged. One wears shorts and a royal blue sweatshirt, another shorts and an olive green sweat shirt, with its hood pulled over his head. No one is wearing traditional clothes.

On the green chalkboard behind the teacher, *Ulke Temane* "House Story" is printed in large balloon letters, outlined in blue chalk and filled in with white. Under the title, the teacher has printed four lines of text from yesterday's children's experience story:

*Ulke takongendo oie **pos** tolimele.*
Pe kolo tolimele. Kolo toko pora siku ulke takolimele.
*Pe **pos** monjiku kokeia kaloko ulke takolimele.*
Pe takoko pora siku kaloko pelimele.

In house building they first cut posts.
Then they clear the spot. Having cleared the spot they build the house.
Then they plant posts, attach rafters, then roof the house.
After they have finished roofing it they light a fire and sleep in it.

The theme for this week is "house."

The teacher positions himself toward the boys' side. He holds Book 13 of the Kaugel Reading Series open to pages 10 and 11: "The Story about Things for Building Houses" (see appendix B3 for a facsimile of the story). Kaugel Reading Series books are small (6.5" × 8"). The children farthest from the teacher can make out the line-drawn illustrations but not the print. This story is not meant to be read by the children. It's a "listening story."

The author of the story has engaged the children's interest by using the names of house-building tools for the names of the characters: three brothers (Hammer, Nail, Saw) and their father (Machine).[48] The children have been enthusiastically predicting actions and outcomes from page to page, laughing, talking excitedly to each other as each page is turned. The teacher turns to the final page and asks what the children see. The illustration shows a hammer, nail, and saw. One girl replies: "Hammer and nail and saw." Then the following exchange occurs:

---

[48]*Masini* 'machine' refers, probably, to an electric power saw or drill run off a portable generator or a gasoline-powered chain saw.

T = teacher, C = children, B = boy

T: *Hmmmm. Manda, Kinie kango te kango Ama. Pirimu, Kango So akupoko piliku aku moloringi. Kinie inie mere nambi teko moloringi kanamili. [Reads from page 16]: "Kinie olio kanokomolo. Ulu i sipe wendo okomo. Kapa ulke takolemele koliamo mele imane takolemele. Ama, pirimu, so kinie masini." Pilikimili?*

Hmmm. OK, now one boy is **Hammer,** [one] Nail, [one] boy **Saw,** [pointing to the picture] those who just understood these few things. Now let's see what is happening down here. [Reads from page 16]: "Now we see. This is the practice that's arisen. At the place where they build houses with **iron** roofs, they use these things: **hammer, nails, saw,** and **machines.**" Do you understand?

C: *Hmmm.*

Hmmm. [affirmative]

T: *Aku **kapa** ulke temaneli tokomolo. **Pirimu, so, ama** melema naa lelanje nambi telka?*

We are reading the **iron-roof** house story. If **nails, saw, hammer,** and things had not been there, what would they have done?

B: *Kou muluni tolemele.*

They use stones.

T: ***Pirimu** naa lelanje nambe telemela? Ulke takolemela molo naa takolemela?*

If there had not been **nails,** what would they have done? Would they have built the house or not?

C: *[unison] Naa takolemela!*

[in chorus] They would not have built it!

T: ***So** naa lelanje?*

If there had been no **saw?**

C: *[unison] Naa takolemela!*

[in chorus] They would not have built it!

T: ***Ama** naa lelanje?*

If there had been no **hammer?**

C: *[unison] Naa takolemela!*

[in chorus] They would not have built it!

T: *Pe lerimuli nambi teringi?*

So what did they do with what *was* there?

C: *Takoringi.*

They built it.

T: *Takoringi. Manda, kinie olionga temane te kanu ombo topo pora sikimulu.*

They built it. OK, now we have come to the end of our story.

(KTPPS classroom visit 2, August, 1995, T9A.8)

The focal point in this exchange is the boy's response to the teacher's "what if" question: "They [customarily] use stones." The boy is speaking from experience. Grammatically, he shifts from the subjunctive to the habitual. He is not hypothesizing. He has seen his fathers and brothers, when a hammer was needed but unavailable, pick up an egg-shaped stone and pound or strike the object—perhaps even nails—successfully. The teacher overrides the boy's observation by enlisting the class in a litany that reestablishes nonindigenous tools to a position of necessity.

The use of stones as common, essential tools for daily life is not that far distant, chronologically, from the KTPPS children and their families. Most of their grandfathers used stone axes. A mere fifty years ago, excellent houses, fences, and bridges were regularly built with some combination of wood and stone implements. Trees still stand in their forests and gardens that bear the signatures of sharpened stone.

In this instance, the teacher has denigrated the cultural importance of stones. An opportunity to talk about the wisdom, strength, skill, and perseverance of their ancestors, who built everything using stone tools, has been neglected in exchange for a reiteration of the superior qualities of the new, introduced tools, echoing the author's words (p. 15): *Yambo kanumune kanoko mini wale munduringi* 'When those people saw that they were amazed'.

In his defense, the teacher could well have been making a case for the context of the story, that of building a house with an iron roof, an undertaking that requires new equipment. Besides, the previous day's lesson had been devoted to traditional house building as attested to by the story on the chalkboard. In addition, the teacher is old enough to know that the story in Book 13 is based on the erection of the very classroom in which he and the children are meeting. He was, perhaps, reemphasizing the wonder that historical event created in those who had experienced it.

The episode above, with its story of nonindigenous house building with nonindigenous tools inside a nonindigenous classroom using the indigenous language, raises the question adapted from Harris (1994) in reference to Aboriginal culture: can Kaugel children learn Kaugel things in Kaugel ways for Kaugel purposes in the context of a "Western-style" school?[49] The answer in the Kaugel case is "perhaps." The form of the classroom and the use of Western materials need not preclude promotion of Kaugel ways if the curriculum and instructional method model the values that Kaugel parents want their children to carry into the future.

The instructional methods for teaching in the KTPPS classroom are patterned on traditional Western models rather than on those of traditional informal Kaugel education and require a conscious effort on the part of the teacher to link classroom activities to community life. Depending on the teachers' level of preparation and energy (which, as noted in chapter 4, frequently is linked to their level of pay), teachers can provide the children with culturally appropriate activities that help them relate the classroom lessons to their own lives. An example is the class visit to a nearby village house that preceded that day's experience story, *Ulke Temane*

---

[49]Harris's question was actually a statement, "Schools as far as possible should do Aboriginal things in Aboriginal ways in Aboriginal contexts for Aboriginal purposes" (1994:144).

'House Story'. Following the short field trip, the teacher opened the discussion by writing the story title on the chalkboard, announcing the topic and asking, "What comes after that, eh? Who knows...?" Below is an edited version of the dialogue that followed, including only the children's responses (and excluding repetitions) (B = boy, G = girl; C = children).

B: *Pos liku aku telemele.*	They get posts, that's what they do.
C: *Kokea [timber]....*	Rafters....
B: *[I] siku marena winju mundulimele kinie unju we panjiku anjilimili.*	They go around up there, collecting timber and standing it up [against something].
B: *Pele lelemele.*	They cut "battens"....
B: *Unju ka.*	[They collect] vines [i.e., rope-like vine]
C: *Kia...toko takolemele.*	They cut *pitpit* to use to thatch the roof.
B: *Ulke takolemele.*	They build the house.
B: *Ga koekolemolo.*	We steam-cook sweet potato in ground ovens.
C: *Kengendelemele...borolemolo.*	They uncover the food and we get it out of the ground.
C: *Pelemele.*	They live in [the house].

(KTPPS classroom visit 1, July, 1995, T8A)

The teacher then had the children repeat the process, including all the elements above, as he wrote the following story on the chalkboard.

Ulke Temane	House Story
*Ulke takongendo oie **pos** tolemele.*	In order to build a house they first cut **posts.**
Pe kolo tolemele. Kolo toko pora siku ulke takolemele.	Then they prepare the spot for the house. Having finished preparing the spot, they build the house.
*Pe **pos** monjiku kokea kalko ulke takolemele.*	Then they plant the **posts,** attach the rafters, thatch the roof.
Pe takoko pora siku kalko pelemele.	After they have finished the roof, they light a fire and live in [the house].

(Field notes 1.24, July, 1995)

The problem with this rendition of the children's "experience" is that the teacher has excluded the only element of the story—other than living in a completed house—that the children have experienced directly: the cooking and the eating of the food. Not only are the children left out, the role of the female members of the community who bring and prepare the food has also been ignored. That this is true is underscored by the fact that the person affix of the verbs used in the chalkboard version of the story—*telemele, anjilimili, takolelmele, lelemele*—are all third person plural. The terms used by the children during the question-and-answer time but excluded from the final version—*koekolemolo* and *borolemolo*—are both first person plural inclusive.

The custom of steam-cooking sweet potato and vegetables for the housebuilders is an essential, not optional, element of the housebuilding process. The preparation and eating of the food is a community event. In the story written on the chalkboard, the housebuilding process has been reduced to a male activity. Although this confirms a pattern of male dominance in traditional Kaugel society, the larger goal of Kaugel cultural maintenance is not served well. The following day, during the scheduled review of Monday's "experience story," each of the three boys present came to the chalkboard and read selected sentences. Then this exchange occurred:

T: *Te nae? Mandopali. Nae nimbe? Ambola te. Ambola te temane teyangi. Naa nimbe? Eh? [Girl's name]! [No response] Nae nimbe? [Second girl's name]? [No response.] Naa ka nini? [Third girl's name]!* — Who else? The next line [of the story] down. Who will read it? Let one of the girls do the story. Who will read it, eh? [name]! Who will read it? [name]? You won't read it either? [name]!

G: *[To other girls] I mere akuna **lain** teko niliku winju-winju pai.* — Start from down at the other end and you read this direction. [In other words, "Don't start with me, I'm not at the beginning of the line."]

T: *Olio pali tere lepo nikimulu kanumele altopo niemili....* — Let's all join together and read [the story] again.

(KTPPS classroom visit 2, August, 1995, T9A)

Since the girls had deferred to the boys during the entire discussion of housebuilding—with the brief exception of references to cooking the after-housebuilding feast—their reticence to participate in the reading activity may simply have been an extension of being excluded from the content. That this was unusual behavior on their part was confirmed by one boy's unsolicited observation at the end of the review lesson: *Ambola paa kolte paa naa niringi* 'Not even one girl has read anything' (KTPPS classroom visit 2, August, 1995, T9A).

The following week's experience story produced a similar lesson, based on the cultural theme of *Yema* 'Men'. Ironically, there was only one boy among the six students that day, making the girls' participation in the activity a necessity. The children's "experience" was merely a discussion of activities that men customarily do. The following exchange illustrates the lack of conscious motivation on the teacher's part to affirm local culture as a feature of the reading lesson.

T:	*Kinie mendo...tene te pilikimili, yemane nambulka ulu telemele?*	Now after this...is one of you thinking of one? What are things men do?
G1:	*Pulue teko panjilimili.*	They break off tangket leaves and wear them.
T:	*Pulue teko panjilimili.*	They break off tangket leaves and wear them.
C:	*Wambale panjilimili.*	They wear the front covering.
T:	*Wambale panjilimili....te?*	They wear the front covering...another?
C:	*Wale pakoli pakolemele.*	They wear shirts.
T:	*Wale pakoli pakolemele...te?*	They wear shirts...another?
G2:	*Unju kola mengi lilimili.*	They get and carry tree branches.
T:	*Unju kola mengi tolemeleka...te?*	They break off and carry tree branches...another?
C:	*Yambo marenga kongono tenjilimili.*	They work for other people's benefit
T:	*Yambo marenga kongono tenjilimilika. Manda. Kinie imbi tokoro kanai.*	They do other people's work, too. OK. Now watch what I'm writing.

Yemanga Temane	Men's Story
Olio kanolimulu keni ulu aisili telemele.	When we observe men they do many activities.
Yemane ulke takolime pe ulu mare ausili telemele.	Men build houses and do many other activities.
Yemane unju kepi melemele pe lopa tolimeleka.	Men carry timber and also hunt marsupials.
Uluma pali yemane mindi telemele.	Only men do all these things.

(KTPPS classroom visit 3, August, 1995, T10A)

In the exchange above, the first girl focuses her response on one of the most obvious differences, traditionally, between men and women, namely, what they wear. Men wear *pulue* 'tangket leaves' as part of any costume at traditional ceremonies, and many of them still wear them for daily activities around home. The other children follow her lead and identify other men's clothing: traditional *wambale* 'front covering' (now usually a length of cotton or synthetic material folded lengthwise and draped over a belt) and *wale pakoli* 'shirt'.[50] Thus, the children have all identified men's things, using traditional terminology. To that, a second girl adds the observation that men carry branches broken from trees. Men carry branches for various purposes: for firewood, for making fences, for housebuilding. The children, in this brief segment, give expression to daily cultural events. Another child adds that some men work for the benefit of others. Although this may be a reference to Apé, who was present with me, and worked "for my benefit," the phrase is descriptive of a highly valued community trait: clan members working jointly, cooperatively, for the mutual benefit of all. None of these contributions to the discussion end up in the "children's experience story."

That the outcome of these language education activities result, to some degree, from the nonindigenous setting in a Western-style classroom, with Western-style instructional patterns, cannot be inferred from the data. What is clear is that the teacher has made no conscious effort to use the children's knowledge of local cultural activities to help them develop positive attitudes toward the local community or to incorporate their thoughts and language into the content of the "children's" story.

At least part of this indifference to cultural maintenance opportunities may be attributed to this teacher's self-admitted disgruntlement over reduced pay for the KTPPS teachers, including himself, that resulted from the almost simultaneous expansion of the KTPPS program, the decision by the Village Services Department to rescind support of TPPS teachers, the KTPPS administrator's enlarged responsibilities with regard to roles with the National Literacy and Awareness Council, the PNG Bible Translation Association Board of Governors, and with SIL programs, and the devaluation of the national currency (see chapter 4). Economy-generated enervation may have its pedagogical ramifications.

For whatever reason, for two consecutive weeks, men's work was portrayed as pre-eminent, in a way that is not cultural, as even the most prestigious of big-men will ascribe his success to the joint efforts of his clan members, including his wives and female relatives who plant, tend, and harvest the gardens, feed and care for the pigs, and nurture and raise the children (cf. A. Strathern 1979:36–37).

One way in which indigenous culture *is* supported in the KTPPS classroom is the frequent opportunities provided by the culturally "near" story content of the Kaugel Reading Series for teacher and students to consider local values and beliefs in a way not available in the community school context. The examples below are selected to sketch the range of cultural discussions elicited

[50]This term qualifies as a loanshift in that it refers solely to shirts and blouses introduced since European contact. The term, literally, means 'the netbag *(wale)* that is customarily put on *(pakoli)*.'

by these stories in KTPPS classrooms; it is not an exhaustive list. The last section of the chapter looks more closely at the KRS as a key factor in promoting culture maintenance in KTPPS classrooms.

The *Wenewene Temane* "An Ogre/Echo Story" (KRS, Book 5, pp. 38–44) provided children with an opportunity to express their knowledge of a traditional animistic cosmology that posits a "middle" world of unseen, mostly malevolent beings. In the story three boys go to a place specified only as "the place where the *wenewene* lives." The *wenewene* is credited with being able to repeat (echo) human speech.

T:	*Pilikimili? Wenewene kolia moloi tena molkomonje?*	Do you all understand? Where do you think the spirit/ogre lives?
C:	*Na waruna… no wanguna!*	Along the river…along the riverbank!
T:	*No waru tena?*	The riverbank where?
C:	*Ambola wangu.*	Banks of the Ambola River.
T:	*Ambola wangu molemo. Nae kanolemo?*	He lives on the banks of the Ambola River. Who [customarily] sees him?
C:	*Olio naa kanolemolo.*	We don't [customarily] see him.
T:	*We molomba niku nikuni?*	You just think he's there so you talk?
G:	*Inie manie molemo.*	He lives down below here.

(KTPPS classroom visit 3, August, 1995, T10A)

The children all burst out laughing at this point because the girl refers to the tiny creek just below their classroom. At the end of the story, the teacher raises a quasi-metaphysical problem for the children:

T:	*Kango wenewene molorumuna naa pulkanje nambi telka? Ungu manda manjilka molo naa manjilka?*	What would have happened if the boys had not gone to where the *wenewene* lives? Could he have been able to reply or not?
C:	*[loudly] Naa manjilka! Naa manjilka! Naa manjilka!*	He couldn't have replied! He couldn't have replied! He couldn't have replied!
T:	*Naa manjilka!*	He couldn't have replied?
C:	*E-e-e-e-e-h!*	Ye-e-e-e-s!
T:	*Pe molorumuna puringi ili nambi terimu?*	What did he do when they went where he lived?
C:	*Manda manjirimu.*	He replied!
T:	*Kolia tena molorumuna puringi?*	Where did the boys go?
C:	*Ambola wangu.*	The banks of the Ambola River.

T: *E-e-eh? Ambola wangu. Kango teka kangoma?*
     Polina: Aika kangoma
T: *Aika kangoma! Manda....*

Ye-e-e-s? Banks of the Ambola River. Where are the boys from? They're Aika boys.
Aika boys! Okay....

(KTPPS classroom visit 3, August, 1995, T10A)

Although neither the boys' clan nor the river are named in the story, once again the children view the place and characters of the story as culturally near; they are boys playing the games they themselves play, on the banks of their own river. The reason for that may simply be that the stories were written in this place, for Kaugel children, by young people and adults who have shared the same experiences. That the writing process also produced stories that children in other parts of the Umbu-Ungu-speaking area can also view as near to them is attested to by the teachers cited in the section on the KRS at the end of this chapter: from Purare (the original school), Pulumungu (on the road to Mt. Hagen), Topé (across the Basin), Malke (on the slopes of Mount Giluwe), and Kalapolo (the next clan up the Basin Road from Aika).

Curriculum and Instruction in the Classroom

Oh...akuli manda nikinulinga aku ulu kanolemolo, ulu akuli olio **Tisa's Gaede Boku** *te lelemo. Akuna olio* **bihainim** *tepolie mele akuma yunu alsi ulsu oliemo akunaka olio* **bihainim** *tepo teltele pulimulu. Ulkelinga oliomo kinie ulkelinga telemolo, tepe mako kepe nindi melu kepe o-oga mundu kepe kongi ka kepe ulu kaliema ausipe ne* **boku**na ka *olio* **bihainim** *tepolie teltele pulumulu. We olionga konupuna te pilipu aku sipe naa telemolo.* **Wiki**manga ne **boku** *akuna yu mako topa pelemo aku lika* **bihainim** *tepo teltele pulumulu.*

Oh...you are talking about this practice [of doing experience stories], which we've been looking at, which is in the *Teacher's Guide Book*. For these [instructional] procedures, we follow what's in there, taking [the lessons] out one-by-one, and putting them into practice. When it's time for the house topic, we do something about houses, or for making fire [traditionally] or for trapping, or sweet potato mounds, or looking after pigs, we follow the book for all that kind of thing, and that's what we do. We don't just make up something based on our own feelings. No. What is marked in the book for each week, that's what we follow, that's what we do.

(KTPPS teacher interview, October, 1995, T14B)

The teacher refers to the *Buk Bilong Tisa* "Teacher's Book" for the KTPPS program. The lessons follow a daily and weekly pattern, repeated each week with a different cultural theme and different story content but the same pattern of instruction. The lessons on the photocopied sheets follow the two literacy acquisition tracks—one whole-to-part, the other part-to-whole—summarized in chapter 4.

Set out on large foolscap (8" × 13") sheets like a calendar grid, with five rows of six columns, the "Book" (actually mimeographed pages since there were not enough books to go around) contained in its pages all the teacher needed to prepare minimally for each day's lessons. The theme for the week is printed at the top of the grid. Headings across the top include the days of the school week, while down the left-hand side, in balloon letters, are the four components of the Story Time track, written in Tok Pisin: Children's Experience Story, Listening Story, Reading a Story, and Writing a Story. The next page is laid out similarly, with the four Word Time components printed down the left-hand side: Key Word, Hearing Syllables, Big Box, Writing Words.

The individual cells of the lesson plan grid provide the teacher with only the barest of information. For example, the "Listening Story" box might say only "Mark's Story. Book 6, pp. 29–37 [in the KRS]." The Key Word box might have a single word and syllable (e.g., *tepe, pe*) and a reference to a page in the teacher's workbook. The Big Box grid might have only the syllables for the lesson (e.g., *mo, mbo, no,* etc.). The teacher I observed most frequently rarely went beyond the instructions in the teacher's book.

The original *Buk Bilong Tisa* had a long introductory section in which the various components of the lessons were described, including suggestions for variety and creativity in instruction. When the original supply of teacher's books were depleted, only the lesson instructions were photocopied, not the introductory material. It is questionable whether the original KTPPS teachers made much use of the introduction section but for the teachers that came later that option was not available. The current format was meant to make the lesson content easily accessible to the teachers and depended on training programs to provide the necessary procedural knowledge. That feature makes it possible for the teacher to present the rudiments of a language education lesson without demanding long preparation time. In one of the classrooms I observed, the teacher would walk over to the small counter in the corner between lessons, to the place where he kept his teaching materials. He would look at the instructional page to locate the next part of the lesson for that day (for example, the Listening Story), go to his stack of KRS books, snatch the book he wanted, then go back to the waiting children before they became too engrossed in their own discourse. There was no indication that the teacher had done any pre-class preparation.

Children's talk

The lack of opportunity for children to engage in conversation in some KTPPS classrooms is another potential problem in an educational innovation that aims, at least in part, on promoting language and culture maintenance. In an address on literacy and biliteracy in Asia, Marie Clay (1995) makes three observations about language and literacy: (1) even in monolingual communities, children enter school at different levels of language use, (2) some children will have had experience with written language and some not, and (3) some written material will be difficult for the children because it is written in a "language variety" that no one uses in everyday speech (p. 8).

> So we have to think hard about the materials we put into the books for children who are beginning literacy learning. Can they talk about that material? (because we need to have them talking), and how will their language variations interact with what has been written into the reading books?

The most animated and extended talking observed in the KTPPS classroom revolved around the stories of the KRS. One observation had the children simultaneously shouting out answers to the teacher's requests for predictions of story content on the basis of the illustration in the book of a man and his hunting dog.

Language socialization, however, involves more than allowing children to shout out answers to the teacher's questions about a particular story. It also involves encouraging them to think about (and critique) their own life situations, to draw meaning from the classroom lessons and relate them to what they already know. For the most part, I did not see this happening in this particular classroom.

A teacher's problem

At least one KTPPS teacher admitted to not understanding the purpose of the Big Box lesson, and asked specifically for my assistance. The Big Box exercise uses a grid of four rows of three or four columns, each cell containing a syllable already learned by the children.

no	ka	mba
me	na	pa
mbo	te	ko
pe	ma	ta

Figure 6.2. Sample Big Box grid.

The teacher is instructed to use the grid to give students practice in combining syllables to form words. In spite of his protests otherwise, this particular teacher did this lesson effectively in the classes I observed (without any advice or suggestions from me). His actual problem was with the Key Word lesson, in which the children are presented a new letter and/or syllable that is part of a word, usually accompanied by an illustration. The pattern for using the key word *tepe* 'fire' to highlight a specific syllable is shown in figure 6.3.

1   **tepe**

2   te   pe

3   tepe   6   te
4   te pe   7   te pe
5   te   8   tepe

Figure 6.3. A key word lesson for *tepe* 'fire' as written
on the chalkboard.

The teacher printed the word *tepe* neatly on the chalkboard (1) then, using his pointer-stick, he read the word to the children as it is normally spoken, directing the children to read the word with him. He then wrote the word again, separating the two syllables, *te* and *pe,* drawing a box around each one (2). Tapping each of the boxes with his pointer, the teacher read each syllable distinctly, then invited the children to join in reading them with him. Next he wrote the word *tepe* off to the side, reading the word at normal speech speed when he finished (3). After the children read the word with him, the teacher wrote the word again, separating the two syllables, carefully keeping the *te* syllable in line with the *te* of *tepe* above it (4). Tapping each syllable with his pointer he read the syllables, then invited the children to join in. Then he wrote the single syllable *te* and read it with the children (5).

At this point, the teacher placed his pointer on the chalk tray and, standing close to the chalkboard, clapped the syllables as he reads *tepe* at normal speech speed, then putting his hands near the syllables in the boxes (2) he read and clapped in staccato. He then went to the word written below (3) and read and clapped at normal speech speed, then the staccato claps as he read the divided syllables (4), then the single clap with the syllable *te* (5).

The teacher then invited individual children to come to the board to repeat the pattern he had just demonstrated, tapping and clapping, respectively, as they read the word and its syllables (the step-by-step procedure that, as far as I could determine, he had been taught during the provincial training course he attended).

It was at this point that the lesson started to unravel. The children had not understood the connection between the tapping and clapping and the number of syllables in the key word. They read subvocally or not at all as they tapped and then clapped the patterns, the rhythmic pattern that the teacher had demonstrated fading into a single tap and clap per line. The teacher did not correct the children or attempt to have them do the exercise with him. After each attempt, including those in which the children clearly did not understand the meaning of what they were to do, the teacher commended the child and directed the class to applaud. He displays here the cognitive confusion Stringer and Faraclas (1987) anticipate if the same teacher teaches both tracks of the method. In the multi-strategy approach they developed, the authors require that each class has two teachers, one teaching only the story track and the other teaching only the word track (1987:8).

The strict division between the two tracks is characterized as the difference between teacher-as-model and teacher-as-trainer. In this KTPPS classroom, the emphasis of a teacher-as-trainer as one who "corrects mistakes" and "stresses accuracy" had been largely replaced by a teacher-as-model who "teaches by doing" and "encourages" the learners (p. 12). Ironically, when one girl finally—but wordlessly—clapped out the rhythm of the chalkboard display just as the teacher had demonstrated it, she was neither commended for that partial success nor encouraged to say the syllables aloud.

When the KTPPS curriculum was initially developed from the model that Stringer was at that time piloting in the neighboring Enga Province, the prohibitive cost of having two teachers for each classroom—one trained in the "whole language" approach and the other in a part-to-whole approach—forced Rambai, with the limited funding available for teacher subsidies, to train

KTPPS teachers to do both tracks.[51] The struggles observed in the class-room are quite possibly a result of confusion over the teacher's role—as predicted by Stringer in her emphasis on using one teacher per track. On the other hand, the problem may arise from the malaise brought on by no/low teacher pay as indicated in an interview with one teacher.

Q: We ulu pulu te kangambolama piliku kaiyu naa telemele molo liku kaiyu naa telemele ulu pulu akulinga kinie nuni ulu te kinie kapola konde topa mele i sipu telemola kinie kangambola manda pilimila, manda molemele niku aku nini te nomanona pilinu lemo kamu nikinu kalialenga niku we opeme toko niani nimbu pilikiru.

I would like you to expand [lit., sew together] on what are some of the different, new things you do to help the children understand something that they are not understanding well or a lesson they are not doing properly, so that they will be able to be content.

*A: Akuli nikiru kanuli. Te olio ulu temololenga enembo tolemo ulu ili.... Olio teko nomanokondo kaiyu naa panjilimili. Aku kou **mone** sili ululi kinie kapola naa telemo ulu ilini olio tepa uru panjilimu. Akulini kinie ne ulu **lesen** akuna pali ulu olio temololenga olio pali kolte enembo mele tolemo. Olionga pengena kamu we bulu bala telemo. Aku telemolene olio sumbi sipu ululi naa telemolo pe kangambolama naa pilingi lemo ne akulinika naa pilimili. Pe olio pali **lesen** akuma pali we teltili pumulu ulu akuli pilimulu kinie olio enembo mele tolemelene naa telemolo.*

There's just one explanation for the way we are doing this [teaching]: we're tired.... People are not doing anything to encourage us. That is, they are not paying us properly, and it is that practice that makes us sleep [on the job]. Because of that we [teachers] are tired of doing these lessons. Our thoughts are constantly struggling back and forth. Given that [state of mind] we do not teach properly. So, if the children don't understand then they just don't understand. The impetus for doing these lessons is with us [teachers], and we are all tired.

(KTPPS teacher, interview, August 1995, T14B)

Tired teacher syndrome: as a theory it has explanatory power, accounting for the teacher's tolerance of the children's lack of understanding, for his un-enthusiastic development of cultural themes in the children's experience stories, and his disenthrallment with the program in general. What it glaringly does not account for is why this and other teachers continue to teach, to come in the morning and ring the bell for the benefit of a handful of children, for what amounts to about seventy-five cents a day.

---

[51]In contact with various *pri skul* program directors from around the country, Rambai, my wife Susan, and I learned that this KTPPS approach coincided with what the others had been forced to do as well. Research comparing the method using one or two teachers would be helpful to those contemplating its use in the future.

For their part, the children's parents provide little encouragement for the *pri skul* teachers. In fact, they present an ethical dilemma because, technically, the school fees the parents are expected to pay are to be turned over to the KTPPS director and pooled together with bakery income for teachers' subsidies. At least one teacher confessed to pocketing the school fees when, infrequent as it might be, a parent brings in one, two, or three kina (of the K5 annual school fee).

Thus, the burden the teachers carry as *namel manmeri* plays out even in this aspect of their lives. Caught between their sense of responsibility to the children and to the program for which they labor with the meagerest of material compensation, even the little money they collect sometimes comes weighted with guilt.

Rambai Keruwa, the KTPPS director, is fully aware of the teachers' situation. When asked about the financial future of the program he responded:

> My one solution...one hopeful thinking now is that my teachers, after struggling voluntarily for quite a number of years, they need to be rewarded for what they have been doing. If we cannot secure any outside funding—like provincial or local government—and the parents are not willing to appreciate the fact that [the teachers] are voluntarily helping our children at the start of their education.... [Rambu's voice trails off.] I would very much like to see they are rewarded for what they are laboring for. (R. Keruwa, interview, July 29, 1995, T5.17)

Rambai's hope was that the government's new education reform would eventually accept his long established *pri skul* program into the elementary level and provide the teachers with the remuneration their efforts deserve (R. Keruwa, July 29, 1995, T5B.18). That hope was fulfilled, in part, in the following year when his application to register the individual KTPPS programs with the Provincial Division of Education for inclusion in the new elementary level was approved, with eight of the fourteen teachers accepted for 1997, including the teacher described above (R. Keruwa, personal communication, April 20, 1996).

Meaningful Materials: Kaugel Reading Series

Teachers and the KRS

When I asked Rambai about the rapid expansion of the KTPPS program from three preschools to fourteen between 1992 and 1995, he replied that the availability of the Kaugel Reading Series (KRS) provided him with the confidence to expand, especially when he thought (mistakenly, as it turned out) that the Village Services Department would provide subsidies for teacher salaries (chapters 3 and 4) (personal communication, July 29, 1995, T4.18). The KRS provided each new school with a relatively large repertoire of mother-tongue literature. The books, along with a supply of chalk, a large chalkboard, and individual lapboards for the children, furnished the teachers with their essential—occasionally their only—instructional materials. That the KRS stories also engaged the interests of both children and teachers re-emphasized their value to the program.

The teachers, interviewed individually and in a group, express a general approval of the KRS as relevant to the children's interests and needs in language education. Their use of the books for both shared reading and listening stories ensures that a large number of the ninety-six stories will be part of the children's KTPPS experience.

On a visit to one KTPPS classroom, Apé and I arrived in the middle of a shared reading of *Kango Tende Lopa Tomu Temane* 'Story About [how] Tende Killed a Marsupial'. An animated conversation was taking place about how the boy climbed a tree to knock a possum from its arboreal refuge so that his hunting dog could kill it on the ground. This story happened to coincide with the news that a local man had been injured falling from a tree while trying to knock down a possum, just like the boy in the story. This is a case where the "experience near" nature of the KRS stories allow the teachers to relate them to the real life happenings in the local community.

Teachers' enthusiasm for the books focuses mainly on the stories' effect of stimulating the children to engage in meaningful, enjoyable dialogue, not necessarily in their usefulness in mother-tongue literacy acquisition. But, others have noted that the books also had a positive effect on the children's desire and ability to read.

Pe aku kinie Umbu-Ungu kundu kinie ne, Umbu-Unguna **boku** *kepe aku sipemanga kanombo kinie komindi ka lerimumu....*	[The children] when it was time to read the Umbu-Ungu books in local language, they did quite well....
Aku pe kanopo akundu kinie, yambo kendo, **skul** *ya oliolio, kangambolama ya oliolio* **nesimi** *mele tepo* **skul**una *mundukumulu akumuni, kangambolama komindi lelkaka none tekemo.*	When I saw [them reading], when we ourselves were still "nursing" the children in school the children appeared to be reading quite well.

(KTPPS teacher, personal communication, November 5, 1995, T36A)

The "nearness" of the cultural content of the KRS is one of the key factors in its usefulness for Kaugel language and culture maintenance. The cultural nearness of the content is almost surely the result of the fact that all of the KRS stories are native-authored. That assertion will be demonstrated by exploring one culturally near topic in more detail.

Content of KRS

The topic most frequently featured in the KRS is food. In fact, 80 percent of the ninety-six stories in the series make direct reference to food.

Table 6.6. Food as a feature in Kaugel Reading Series

Level	Total books	Food-as-feature
1	30	23
2	27	21
3	25	22
4	14	11
KRS total	96	77

The foods mentioned throughout the series are: *ga* 'sweet potato', *lopa* 'marsupial', *oma* 'fish', *kera* 'bird', *langi* 'food', *kongi* 'pig/pork', *kumaka* 'mouse/rat', *kemu* 'vegetable greens', *unju mongo* 'fruit', *me* 'taro', *mingi wawa* 'squash', *ame* 'breast milk', *kanapa* 'corn', *londea* 'frog', *po* 'sugar cane', *no* 'water', *amu* 'pandanus nuts', and *kula* 'edible wild sugar cane'. The following food items were mentioned only once in the series (which is not necessarily an indication of their relative importance in the minds of the KRS authors): *api* 'local salt', *kapisa*, 'cabbage', *nonda* 'mushrooms', *kengepa* 'edible green leaves', *kera mulu* 'bird's egg', *kaliepo* 'peanuts', *palu* 'wood beetle', *tauwa* 'banana', *lkepa* 'indigenous spinach', *kuni* 'parsley', *kera walipe* 'bat', *komba* 'edible green, near water', *girisi* (TP) 'butter, margarine', *oma akena* 'eel', *kewa no* 'soda/lolly water (lit., foreign water')', *mamuli* 'berries', and *pamba kuni* 'edible ferns'. The high proportion of stories incorporating food as a subject in the KRS is consistent with the high regard in which food is held by highlanders in the Kaugel area.

> In section 3.1.5 we sketched the importance of food (Ku Waru *langi*) to Nebilyer concepts of personal identity and relatedness. We observed there that Nebilyer ideas of consubstantiality are not based on genealogy but rather on the assimilation of nutritive substances (*kopong*, Tok Pisin *gris*) which ultimately derive from the ground and are absorbed through eating foods. *Related to indigenous notions of substances as derived from food is intense interest in what people eat. This is a subject of fascination beyond anything an outsider might*

imagine. People are perpetually interested in what others eat and in gifts of food, even more so if the foods are delicacies and thus tokens of special recognition. (Merlan and Rumsey 1991:232; emphasis added)

Not surprisingly, sweet potato, the staple food in the Kaugel area, is at the top of the list, having been mentioned in one-third of the ninety-eight stories in the KRS. The frequent reference to *lopa* 'arboreal marsupial' can be explained by the very high degree of prestige accorded to successful hunters. That and the excitement of the hunt for *lopa* is at least equal to the animal's food value in accounting for its prominent place.

The presence of *oma* 'fish' in half a dozen stories requires a closer look. Fish (including eels) were a traditional but rarer food item. They play main roles in several clan myths of origin. Catching fish is mentioned in five of the stories. These need to be contrasted with two references to tinned fish, a product imported from overseas that is a common item in every local trade store and a more likely ingredient than fresh fish in local meals for most residents of the Tambul Basin.

More surprising is the absence of any reference to rice, which is the invariable accompaniment to tinned fish. One possible reason for this is that *raisa* 'rice' is a loanword from Tok Pisin and English, but *oma* is the traditional term for fish. Eating tinned fish and rice is a nonindigenous cultural adaptation, associated with the new ways, **lo** te- 'doing *lo*'.

Kera 'bird', *kongi* 'pig', *kumaka* 'rat/mouse', and *kemu* 'vegetable greens' are all common foods for children, with the hunt for *kera* and *kumaka* taking up large parts of each day—especially among boys—a likely result of the chronic shortage of protein in the Kaugel people's traditional diet.

Table 6.7 sets out the story texts of the KRS in terms of their relationship to traditional culture: "Traditional" makes no reference to introduced items or activities, "Nontraditional" refers primarily to introduced items or activities, and "Both" makes reference to both traditional and nontraditional items and activities.

Table 6.7. KRS story texts' relationship to traditional and
nontraditional content

Level	Traditional	Nontraditional	Both
1	21	0	9
2	22	1	4
3	18	1	6
4	14	0	0
Total	75	2	19

In the development of the Kaugel Reading Series, general topics of cultural interest were suggested to the authors, but no restrictions were made with regard to the content of the stories. Therefore, authors had the freedom to feature those aspects of community life that they considered of interest and importance to themselves and the children. In retrospect, this freedom seems to have been a very productive feature of the literature development process. This is especially true because the expatriate team of "literacy advisors" (my wife and I) were at that time unaware of the cultural significance of food and would not have given that much space to what turned out to be a chief cultural concern in the language area. Such freedom for local authors allows for the possibility of developing literacy materials that do not suffer from what Rogers calls "concept distance" or "cultural otherness."

> Every learner places the material with which they are confronted at a specific location within their own sense of reality. The distance between where they place this new material and where they place themselves is usually expressed in terms of space (it is of "remote interest" or a matter of "close concern," etc.) or in terms of social relationships (it is "alien," etc.). (1992:140)

Although Rogers observes this phenomenon with regard to adult literacy related to development projects in the Third World, his conclusion warrants investigation in literature development for pre-primary mother-tongue education in traditional societies, namely, that if literacy material

> is placed far from themselves, these practices are regarded as "culturally other," and thus learning them will be more difficult; on the other hand, if they are placed close to themselves within their picture of reality, learning will be facilitated. (1992:140)

That children in the Purare KTPPS classroom are placing the KRS stories "close to themselves" is evidenced by their giving local clan and place names to characters and events in response to questions by the teacher when that specific information is not included in the stories:

Referring to a Children's Experience Story on the topic of "house"

T: *Pos melema tena lipulimili?*   Where do they go and get the posts
                                             and things?

C: *Lakuraka...kondena!*   Lakuraka...in the forest! [*Lakuraka*
                                             is the name given to the Aika clan
                                             area of the forest near Murmur Pass,
                                             but not mentioned in the children's
                                             text.]

(KTPPS classroom, July 31, 1995, T8A)

Referring to "Mark's Story" in KRS, Book 5

T: *[referring to main character in story]*   Who is the boy?
    Kango nae?

C: *Mako!*   Mark!

T: *Mako...teka kango?*   Mark...a boy from where?

C: *Korika!*   Korika! [clan adjacent to Aika, but
                                                not mentioned in the text]

(KTPPS classroom, July 31, 1995, T8A)

Referring to the "Echo Demon Story" in KRS, Book 5

T: *Pilikimilii? Wenewene kolia moloi tena*   Are you understanding? Where does
    molkomonje?   the *wenewene* demon live?

C: *No waruna...na wanguna...*   By the river bank....by the river
                                               bank....

T: *No waru tena?*   A river bank where?

C: *Ambola wangu.*   Banks of the Ambola River.

(KTPPS classroom, August 7, 1997, T10A)

In the first example, the children's naming of a locally familiar forest area as the setting for the collection of housebuilding materials is not surprising, since they had composed their "house story" after viewing a house belonging to the family of Aika Siminji, a person well-known to the children and who owns forest at Lakuraka. This highlights the advantage of the children's language experience story lesson in creating culturally-near texts for the children's early reading attempts.

The second and third examples relate specifically to stories in the Kaugel Reading Series which the children clearly perceive as culturally near, giving local names to story characters and settings. Their perception of closeness is a result of the familiarity of the story content with the children's own life experiences.

Another possible explanation for the excitement and interest generated by the stories is that since they were written by local authors, they have been taken from real life experiences that are well-known in the area. However, the fact that the stories were composed between 1984 and 1987 makes it unlikely that these six- and seven-year-old children had actually heard oral accounts of the stories' content. The fact that children in *pri skuls* throughout the wider area demonstrate the same enjoyment also indicates that their appeal is based on more than acquaintance with the original characters on which the stories might have been based. Thus, it is safe to conclude that the "culturally close" nature of the stories accounts at least in part for the widely expressed satisfaction the KTPPS teachers perceive in the children's reaction to the KRS material.

To summarize, the analysis of lexical borrowing and code-switching in a KTPPS classroom demonstrates that the mother tongue enjoys a preeminent place in the realm of spoken and written language. Limited in both variety and frequency, the kind of wholesale lexical borrowing that sometimes indicates significant language shift is largely missing from the KTPPS classroom. This is in stark contrast to the same phenomenon in church and Sunday school-related activities observed in the Tambul Basin. As discussed in chapter 4, the community schools, to which KTPPS "graduates" go after their year of *tok ples* education, demonstrate, at best, a passive approval of Kaugel language and culture. At worst, they offer many models for language and/or culture shift.

The problems with curriculum instruction in the classroom can be attributed to inadequate training and supervision which accounts for one teacher's confusion over his dual role as "model" and "trainer" and to the loss of teacher motivation due to the lack of remuneration for time and effort. The KRS literacy materials themselves were appropriate and appreciated by teachers and students. Analysis revealed that the KRS is a major factor in promoting the language and culture maintenance goal of the KTPPS program.

The Kaugel home remains the primary sanctuary for L1 maintenance, with secondary support from some local social institutions, but by no means all of them. The major language shift observed in local churches, the well-attended video house at Kalapolo, the community schools and private Christian school are chipping away at the viability of the immediate community as a haven for maintaining traditional language and cultural values. The KTPPS, therefore, provides a needed auxiliary domain for the L1, assisting the home in providing support for local language and culture. For the KTPPS program to be effective, however, the teachers need additional training to enable them to understand the language and

culture maintenance goals enough to take advantage of impromptu opportunities as they arise in the KTPPS classrooms. In addition, the community and government need to demonstrate a greater commitment to
the support of the mother-tongue teachers, to provide them with adequate financial remuneration or, if that is impossible, to provide their
families with the food, firewood, and assistance (gardening, etc.) that will
help the teachers know they are appreciated (rather than feeling shamed
as they do now). Clearly, this is a task for the *namel manmeri,* who know
and appreciate the wisdom of the past well enough to act on its behalf in
the present.

7

Conclusions

The VCR and a 24" color monitor sit inside a plywood box/cabinet, the open door of which has a large hasp lock. The cabinet sits atop a (presumably) empty 44-gallon petrol drum. To the left of it, seed potatoes in 50 kg. sacks have been piled on the dry-grass covered dirt floor. To the right of the video equipment are stacks of Coke cartons, each filled with a mixture of empty Coke, Fanta, and Sprite bottles. The volume of the video is loud enough to override the boisterous banter of the large circle of card players near the entrance of the *haus piksa* 'video house'. I can see the screen clearly from thirty feet away. I've come here with Apé's grade 6 son, Mark, San, my landlord's 20-year-old niece, and 4-year old Maia (short for Jeremaia).

A video of PNG's top twenty hits captivates most of a group of about twenty. PS2 from Hanuabada in the National Capital District perform music in a contemporary light rock mode with wailing guitars and electric piano, as Motuan women sway in grass skirts in traditional rhythm. The owner's 13-year old son sits on my right, with a young man in his late teens on his right. The younger one is now more fascinated with my note taking than with the video. I learn later that he is a student at the private Christian school. The video performers pause for a commercial...*Pepisi Jeneresen* 'Pepsi Generation'. The two youths sing along:

Nupela laik bilong jeneresen	There's a new preference for this generation.
Nupela stail bilong jeneresen	There's a new style for this generation.
Em Pepsi long PNG!	It's Pepsi for PNG!

> The older youth now tells me the story line of a video song by a
> Rabaul (East New Britain) singer code-switching between Tok Pisin
> and English..."He goes around with a girl all over town so everyone
> thinks they're married, but when he goes to her village and she's
> asked who the guy is she says she doesn't know him," which elicits
> a plaintive refrain from the singer: "Shame on you!"

> The next song is also by a Rabaul group, singing in Kuanua, the lo-
> cal mother tongue. The two teenage boys, faces lively, eyes focused
> on the screen, enthusiastically sing along in Kuanua, from mem-
> ory.... (Field Notes 4.11, November 17, 1995)

As an epilogue to the episode excerpted above, I left for home by myself
shortly after the opening scene of a hoodlums-with-machine-pistols-
chasing-young-long-haired-guitar-player genre, with already a dozen or
so little hibiscus buds of whatever kind of imitation blood the film makers
used blooming in widening circles on the hoods' white shirts. Everyone on
the screen was speaking Spanish and, to my knowledge, no one in the *haus
piksa* noticed me leave.

Summary of Findings

I began this case study with the assumption that the people involved in
the Kaugel Tok Ples Pri Skul program experience tension between their
goal of preparing their children for a successful experience in the English-
language formal education system and simultaneously developing the
children's appreciation for and ongoing use of the local language and culture. The underlying question of this study has been how and to what extent the KTPPS has served the community in achieving these two goals. In
the search for answers to that question, two key aspects of how the Kaugel
people perceive themselves became apparent: they view themselves as active participants in the shaping of events that impinge on their own lives
and the life of their community, and the generation currently in leadership view themselves as *namel manmeri* 'in-between people', in a favorable
position to negotiate the exchanges between the two cultures, having experienced both in a way the younger generation has not, cannot.

I wanted to learn how the KTPPS program has been sustained through
ten years despite a number of serious setbacks; how the program has
served the goals and purposes of the people themselves; and how the
members of the local communities, especially the parents, resolve the tension between their desire for their children to succeed in school and their

desire for the children to continue to respect and appreciate their mother tongue and local community values.

The context in which the KTPPS program originated and expanded was described in chapter 3: a social, economic, cultural, political, linguistic, and educational environment in a state of flux. Emphasis was on the significance of the people's interactions with expatriates and their Western culture and the ways these interactions have had an impact on the Tambul Basin. I presented the views of previous ethnographers—supported in my own data—that people in the area display an ethnocultural predisposition to act, to enter into and shape events in order to accomplish individual and community purposes (Merlan and Rumsey 1991; A. Strathern 1979a).

Chapter 4 focused on the KTPPS program itself and the way in which it developed through the collaboration of Rambai Keruwa, my wife, and me as a response to local concerns about the impact of the formal education system on Kaugel children; Rambai as KTPPS director and a principal actor in the KTPPS story, the role his traditional upbringing and formal education has played in the program, and the tensions he experiences because of his multiple responsibilities; the growth of the KTPPS as a community-based program, having started and expanded with community participation; the strengths of the program, focusing on Rambai's leadership and the teachers' perseverance and on the critical importance of adequate and culturally relevant literacy materials (the Kaugel Reading Series); and the weaknesses of the program, including poor instruction (perceived by the teachers themselves as a result of their malaise over poor or nonexistent pay and inadequate supervision) and the damage caused by rapid expansion of the program based on the national government's broken promises regarding teachers' subsidies. The chapter concluded by linking the current KTPPS program to the government's newly initiated mother-tongue elementary schools as part of the national education reform.

The attitudes of parents, teachers, and children with respect to Umbu-Ungu language and culture were studied in chapter 5. Emphasis was on the tension that arises from people's desire for access to the material resources perceived as open to those who succeed in the English education system and their desire to maintain what is perceived as good and essential from the indigenous language and culture. Although participants in the study expressed many concerns with regard to loss of culture and especially traditional values, few acknowledged that the language itself might be endangered. Yet, it was clear from the data that signs of language shift *do* exist (e.g., church services, the *haus piksa*, children's attitudes of disrespect to parental authority, and community leadership).

Thus, the *namel manmeri*, who view themselves as choosers, taking and leaving, aware of new possibilities and new manners of individual and social action, may be unaware of—and, therefore, passive toward—the evidence that their language is threatened.

Chapter 6 began with an analysis of language use in the Purare KTPPS classroom, finding that the children exhibit some marks of a developing, but not extensive, bilingualism. Teachers' and children's limited use of lexical borrowing and code-switching lends support to a favorable view of the KTPPS as a medium for Umbu-Ungu language maintenance. I then looked at the way traditional culture and values are promoted in the classroom. A significant result of this analysis is the understanding of the role that the Kaugel Reading Series has played in promoting Kaugel culture and language through content that is consistently "culturally near" and language that, for the most part, leads the children into an enjoyment and appreciation of traditional ways. Problems regarding curriculum and instruction were also discussed. For the most part, these could be attributed to the teachers' inadequate grasp of the part-to-whole aspect of the literacy method, inadequate training and supervision, and the teachers' indifference toward the children's learning as a result of their resentment over inadequate remuneration.

Community Awareness of Language Shift Necessary for Preemptive Action

If people in the Tambul Basin are not content to "fold their arms and watch" events unfold, but are predisposed to take action when confronted with problems and possibilities, then an awareness of the language situation described in chapters 5 and 6 should encourage them to take practical steps to prevent further erosion of language and culture domains. Indeed, if their language and culture are not to be lost, they must take further action beyond the maintenance of the KTPPS program. Experiences in other parts of the world have demonstrated that, although the program is effective in a small way, it cannot, on its own, offset the strong and constant pressure from Tok Pisin and English that inundates the children's local culture through English-language school, church, and community enterprises like the *haus piksa*.

A community awareness program is clearly needed, one based on an assessment of language shift indicators by the community members themselves. In table 7.1, the "factors contributing to language shift" that were presented in chapter 1 (table 1.2) have been divided between those that are currently observable in the Tambul Basin and those that are not yet apparent.

Table 7.1. Language shift factors present in the Kaugel language situation

Observable	Not observable (yet)
Sociocultural	
Occupational shift, rural-to-urban*	Long stable residence in dominant
Easily accessible travel out of L1 area	L2 area
[Wage] employment requires L2	Small number of scattered speakers
Ease of social, economic mobility*	Homeland remote
Access to L2 mass media*	L1 home community losing vitality
Social institutions in L2 open to L1	Military service in L2 open or
Marriage outside L1 allowed	required
Potential community leaders alienated by education	Ethnic discrimination in social and economic arenas leading to denial of ethnic identity
Cultural	
Cultural and religious activity in L2*	Ethnic identity defined by nonL factors
Few nationalistic aspirations	Self not defined by shared L1
Emphasis on L2 education	High emphasis on individual, low emphasis on family, community ties
Acceptance of L2 education	Culture and religion similar to that of L2
Linguistic	
Widespread bilingualism	L1 is nonstandard; not in written form
Mother tongue not the only homeland language	Use of writing system which is expensive to reproduce, difficult to learn
L1 of little or no international importance	No tolerance of new terms from L2; conversely, indiscriminate lexical borrowing from L2 resulting in L1 loss
L1 considered inferior to L2*	
Little or no L1 literacy **	

* = limited
** = increasing in L1 literacy as a result of the NDOE's three-year elementary level of pre-primary education and adult L1 literacy in conjunction with the publication of Umbu-Ungu NT

As table 7.1 demonstrates, the observable indicators of language shift are numerous enough to cause concern. Given Fasold's (1984) warning that the later stages of language shift are easier to detect but more difficult to reverse, these findings indicate that the local Kaugel community needs to become aware of their rapidly changing language and culture situation so they can begin taking steps to reverse what might otherwise become an irreversible shift.

To that end, towards the end of 1995, during a three-day KTPPS teachers' conference at Tambul, I conducted a "language awareness" session in which I wrote a condensed set of the language shift factors on the chalkboard and asked the teachers whether they had observed any of the conditions listed. The result was a long discourse on language shift as observed by one of the teachers.

Planti man meri ol i go aut skul, skul na i go aut, na ol i no save tingting long kam bek long ples bilong ol, as ples bilong ol. Ol i stap aut long wanem hap ples ol i wok long en. Ol i sindaun longpela taim. Krismas tu, **holidays** *tu. Ol i no tingting long kam bek, na... Ol i stap long dispela. Ol i yusim* **Inglis** *na* **Pidgin** *- em min olsem* **main language** *bilong ol - ol tok ples bilong ol i stret. Na taim ol i-, wan wan taim ol, samting ol i kam bek long ples nabaut, ol pikinini bilong ol tu i no save tingting-, harim tok ples bilong mipela, it's Umbu-Ungu. Na ol i save toktok long* **Pidgin** *o* **Inglis.** *Wanem samting yu askim tu, ol i no inap harim. Ol i no inap bekim tu. Tasol yu wokim long Tok Pisin, em ol bai bekim. Na yu wokim long Tok* **Inglis,** *em ol bai bekim. Em dispela* **system** *em i kamap tru long en na* **point** *i stap antap.*

Lots of people finish school, leave the area, and don't come back and don't think about returning. They stay where they work. They stay a long time and don't come back even for Christmas or [other] holidays. They don't think about coming back. They live there and they use English and Tok Pisin as their main language, their mother tongue. On the occasions they return here, their children don't understand Umbu-Ungu, they speak Tok Pisin or English. If you talk to them in Umbu-Ungu, they don't understand; they can't respond. But if you speak to them in Tok Pisin then they'll respond in Tok Pisin. If you speak in English, they'll respond. Truly, that process has appeared, that point on top [i.e., the one written at the top of the chalkboard].

*Na wanem samting ol i tingting bihain long mekim bilong kamapim dispela tok ples bilong yumi stret Umbu-Ungu i kamap olsem bihain pikinini ol manki i stap long en na ol i bai kisim dispela tok ples. Em i orait. Na em i no ken lus olgeta olsem dispela point yu putim antap. Em samting tru **happen** na yumi mas traim painim sampela rot long kisim tok ples i kam bek. Em tingting bilong mi na lukluk bilong mi tu. Em **point** bilong mi.*

The way to ensure our mother tongue Umbu-Ungu for the future is to ensure that all the children and youth learn it.... That's the truth. It's happening, and we must find a way to retrieve our mother tongue. That's what I think and what I see. That's *my* point!

*Na long **point two** em wankain. Planti man i marit ausait em dispela **same problem**. Ol i statim-, planti taim ol i-, man i save stap long ples bilong meri. **OK**, na ol i yusim dispela tok ples bilong meri o **Pidgin** na **Inglis**. Sampela taim ol i no-, em olsem **same** toktok mi wokim hia. Ol i no save tingting long kam bek long ples bilong ol stret. So planti taim ol i stap long ples bilong-, narapela ples na...tok ples i no save kamap stret. Olsem ol i stap long dispela hap ol i yus long **Inglis** o **Pidgin** na tok ples bilong narapela, olsem- Sapos man i go stap long ples bilong meri em bai kisim tok ples bilong meri. Na sapos meri i kam stap long ples bilong man em bai kisim tok ples bilong meri-,ah, man na dispela narapela tok ples bilong narapela bai lus...olsem bilong man o meri. Wanpela bilong tupela bai lus. Na i **happen** nau.*

And the second point is like the first. Lots of men are marrying outside [the language group]. It's the same problem. Lots of times the man stays at the woman's place, so they use her language or Pidgin and English. Same as above, they don't think about coming back here. So, they live elsewhere and [even if they use Umbu-Ungu] they don't speak it properly. They use English or Tok Pisin or use a different vernacular. So if the man goes and lives at the woman's place, they use her language. If the woman comes to the man's place they use his language. Whichever way, one of the languages is lost, either the man's or the woman's. It's happening now!

*Olsem na moabeta if yu bringim dispela tok ples bilong yumi kam bek long dispela kain **system** olsem nau mipela toktok pastaim na yumi save...tok pri-skul nabaut. Na bringim i kam bek bai gutpela. Em tingting bilong mi. Tingim tasol.*

Therefore, it will be better to bring Umbu-Ungu into this kind of "system" that we know about here, all these *tok ples* preschools. If we bring the language back, that's good. That's my opinion. Just a thought.

Long lukluk bilong mi, laik pinis nau. [If we don't bring the language back]
Tok ples bai pinis. Olsem yu tok hia, as I see it, the mother tongue will die.
*bihain long **Two Thousand** yia, **Two*** Just like you're saying here, later, in
***Thousand** o...nau long '**Nineties** olsem* the year 2000, it will die. Why? Be-
1999 samting em bai pinis...yu luk olsem cause lots of young men and women
bai pinis. Bikos planti manki, manmeri i are going to school and leaving the
go aut skul yet na man i stap long ples area, and the number of us left here is
em i go liklik, nabaut na ol i go liklik.... dwindling.
  Bikos long sait long skulim bilong mipela In our [pre]schools now, when we ask
long nau olsem taim mipela askim ol long the children to bring a legend of some
*bringim sampela **legend** samting o stori* sort, or a story about our ancestors,
tumbuna bilong bipo no gat wanpela we don't have a single child who
manki save kisim dispela kain stori i kam. learns these kinds of stories. Their par-
***His** papamama insait long haus ol i no* ents don't teach them to them at
save lainim. Ol i no save kisim i kam. Na home. So the children don't bring
mipela yet i traim long mekim up sampela them [to school]. We [teachers] try to
kain stori olsem na save skulim ol long make up the stories ourselves. When
kain samting olsem-... Na taim mipela we tell these stories these days, I ob-
wokim long tok ples ating planti bilong ol serve the kids and think that they are
*long nau long **nowadays** mi lukim ol* not happy with Umbu-Ungu. They like
manki no amamas long tok ples tu. Ol i English or Tok Pisin. Now this practice
*laikim **Pidgin** o [inaudible] **Inglis**. Na* we're doing will result in the loss of
*dispela **system** yumi mekim bai tok ples* the mother tongue.
bai tok ples bai i go daun.
(Steven Kot, group interview, November 21, 1995, T56A)

Not all the KTPPS teachers shared Steven's alarm regarding the children's lack of knowledge about traditional stories and legends. Bob
Golipu, KTPPS teacher at Malke, stated (translated from Tok Pisin):

> [The children] like to do the ancestors' stories. One will bring one
> [to *pri skul*] and another [child] will bring another [story]. In the af-
> ternoon they will go and ask their parents to tell them another
> ancestor story. We do that and the children really like sharing those
> stories with each other. (Bob Golipu, group interview, November
> 21, 1995, T56A)

During the nine sessions I observed at one KTPPS location, however,
the teacher repeatedly asked the children to share a legend or story from
the ancestors, but without success, the children's typical response being
Te naa pilimulu 'We don't know any'. I suspect the children do know stories, but that they do not know as many of them or as well. Steven Kot's
discourse, therefore, is not an expression of all the teachers' experience.
   His thoughts do relate to the findings of chapters 5 and 6. The English
language schooling that commands so much attention and so much of

Kaugel families' limited financial resources is perceived as ushering Kaugel children out of their home language and culture into a new, distant way of living that is perceived in the Tambul Basin community as still somewhat incomprehensible, to be desired or avoided depending on who is speaking and in what context. This is the tension that characterizes each of the language and culture maintenance issues discussed in this study. Parents like Siminji and Akia, who see their children's acquisition of English as the road to a way of life that's far better (*olando olando pungi* 'they will go higher and higher') are countered by those who, like Councilor Dopenu, see primarily the disintegrative aspects of schooling on the life of the local community. To borrow the imagery in the quotation above, the language seems to be flowing away like water, or—to reach back to Dopenu's image of Umbu-Ungu as the pulse of the people—like blood.

Community Action in Reversing Language Shift

In table 1.3 of chapter 1, I presented Fishman's (1991) "heuristic device" for discussing the process of reversing language shift (RLS). It describes eight stages in the movement of the mother tongue from a seriously endangered "weak position" to the "strong side" of language maintenance though these are not discrete entities but "overlapping and interacting" stages (Baker 1996:72–73). According to Fishman, the L1-dominant home is the pivot around which all language planning strategies must revolve.

Stages 6 and 5 in table 7.2 represent my estimate of the Kaugel community's current position. Questions arise immediately. First, although the Kaugel home is still a safe haven for Umbu-Ungu dominance, the "community" that figures prominently in Stage 6 is more ambivalent, with some community members voicing extreme concern over the ramifications of the loss, especially of traditional cultural values, and others voicing a willingness to let the language and culture go in favor of the "good new ways." A concern voiced by several community members is that the English-language schools within their midst have powerful and undesirable socializing influences upon their children. One conclusion drawn from this discussion is that if the home is to retain its language vitality in such a context it will need help from other social institutions within the community.

Table 7.2. Kaugel Language situation on Fishman's (1991)
adapted scale

Weak side

Stage 8	Stage 7	Stage 6	Stage 5		
So few flu-	Older gen-	Language	Language	> > >	Education
ent speak-	eration uses	and identity	socializa-		reform:
ers that the	language	socialization	tion in-		
community	enthusiasti-	of children	volves		
needs to	cally but	takes place	extensive		
re-establish	children are	in home,	literacy,		
language	not learn-	community.	usually in-		
norms; re-	ing it.		cluding L1		
quires out-			schooling.		
side experts					
(e.g.,					
linguists).					

	Strong side			
	Stage 4	Stage 3	Stage 2	Stage 1
> > >	3-year	L1 used in	L1 is used	Lower gov-	"...cultural
	mother-	children's	in work-	ernmental	autonomy is
	tongue	formal edu-	places of	services and	recognized
	elemen-	cation in	larger soci-	local mass	and imple-
	tary level	conjunction	ety, beyond	media are	mented"; L1
		with na-	normal L1	open to L1.	used at up-
	grades	tional or of-	boundaries.		per govern-
	EP, E1,	ficial			ment level.
	E2	language.			

Although the KTPPS program provides *some* Kaugel children with *some* degree of Umbu-Ungu literacy, it can hardly be characterized as "extensive." As currently constituted, the KTPPS program is not likely to assume a larger role in the language socialization of Kaugel children, even if the community wants it.

The formal education system, developed from the one instituted by the Australian colonial administration, has proven to be a one-way passage out of the traditional culture to a kind of cultural no-man's land. Of potentially vital importance, in terms of Fishman's RLS scale, is the planned education reform. The National Department of Education, through the reform, plans to introduce a three-year pre-primary program of mother-tongue education to increase access to and relevance of early education for Papua New Guinean children. The plan calls for a great deal of local community input and control, with the NDOE providing basic teacher training, teacher salaries, and basic materials. The third conclusion points to the potential benefit that should result as the existing preschools in the KTPPS program are accepted by the NDOE for elementary level, thereby providing the community an increased capacity for Umbu-Ungu language socialization.

These three conclusions—however tentative they may be—form a rough framework for language planning at the local level. If English-language schools, Tok Pisin churches, and other enterprises in the community are exerting a powerful socializing influence on the children, then the promotion of systematic community awareness of the vital role that Kaugel homes and immediate environs play in maintaining Umbu-Ungu vitality is a necessary first step. Rambai, Apé, Karoma, Local Government Councilors like Dopenu, church leaders like Kopatoli, the KTPPS teachers, and the other *namel manmeri* have shown their preference for and experience in taking action to ensure the well-being of the community. They are the logical leaders for a language and culture maintenance movement.

Suggested course of action

With respect to status planning (Hornberger 1994), community leaders can identify the domains in which the use of the mother tongue is the most natural and appropriate. Those domains can then be set aside or "dedicated" for supporting the retention—or, where already fallen into disuse, reintroduction—of the mother tongue. In the Umbu-Ungu context, these would most likely be the church, the home, traditional community events, the KTPPS and, in the near future, the elementary grades that are to be incorporated into education reform.

The strong influence of Christian churches in the area and the close ties that exist socially and educationally between the home and the church make it a vital partner in any language and cultural maintenance effort. The importance of the KTPPS as an adjunct to the home and church in language and culture maintenance and as a link with the formal education system was demonstrated throughout chapters 4–6. The program's success in surviving several potentially disastrous situations attests to the presence of a resilient infrastructure. No physical or legal constraints require KTPPS teachers to continue holding classes. That they do suggests strongly that they see potential in the program for their future and the children's. The existing administration, training, instructional method, and materials should provide an adequate bridge for incorporating the existing KTPPS program into the elementary level. Rambai's long-established relationship with the Provincial Education Division, his knowledge of the educational system, and his reputation as a mother-tongue literacy educator should also facilitate a smooth transition for most of the fourteen Kaugel preschools into the formal system.

The new elementary classes, which will increase the pre-primary mother-tongue component from one to three years, should provide another significant domain for mother-tongue usage. In preparation for the incorporation of the KTPPS classes into the elementary system, an important element of corpus planning—developing mother-tongue literature—can be undertaken almost immediately. Local community support for a project of this type was expressed by Councilor Dopenu, a voice of concern with regard to language and culture shift.

Naa pilikimili ulu ilinga penga kepe umbuni pembalenga olione kapola umbunga ulu pulu akulinga temane topo kinie uluma i sipe pelemo i sipe terimulu nimbu kinie olio **bokure** *kepe topolie kepe tenga nosilimulanje temanele lelkanje kapolalenga. Penga kangambola ongimane kapola* **bokuna** *kanoko kinie i teringi lemo niku kinie kanoko ulu akuli teko mengo pangi.*	[The people] don't think that there's going to be a problem in the future [i.e., the old customs being lost] because they can still talk about them and tell the stories, but what I think would be good is if we would write a book now of the customs and stories. Then, the future generation of children can read them, understand them, and carry them on.

(Councilor Dopenu, interview, November 17, 1995, T53.5)

Rambai's ability to access local community "funds of knowledge" (cf. Moll 1992) for use in the development of KTPPS curriculum and literature suggests that a plan for community control of elementary curriculum is possible (within the limits allowed by the NDOE). Community control of the content of their children's education is a necessity (as noted also by Harris 1994) if true cultural maintenance is to accompany retention of the mother tongue. In that respect, the 17-volume Kaugel Reading Series provides an excellent building block for an Umbu-Ungu language-based education program. A language and culture-shift awareness component can be incorporated into KTPPS teachers' pre-service and in-service training courses to help them understand the process of language shift and the steps they can take in the classroom to privilege Kaugel culture values and the language that best encapsulates those values.

But the schools, even with support from the churches, cannot be expected to shoulder the responsibility for language and culture maintenance. As noted in chapter 1, the history of resuscitating moribund languages through formal education systems is grim. Ireland provides an example of a government-initiated language maintenance effort using the formal education system failing, to a certain extent, precisely because the language shift to English continued unabated in Irish homes (Benton 1986). If a language and culture maintenance effort in Kaugel is to be successfully implemented, the *namel manmeri* will need to recognize that the home and community, as sanctuaries for Kaugel language and cultural values, are the key domains and need to be encouraged and supported.

This is not to say that Kaugel parents should resist a practical bilingualism that affords their children access to the benefits of English education. The suggestion is that the children also need to be have opportunities to learn the values that are important to sustaining community life. Without it, the children may well leave Umbu-Ungu altogether for the lure of English and Tok Pisin and the popular world culture they represent. The world of the Kaugel traditions will be beyond them. As Aika Kopatoli remarked, *Akuma akulinga naa pilingi. Enenga ungu lupa pilingi* 'They won't be able to understand [the old traditions]. They will only listen to their own strange thoughts' (Group interview, November 14, 1995, T47A.31).

Namel Manmeri: Past, Present, and Future

In the narrative that began chapter 1, Karoma came to the mission school to fetch the young Rambai because the community leaders, surveying the changes occurring around them, had arranged for the *sandallu* youth initiation. Their purpose was to effect community control over the eyes through which Rambai's generation would see the world. Rambai's personal history seems to confirm their wisdom, as he and Karoma and other initiates continue to provide culturally appropriate leadership for the community.

The dilemma they face in the process of promoting the community's welfare through commerce between widely differing cultures is well illustrated in the episode that opened this chapter. There at the Kalapolo *haus piksa* another "ceremony of initiation" takes place for the children and youth of the Tambul Basin, with language and customs from a distant land carried into the local community in the pocket of a video entrepreneur. None of the community leaders, including the children's parents, preview the contents. No one knows "through whose eyes their children see the world" after a long night of viewing. The chances of any of the young viewers concluding from the videos that they have been chosen to have "responsibility for the community" seem remote if not impossible.

During the final meeting of the Purare Community School Board of Management, the chairman, David Serowa, submitted a plan for an Aika-Korika-Kengelka Community Center. Its physical form strongly resembled the wood-frame, corrugated iron roofed buildings at the Evangelical Bible Mission station where David works as a construction supervisor. My first reaction when I saw it was, "How can this rural American architecture contribute anything to Kaugel language and culture maintenance?" When I asked Rambai about it later he replied as follows:

Ating...liklik samting em Devid i laik putim moa long em i no gat long **plan** *bilong em. Long* **entrance** *bilong go aut, em laik entrance kamap olsem wanpela haus* **lapulka.** *Tru tru haus man. Em long makim dispela. Na em no wokim long plan bilong em.*

That's probably one of the details that didn't get into David's plan. He wants to make the entrance/exit to resemble the front of a *haus man* [lit., fathers' house]. Like a real men's house. To give it its identity, but he didn't draw it into the plans.

Na narapela...samting tru mi ting long piksa we em bin putim long en, em bai makim olsem wanpela haus i no tru tru haus man. Tasol dispela tingting long bungim man bilong kam na toktok na sindaun, em tasol bai makim olsem ol **aim** *bilong ol. Makim sampela, tru i gat... sampela ausait samting, piksa na lukluk bilong em em bilong ausait...* **some materials,** *kapa haus, em bilong ausait. Tasol, we ol yus long en, em laik strongim tingting bilong haus man....*

Something else...it's true that in his drawing the building doesn't really look like a real men's house. But the idea of gathering men to come and sit and talk together, that's what he's aiming for. Looking at the drawing, true, it's not indigenous...some materials, iron-roofed house, that's nonindigenous. But the way they will make use of it, that will reinforce the underlying idea of the men's house.

Ol man [tok olsem]: Wanem kain haus yu mekim em mipela no wari tasol long as yu tok...em bai yu kamap wanpela ples bilong makim haus man bilong mipela.... Tasol dispela [David] laik kamapim wanpela samting klostu olsem dispela bilong bungim mipela long kam toktok long wanem hevi—problem—o wanem gutpela samting. Em, em bai makim haus man na mipela amamas.

The men say this: Whatever kind of building you construct, we're not concerned about that. But, respecting your purpose, we can see you are developing a substitute for our men's house. So David wants to develop something similar that will provide a place for us to meet and talk about troubles—problems—or something good. That's like a men's house [for us] and we're happy and excited [about it].

(Rambai Keruwa, interview, December 12, 1995, T63A)

Rambai's explanation suggests that the community leaders are already aware of the need for a place to gather people together in order to talk over community concerns including, I presume, their concerns regarding the Kalapolo *haus piksa* or the effect of the English-language schools on their children's and young people's behavior.

Apé confirmed Rambai's interpretation of the plan's rationale, comparing the building to PNG's House of Parliament which is architecturally styled after a Sepik region *haus tambaran* 'ancestral spirit house'. David's plan to make the entrance of this community center after the fashion of a men's house seems to make this same connection between the old and the new.

When the plan for the center was presented to the community at the Purare Schools Closing Day, Tendi, one of the Aika big-men, made an enthusiastic speech, which Rambai later recounted for me.

*Na bihain Tendi i tok...em tok, Em gutpela tingting yu kamapim na tru klostu dispela tingting long haus man i laik dai na em, em, yu wokim dispela plan na tingting long kamapim haus man long hia. Em gutpela tingting yu gat. Na em tok, bipo taim mipela stap taim bilong mipela, lukim, long Tambul i go long Tomba na i go klostu long Walia, em dispela rot em mipela man tasol go mekim. I no wanem samting, **machine** i kam mekim, nogat. Mipela yet i go mekim nau. Na nau em planti ol yusim dispela rot na amamas. Tasol i no gat wanpela **masin** wokim. Em day and night mipela mas kam bek kisim kaikai go bek slip katim...*

Later Tendi spoke. He said [to David Serowa], "that's a good idea that you've come up with because, truly, the [traditional] idea of the men's house is almost dead, so you have made a plan to build a 'men's house' here. That's a good idea you have." Then he said, "In the past, back in our days, just we men went and made the road from Tambul to Tomba and then close to Walia. There was no, what do you call it, machine that made it. No way. We went and made it by ourselves. Now many people happily use the road. But there wasn't a single machine that helped make it. Day and night we would come back [home] eat, sleep, cut firewood....

Na taim ol toktok long mipela long kisim waisan, em mipela mas kisim dispela amu, diwai, katim na mekim hol insait long hollow. Em mipela givim ol wanwan mama, tokim ol long go long wara na karim ston i kam. Mipela rausim graun, em mipela mekim na mipela hat wok tasol nau, sori, nau yu gat kar long kisim wanem samting i stap longwe kisim i kam. Nau yu ken yusim gutpela rot i stap pinis long en.

When they told us to get sand, we had to get the pandanus trees, split them and hollow out the core. Then we'd give those to the women to carry down to the river to get stones to carry back up [to the road]. We dug up the ground, and doing that was hard work, but now, sorry, you all have vehicles to use to go and get whatever you want and bring it here. You use this good road to do that.

*And wanem haus yu tok long en, em, sapos wanpela haus man tasol yu toktok em mi gat tubel, tasol nau yupela olgeta Aika, Korika-Kengelka bungim tingting na bungim mani na bungim **strong** bilong*

And, whatever building you're talking about now—if it's [really] a *haus man* you're talking about I have mixed feelings about that—but now, all of Aika and Korika-Kengelka, put your minds

yupela na bungim wanem narapela re-	together and collect your money and
sources yupela gat long em, putim em.	gather your strength, and gather to-
Em tok, em liklik samting. Gutpela yu	gether whatever other resources you
autim dispela tasol em liklik samting na	have." He said, "This is no big deal. It's
mi laik strongim yupela. Yupela mas	good that you have announced this but
yusim bun bilong mipela ol man. Na	it is not a big deal, so I want to encour-
mipela mekim dispela wok.	age you. You must use the strength of
	all of us men and we will complete this
	work."

(Rambai Keruwa, interview, December 13, 1995, T63A)

Tendi alludes to the road that he and his peers constructed with dig-ging sticks and a few spades in order to connect Tambul to the road that was being similarly constructed to connect Mount Hagen and Wabag. From the vantage point of thirty years, the monumental labor they ex-pended on that project can be seen to have opened a metaphorical as well as a physical road to new possibilities. Therefore, Tendi encourages the young leaders to be bold in their plans for a building that will likely cost in excess of K50,000. Compared to making a road with sticks and carrying sand and stones in the hollowed out trunks of pandanus trees, this build-ing is a little thing, he says.

The locations in which traditional education took place are past or pass-ing. Tendi and his age-mate Pangu live in the last of the original style men's house. When they die, no more traditional men's houses will be built. Tendi sees nothing incongruent in replacing the traditional *form* with a new one. It is the purpose and content of the form that is important, as can be inferred from Tende's comments about meeting together as a community in unity, cooperating, sharing resources for the community good. These, he says, are what need to be preserved.

For the *namel manmeri*, the Kaugel Tok Ples Pri Skul program can serve as a kind of interim medium of community education, another way in which they can affect their children's future. The children who attend learn how to learn in their mother tongue and to enjoy the stories of Kaugel life as it was and is. In a modest way, the KTPPS has aided the home in maintaining the language that best defines who Kaugel people are and who they are to become. Whether the program will continue as it has, or whether it will become part of a larger mother-tongue program within the elementary level is yet to be determined. What seems most cer-tain is that Rambai and the other *namel manmeri* will be actively engaged in shaping those events.

Appendix A

Appendix A1

Interviews

Tape	Sex	Role	Place/date	Clan	Residence	Interviewer*
1A	M	Parent	Purare 7/24	Aika	Kikuwa	AK (DM)
22	M, F	Parents	Purare 8/31	Aika	Purare	AK (DM)
26	M	Parent	Kalapolo 9/20	Kengelka	Kalapolo	DM (SM)
42	M, F	Parents	Mt. Hagen 11/08	Aika	Mt. Hagen	DM(AK)
47	M, F	Parents	Purare 11/14	Aika, Korika	Sakaleme,Purare, Pomboli, Kalapolo	AK (DM)
53	M	Parent	Purare 11/17	Aika	Pomboli	AK (DM)
54A	F	Parent	Sakaleme 11/19	Aika	Sakaleme	AK (DM)
54B	F	Parent	Kikuwa 11/19	Aika	Kikuwa	RK (DM)
1B,2,3,4,5,6	M	KTPPS director	Purare 7/26 to 7/29	Aika	Kikuwa	DM
14A	M	PS teacher	Purare 8/10	Aika	Pomboli	AK (DM)
14B	M	PS teacher	Purare 10/12	Aika	Pomboli	AK (DM)
25	M	PS teacher	Alkena 9/21	n/a	Alkena	AK (DM)
27B	F	PS teacher	Maripena 10/02	Tendepo	Maripena	AK (DM)
36	M	PS teacher	Kulipena 11/05	Korika	Kulipena	AK (DM)
38A	M	PS teacher	Pulumungu 11/06	Kanimbe	Pulumungu	AK
56	M, F	PS teachers	Tambul 11/21	n/a	Tambul	DM,RK
29AB	M, F	CS teachers	Tambul 10/04	n/a	DM (AK)	40
40	M, F	CS teachers	Yombikuli 11/07	various	Yombikuli	DM (AK)
23	F,F,M	Children	Purare 10/13	Aika	Purare	AK

*Initials in parentheses ( ) indicated presence as observer, not as interviewer; AK = Apé Kolowa, DM = Dennis Malone, SM = Susan Malone, RK = Rambai Keruwa.

24	M, F	Youth	Purare 9/30	Aika		AK (DM)
41	M, F	Children	Baisu 11/08	Aika		AK (DM)
32	M	ERCordWHP	Mt. Hagen 10/16	Kulka	Mt. Hagen	DM, RK
Not Taped	M	CS inspctr	Tambul 10/02	Baiyer	Tambul	DM
Not Taped	M	REU director	Port Moresby 7/10	n/a	Port Moresby	DM
59	M, F	SIL team	Purare 12/03	Expatriate	Purare	DM
Not taped	F	ACE principal	Tambul Bible School 12/07	Expatriate	Tambul	DM

Appendix A2

Classrooms

Tape	Date	School	Place	Language MOI	Lessons
8	7/31	KTPPS	Site 1	Umbu-Ungu	MT literacy
9	8/01	KTPPS	Site 1	Umbu-Ungu	MT literacy
10	8/07	KTPPS	Site 1	Umbu-Ungu	MT literacy
11	8/07	KTPPS	Site 1	Umbu-Ungu	MT literacy
12	8/08	KTPPS	Site 1	Umbu-Ungu	MT literacy
13	8/09–8/10	KTPPS	Site 1	Umbu-Ungu	MT literacy
18	8/22	KTPPS	Site 1	Umbu-Ungu	culture (flutes)
27A	10/02	KTPPS	Site 2	Tok Pisin	MT literacy/maths
37	11/06	KTPPS	Site 4	Umbu-Ungu	MT literacy
28	10/04	CS, 2A	Site 3	English/Tok Pisin	Language/maths
39A	11/07	CS, 1	Site 5	English/Tok Pisin	Language/maths
39B		CS, 4	Site 5	English	Science
49	11/16	CS, 1	Site 6	English/Tok Pisin	Language/maths

Total time for KTPPS: 450 minutes
Total time for CS:180minutes

Abbreviations:
MOI = Medium of instruction
KTPPS = Kaugel Tok Ples Pri Skul
CS = Community School
MT = mother tongue

Appendix A3

Taped Events

Tape	Date	Place	Activity	Participants
7	7/31	Kikuwa	Father teaching his 12-year-old son string games	Father, son, daughter, mother, researcher
15	8/29	Purare	Two children relating day's activities to father of one of the children [natural setting]	Father, daughter, nephew
16	8/20	Pomboli	Sunday school	SS leader and SS children
17	8/20	Pomboli	Church service	Pastor, worship leaders and worshipers
19	8/23	Purare	An evening of flute-playing in the men's house	Four men playing flutes, clan leader, several drop-ins, researcher
20	8/27	Kikuwa	Sunday school	SS leader and SS children, researcher
21	8/27	Kikuwa	Church worship service	Pastor, Bible school students and worshipers
29A	10/04	Tambul	Grade 2A students reading Umbu-Ungu story	Grade 2A students
30	10/07	Tambul	Grade 6A students reading MT and English stories	Grade 6 students
31	10/07	Purare	A grade 1 boy relates several stories in Umbu-Ungu	Grade 1 boy and younger children
33 and 34	11/04	Kikuwa	Compensation payment to Kulumindi-Yapo clans	Local community members, local government representative, K-Y clan members
38B	11/06	Pulumungu	Children singing songs with Umbu-Ungu lyrics	KTPPS students, researcher, local community bystanders
46	11/04	Purare	Student relates his understanding of a local event	Grade 5 student, two younger boys, researcher
50, 51 and 52	11/16	Purare	Purare CS Board of Management meeting	Members of board, CS head teacher, researcher

58	11/28	Tambul	Umbu-Ungu New Testament dedication	Church and government leaders, Kaugel community members, visitors
60	12/05	Purare	CS/KTPPS end-of-year School Closing	Local clan leaders, clan members
61	12/06	Yombikuli	CS/KTPPS end-of-year School Closing	Head teacher, staff, board members, parents, students, community leaders
63	12/13	Purare	Debriefing of Purare School Closing	Apé Kolowa, Rambai Keruwa, Dennis Malone

Appendix A4

Interview: Adults

Who conducted the interview?_____
    Date:_____
    Place:_____
    Tape number:_____

1. Your name?

2. Male or female?

3. Age?

4. Church?

5. Birthplace?

6. Other places of residence?

7. Which language did you learn first?

8. Do you understand another language?

9. How many children do you have? Did your children go to Kaugel preschool? Did your children go to community school? What grade did they complete?

10. Did you attend English-language school? If you did not attend English school what caused you not to attend?

11. Do you work for wages? If you don't work for wages, how do you get money?

12. Have you traveled around to see other places [coastal areas or to Caucasian countries]?

13. Do you read English? Do you read Umbu-Ungu? Do you read Tok Pisin? Do you read some other language?

[Start tape recorder here: names, day, date, place]

I.   What thoughts do people express about speaking Umbu-Ungu?

Some people say that their children should only learn the white people's language [English] in school. What do you think?

If a relative of yours comes from a distant place like Ialibu, and asks you what they do in the Umbu-Ungu [pre-] school, what would you reply to them? Would you be able to tell them what work is done in the Umbu-Ungu school?

If the Umbu-Ungu schools were ruined and ceased to operate, what changes would occur for the children and the community? What do you think?

What do the community school administrators and grade 1 teachers think about the Umbu-Ungu preschools?

II. What do people think about the old traditional customs?

1.   Some people are saying that the children here are forgetting Umbu-Ungu and the traditional customs. What are your thoughts on that issue?

2.   What kind of behavior do we observe in children that helps us predict how they will do later in life?

3.   Some people say that if the children spend three years in pre-school learning in Umbu-Ungu, they won't learn English properly. What are your thoughts about that?

4.   If the children tire of Umbu-Ungu and speak only Tok Pisin or English, what local customs would change? What would happen to customs like marriage, funerals, pig exchange? If those customs all ceased, what do you think?

[We will ask this question (5) if a parent has some children who went straight from home to grade 1 and some children who went to pre-school first then to grade 1.]

5.   Some of your children went to Umbu-Ungu pre-school first then to community school. Some of your children did not

go to Umbu-Ungu [pre]school but went straight to grade 1 in community school. Since your children have taken two different paths to community school, when you compare them how well did they do?

Interview: Children and youth

Who conducted the interview?:_____
    Date:_____
    Place:_____
    Tape number:_____

I.   Children's and youths' Talk

    1. Name? _____

    2. Male or female? _____

    3. Age? _____

    4. Birthplace? _____

    5. Church/worship? _____

    6. Have you lived elsewhere? _____

    7. Which language did you learn first? _____

    8. Do you speak other languages? _____

    9. Did you attend Umbu-Ungu preschool? Did you attend English language school? What was the highest grade you completed?

    10. Do you read Umbu-Ungu? Do you read English? Do you read any other language?

II. What the children/youth think about the Umbu-Ungu language

    Some people say that children should do only English-language school. What do you think?

III. What do they think about people following urban life styles?

    Suppose your father and mother went to work on the coast and took you with them. You all went to live permanently on the coast. What good local customs would you *not* be able to do?

IV. Umbu-Ungu school [Kaugel preschool]

Suppose a stranger came here from a distant place. When he sees our Umbu-Ungu school, he asks you what kind of things do you do there? What would be your reply to him/her?

V. When you come back to this place what kinds of local activities do you think you would like to do?

Interview: Teachers

I. Teacher information

  1. Name

  2. Clan

  3. Residence

  4. Gender

  5. Marital status

  6. Children

    Boys?

    Girls?

  7. Church/worship?

  8. Do you speak Umbu-Ungu?

  9. Do you speak any other languages?

  10. What was the highest grade in school you completed?

  11. Where do you teach preschool?

  12. Where did you do teacher training for Umbu-Ungu preschools?

  13. How long have you been a KTPPS teacher?

II. Teachers' work

  1. Tell me about the things you do when you teach the children.

  2. Tell me any stories about the good things that happen in your school.

3. Tell me any stories about things you observe that are bad or cause problems.

4. Who supervises you when you teach? Who helps you with your teaching responsibilities? What kinds of things does(do) s/he(they) do?

5. Who chose you to be an Umbu-Ungu preschool teacher?

III. Umbu-Ungu school activities

1. What preschool activities do you think should be retained?

2. What kind of fruit do you observe in the students? Is it observable now or in the future?

3. What do you think needs to be done in order to improve and strengthen the preschools?

4. Which of the traditional customs do you think the children really enjoy doing [in preschool]?

Appendix B

Appendix B1

The Cabbage Story

Kapisa Temane

Mutenke Kristen temone imu torumu.

Kapisa mulu mare molkomele.

3   4

Ye anda teme te wa tokomo.   Kapisa pulu ambomo lombili okamo.

5   6

Lombili omba ye anda
kanumu kopene tokomo.

7

Kanu kinie kapisa mulu
kanumu perele-marele pukumu.

8

The Echo Ogre Story

Wenewene
Temane

Rambai Keruwa temane imu torumu.

Kangoma wenewene molkomo
koliana puku molongi.

38   39

Kango te waaa nimu kinie
wenewene waaa-la nimu.

Kango te owa mele kalle nimu.
Wenewene owa mele kalle-la nimu.

40   41

Kango te lupane wi manie naiye nimu. Wenewene wi manie naiye-la nimu.

42

Kango te we molkomo nimu kinie wenewene we molkoro-la nimu.

43

Wenewene ungu sumbi sipe pilimo.

44

A Story about Housebuilding Things

Ulke Takolemele
Melemango Temana

Mana Tapuyeni temane imu torumu.

Kango yapoka molemeia.
Kango tenga imbi Ama.
Kango tenga imbi Pirimu.
Kanga tenga imbi So.

10

11

Kango Ama ulke takombandó mindi
ambolema. Kango Pirimu ulke takombando
pirimu mindi ambolemo. So ulke
takombando so mindi ambolemo. Ene alleli
kerikeri mindi illimele.

Kango imanga lapamo Masine nilimele.
Kango poko mele mare korolemele kinie
lapane tepa silimu. Lapa yu mele
akumanga te naa korolemo.

12

13

Walse ulke te takomolo melema liringi.
Ulke manle uluma teringi kinle kango
Ama yuni ama ambolorumu. Kango
Pirimuni pirimu ambolorumu. Kango So
so ambolorumu.

14

Lapa Masine yu masine ambolorumu.
Mele te naa kororingi. Ulke kanumu ena
telunga ombe ola purumu. Yambo
kanumune kanoko mini wale munduringi.

15

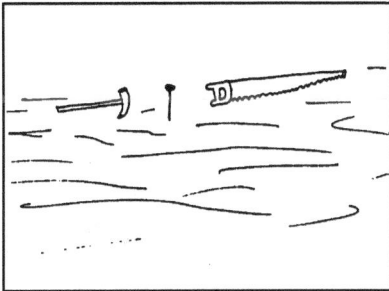

Kinie olio kanakomolo. Ulu isipe wendo
okomo. Kapa ulke takokomele koliamo
mele imane takolemele. Ama, pirimu so
kinie masine.

16

Story about Something Boys Do

Kangoma
Telemele Mele
Temane

Rambai Keruwa temane imu torumu.

Kango kise molkolle kulku luma lepamolo nikimlil. Kango akumanga tene ola angilipelie wi pangi te ki sundu topalie, "Akune pupu kulku luma lepamolol" nikimu.

16

17

We kangoma aku manda ningu enenga lou koya telu telu ningu lilku ambolko pukumili. Ena puku ma pangi tenga nondoko mele pukulle pamba unju talo peke tokomele.

Toko manie panjikulie mimi teko kango tene pamba unju ta ola lipe pilkimu kinie umuni tekemo nimbe kelepa manie mundukumu.

18

19

Pe ma pangina olando pungindu kango talone pamba unju te tarepola teko mekembele. Kango talone unju te tarepola teko mekembele.

20

Pangi muli mulina ola pukulie ene pamba unju tolo manie nosikulie kulku luma lengendo tekemela. Kango talo kumbi lelko eltenga pamba unjune talape tokolo molkombele.

21

Pe elte waruna mando ikisikimbili. Pe kango talo akula tekelo mando ikisikimbili. Puku mere manie kolona ene peya molkolie pe enenga pamba unju kanuma pangina olando wandupundu teko meli pukumili.

22

Aku teko mindi molangi ma pangina era ponie kanumu we pora nimbe ma wendo okomo. Kinie enenga pamba unju kanuma lepeli ene no kolopamolo ningu pukumili. No keto tenga minimbe unju te angilkimu kanokomele.

23

Kango talo minimbe unjune ola
pukumbili. Kango talo manie we
molkombele. Kango talone minimbe
gomo peyanga talo talo ningulu langoko
manie mundukumbili.

24

Kinie no kelo tenga angilkuile enenga
minimbe gomo kanuma kimbuku no
kolko meli kelko ma pangina olando
pukumili. Pangina angilkuile kulku
luma leiko sulke toko nosiringi
akumunga no onde leikemele.

25

Kulku luma lengi kolia kanumu teko
teko silipepe tonjikimili. Aku tekolie
kinie enenge pamba unju noringi tolo
lilku eneme ola talape tolo molkolie
warune mando ikisiku andokomele.

26

Aku siku kara puku pepe perako mindi
molkomele kinie kolia ena we pukumu.
Ene oli pakoko monjili enenga ulkendo
ikisikimili. Enenga lapali kinie
anupilimane manda tengi ningu kapi
ninginje.

27

Appendix B2

Umbungu Kambu Tamili
[The Kaugel Reading Series]

Book	Title	Pages	Author
Red	*Ulke Temane* [House Story]	3–7	Children
1	*Kongi Temane* [Pig Story]	8–12	Children
	Oma Temane [Fish Story]	13–17	Mana Tapuye
	Kongi Ga Nokomo Temane [Story about Pig Eating Sweetpotato]	18–23	Mana Tapuye
	Lopa Temane [Marsupial Story]	24–29	Mana Tapuye
	Mingi Sipe Temane [Water Gourd Story]	30–36	Mutenke Kristen
	Owa te Walo Nosipe Molkomo Temane [Story about the Dog that Had Puppies]	37–41	Mutenke Kristen
	Kango te Kinie Koya tenga Temane [Story about a Boy and a Knife]	42–46	Mana Tapuye
Red	*Pita Kinie Saimono Tolonga Temane* [Peter and Simon's Story]	3–8	John Mane
2	*Kepo Kinie Yunge Yamboma* [Kepo and His Family]	9–21	John Mane
	Kera Porowe kinie Kumaka Tolonga Temane [Hawk and Rat's Story]	22–27	John Mane
	Kanapa kinie Wambie Temane [Corn and Snake Story]	28–32	Mana Tapuye
	Lapa Malo Tolonga Temane [Father and Son's Story]	33–37	Mutenke Kristen
	Lopa Takopo Temane [Opossum Story]	38–42	Children
	Oma Temane [Fish Story]	43–48	Mana Tapuye
Red	*Owa kinie Wa Ye tolonga Temane* [Dog and Thief's Story]	3–8	John Mane
3	*Ambola te Mindili Nokomo Temane* [Story about a Girl Getting Injured]	9–15	Mutenke Kristen
	Kango Talo Kanapa Kalkombele Temane [Story about Two Boys Cooking Corn]	16–21	Mutenke Kristen
	Ambo te kinie Kongi tolonga Temane [A Woman and Pig's Story]	22–27	John Mane
	Api Temane [Salt Story]	28–32	Children
	Kango te kinie Owa tolonga Temane [A Boy and Dog's Story]	33–37	Mutenke Kristen
	Kango Talonga Temane [Two Boys' Story]	38–42	Mutenke Kristen
	Kera kinie Kango tolonga Temane [Bird and Boy's Story]	43–47	Mutenke Kristen

Red 4	*Kapisa Temane* [Cabbage Story]	3–8	Mutenke Kristen
	Ye Anda Nona Pou Nikimu Temane [Story about an Old Man Who Fell into the River]	9–14	Mutenke Kristen
	Ambola Talo Ga Aporale Tekembele Temane [Story about Two Girls Fighting over Sweet Potatoes]	15–19	Mutenke Kristen
	Londea Temane [Frog Story]	20–29	Rambai Keruwa
	Anumu Lemenu tolo Oma Ki Likimbili Temane [Story about a Mother and Daughter Opening a Fish (Can)]	30–36	Mutenke Kristen
	Owa Kuruma kinie Kango Pai tolonga Temane [Dog Kuruma and Boy Pai's Story]	37–42	Mana Tapuye
	Wambie Temane [Snake Story]	43–48	Mana Tapuye

Blue 5	*Owa tenga Temane* [A Dog's Story]	3–7	John Mane
	Ambo tenga Ambolamo Unju Kolane Tomu Temane [Story about a Woman's Daughter Hit by a Branch]	8–13	Mutenke Kristen
	Ambola te Anumunga Ungu Lipe Su Sikimu [A Girl Who Disobeys Her Mother]	14–18	Mutenke Kristen
	Kimi Llapo Temane [Lizard Story]	19–28	Rambai Keruwa
	Kango Makunga Temane [Boy Mark's Story]	29–37	John Mane
	Wenewene Temane [Ogre Story]	38–44	Rambai Keruwa

Blue 6	*Kango Yepoko* [Three Boys]	3–18	Rambai Keruwa
	Kango Tende Lopa Tomu Temane [Story about Boy Tende Killed a Marsupial]	19–26	Rambai Keruwa
	Kowa kinie Kangoma [Kowa and Boys]	27–34	John Mane
	Ambola Teresanga Temane [Girl Teresa's Story]	35–48	John Mane

Blue 7	*Kongi Temane* [Pig Story]	3–8	Mutenke Kristen
	Anumu Lemenu tolo Ka Topukumbili Temane [Story about a Mother and Daughter Going to Get String]	9–17	Mana Tapuye
	Ambola te Ga Akukumu Temane [Story about a Girl Digging Sweet Potatoes]	18–24	Mana Tapuye
	No Polo Temane [Bridge Story]	25–31	John Mane
	Kamako Karimbi Makali Tekemo Temane [Story about Rich Man Karimbi Doing Pig Exchange Ceremony]	32–39	Mana Tapuye
	Mako kinie Yunge Yambomanga Temane [Mark and His Family's Story]	40–48	Mana Tapuye

Blue	*Ambola Talo Kemu Mepuringili Temane* [Story about Two Girls Going to Get Greens]	3–12	Mutenke Kristen
8	*Ambo te Ga Akupe Koerimu* [A Woman Dug Up Sweet Potatoes to Steam Cook]	13–21	Mutenke Kristen
	Kepa kinie Yunge Owa tolo [Kepa and His Dog Story]	22–30	John Mane
	Kango Angenungulu Talonga Temane [Two Boys Wrestling Story]	31–37	John Mane
	Amu Panjilimolo Temane [Story about Planting Pandanus]	38–46	Jack Algo
Blue	*Unju Kaloli Temane* [Firewood Story]	3–8	Rambai Keruwa
9	*Kengena kinie Waina tolo Poniena Pukumbili Temane* [Story about Kengena and Waina Going to the Garden]	9–17	Mutenke Kristen
	Mekene Temane Te Olio Topa Simbe [Mek Is Going to Tell Us a Story]	18–26	Meke
	Ga Mundu Temane [Sweet Potato Mound Story]	27–35	John Nia
	Ma Jiminjimi Telemo Temanemo [The Story about Earthquakes]	36–40	Rambai Keruwa
	Kangoma Telemele Mele Temane [Story about Things Boys Do]	41–45	Rambai Keruwa
Beige	*Anumu Lemenu tolo Londeya Kandupuringili Temane* [Story about a Mother and Daughter Going to Look for Frogs]	3–10	Mana Tapuye
10	*Lopa Posi Temane* [Cat Story]	11–17	John Nia
	Nokeya kinie Pokome tolo Amu Lipukumbili Temane [Story about Nokeya and Pokome Going to Get Pandanus Nuts]	18–25	Mutenke Kristen
	Lou Ilse Telemele Temane [Story about Making Axe Handles]	26–29	Rambai Keruwa
	Kango te Ulke Takorumu Temane [Story about a Boy Who Built a House]	30–39	Mutenke Kristen
	Kango Talo Ponie Unju Langokombele Temane [Story about Two Boys Trimming Garden Trees]	40–49	Mutenke Kristen

Beige 11	*Langi Mongo Koeringi Temane* [Story about Steam Cooking Food]	3–7	Rambai Keruwa
	Kango Talo Kongi Koekembele Temane [Story about Two Boys Steam Cooking Pork]	8–16	Mutenke Kristen
	Kango Apoka Tenga Temane [An Orphan Boy's Story]	17–26	Mutenke Kristen
	No Kendepo Temane [Water Spout Story]	27–31	Rambai Keruwa
	Kera Walipe Temane [Flying Fox Story]	32–40	George P. Miki
	Owa kinie Lopa tolonga Temane [A Dog and Marsupial's Story]	41–48	Children
Beige 12	*Kongi Arili Temane* [Tended Pig Story]	3–11	George P. Miki
	Siri Ga Mundu Terimu Temane [Story about Siri Making Sweet Potato Mounds]	12–18	Mana Tapuye
	Kolape Mingi Temane [Flute Story]	19–35	Rambai Keruwa
	Kemu Komba Temane [Leafy Green Vegetable Story]	36–44	Mana Tapuye
Beige 13	*Sukunga Yambomanga Temane* [Suku's Family's Story]	3– 9	Mana Tapuye
	Ulke Takolemele Melemanga Temane [House Building Things' Story]	10–16	Mana Tapuye
	Kumake Melu Temane [Rat Trap Story]	17–25	Mana Tapuye
	Ambo Ambu tenga Langi Koyerimu Temane [Story about an Old Woman Steam Cooking Food]	26–34	Garu Puli
	Oma Akena Temane [Eel Story]	35–45	Luke S. Diwi
Beige 14	*Wenewene Temane* [Ogre Story]	3–21	Timothy Anzu
	Kango Keloma Unju Lipuringi Temane [Story about Small Boys Going to Get Firewood]	22–28	Mana Tapuye
	Lapa Malo Talonga Temane [Father and Son's Story]	29–35	Mana Tapuye
	Kango Talo Tauno Koliana Puringili Temane [Story about Two Boys who Went to Town]	36–43	John Nia
Green 15	*Owa te Walo Nosipe Molorumu Temane* [Story about a Dog that Had Puppies]	3–10	Mana Tapuye
	*Asi Mara Koke: Owa tenga Temane [Asi Mara Koke: a Dog's Story]	11–17	Mana Tapuye
	*Kunungu Temane [Rain Cape Story]	18–29	Rambai Keruwa
	*Nokindiye Menu tolo Opa Teringili Temane [Story about Nokindiye and His Wife Fighting]	30–36	Mana Tapuye

References

Afolayan, A. 1984. The English language in Nigerian education as an agent of proper multilingual and multicultural development. *Journal of Multilingual and Multicultural Development* 5(1):1–22.

Ahai, N. 1990. The status of literacy and primary education. Papua New Guinea country paper. Report presented at the Unesco Sub-Regional Workshop on Planning Strategies for Literacy and Non-Formal Education. Quezon City, Philippines.

Ahai, N., and M. Bopp. 1993. *Missing links: Literacy, awareness and development in Papua New Guinea.* Report to UNICEF regarding a review of the National Literacy and Awareness Programme and related issues in Papua New Guinea. Port Moresby: National Research Institute of Papua New Guinea.

Akinnaso, F. 1989. One nation, four hundred languages: Unity and diversity in Nigeria's language policy. *Language Problems and Language Planning* 13(2):133–146.

Akinnaso, F. 1991. On the mother tongue education policy in Nigeria. *Educational Review* 43(1):89–106.

Baker, C. 2001. *Foundations of bilingual education and bilingualism,* third edition. Clevedon, England: Multilingual Matters.

Banks, A., ed. 1995. *Political handbook of the world: 1994–1995.* Binghamton: State University of New York.

Benton, R. 1986. Schools as agents for language revival in Ireland and New Zealand. In Spolsky (ed.), 53–76.

Bernard, H. 1992. Preserving language diversity. *Cultural Survival Quarterly* 15–18.

Besnier, N. 1993. Literacy and feelings: The encoding of affect in Nukulaelae letters. In Street (ed.), 62–86.

Bledsoe, C., and K. Robey. 1993. Arabic literacy and secrecy among the Mende of Sierra Leone. In Street (ed.), 110–134.

Bloch, M. 1993. The uses of schooling and literacy in a Zafimaniry village. In Street (ed.), 87–109.

Bogdan, R., and S. Biklen. 1992. *Qualitative research for education: An introduction to theory and methods.* Boston: Allyn and Bacon.

Brenzinger, M., B. Heine, and G. Sommer. 1991. Language death in Africa. In R. H. Robins and E. M. Uhlenbeck (eds.), *Endangered languages* 19–43. Oxford: Berg.

Canale, M. 1984. On some theoretical frameworks for language proficiency. In C. Rivera (ed.), *Language proficiency and academic achievement,* 28–40. Clevedon, England: Multilingual Matters.

Cazden, C. 1992. *Language minority education in the United States: Implications of the Ramirez Report.* Santa Cruz, Calif.: National Center for Research on Cultural Diversity and Second Language Learning.

Cenoz, J., and F. Genesee, eds. 1998. *Beyond bilingualism: Multilingualism and multilingual education.* Clevedon, England: Multilingual Matters.

Clay, M. 1995. Literacy and biliteracy in Asia: Problems and issues in the next decade. *Asian Reading Congress 1995: Selected papers,* 3–18. Singapore: National Book Development Council of Singapore.

Connolly, B., and R. Anderson. 1987. *First contact.* New York: Viking Penguin.

Cooper, R. 1989. *Language planning and social change.* Cambridge: Cambridge University Press.

Crystal, D. 2000. *Language death.* Cambridge: Cambridge University Press.

Cummins, J. 1979. Linguistic interdependence and the education development of bilingual children. *Review of Educational Research* 49(2):222–251.

Cummins, J. 1981. The role of primary language development in promoting educational success for language minority students. In California State Department of Education (ed.), *Schooling and language minority students: A theoretical framework.* Los Angeles: California State Department of Education.

Cummins, J. 1984. Bilingualism and cognitive functioning. In S. Shepson and V. D'Oyley (eds.), *Bilingual and multicultural education: Canadian perspectives,* 55–67. Avon, England: Multilingual Matters.

Cummins, J. 1986. Empowering minority students: A framework for intervention. *Harvard Education Review, 56*(1):18–36.

Cummins, J. 1993. Bilingualism and second language learning. *Annual Review of Applied Linguistics* 13:51–70.

Cummins, J. 2000. *Language, power and pedagogy: Bilingual children in the crossfire.* Clevedon, England: Multilingual Matters.

Cummins, J., and M. Danesi. 1990. *Heritage languages: The development and denial of Canada's linguistic resources.* Toronto: Our Schools/Ourselves Education Foundation and Garamond Press.

Davis, P. 1994. *Literacy acquisition, retention, and usage: A case study of the Machiguenga of the Peruvian Amazon.* Ph.D. dissertation. University of Texas, Austin.

Delpit, L., and G. Kemelfield. 1985. *An evaluation of the Viles Tok Ples Skul scheme in the North Solomons Province. ERU Report No. 51.* Port Moresby, Papua New Guinea: University of Papua New Guinea.

Department of Education. 1986. *Philosophy of education for Papua New Guinea* [The Matane Report]. Waigani, Papua New Guinea: Department of Education.

Department of Education. 1990. *Curriculum guide for tokples preparatory schools, trial draft.* Waigani, Papua New Guinea: Department of Education.

Department of Education. 1991. *Education sector review: Executive summary.* Waigani, Papua New Guinea: Department of Education.

Department of Provincial Affairs and Village Services. 1995a. *The government's policy for Village Services.* Policy paper presented to the Fifth National Parliament. 12 August, 1992.

Department of Provincial Affairs and Village Services. 1995b. *Village Services Division 1995 draft policy paper.* Port Moresby, Papua New Guinea: Department of Provincial Affairs and Village Services.

Dolson, D., and J. Meyer. 1992. Longitudinal study of three program models for language-minority students: A critical examination of reported findings. *Bilingual Research Journal* 16(1 and 2):105–157.

Dorian, N. 1981. *Language death.* Philadelphia: University of Pennsylvania Press.

Dorian, N. 1993. A response to Ladefoged's other view of endangered languages. *Language* 69(3):575–579.

Downing, J. 1984. A source of cognitive confusion for beginning readers: Learning in a second language. *The Reading Teacher* 366–370.

Duranti, A., and E. Ochs. 1986. Literacy instruction in a Samoan village. In B. Schieffelin and P. Gilmore (eds.), *The acquisition of literacy: Ethnographic perspectives,* 213–232. Norwood, N.J.: Ablex.

Dutcher, N. 1982. *The use of first and second languages in primary education: Selected case studies.* World Bank Staff Working Paper No. 504. Washington, D.C.: The World Bank.

Edwards, J. 1981. The context of bilingual education. *Journal of Multilingual and Multicultural Development* 2(1):25–44.

Edwards, J. 1985. *Language, society and identity.* Oxford: Basil Blackwell.

Edwards, J. 1992. Bilingualism, education, and identity. In J. Gimbel, E. Hansen, A. Holmen, and J. N. Jorgensen (eds.), *Papers from the Fifth Nordic Conference on Bilingualism,* 203–210. Clevedon, England: Multilingual Matters.

Eisner, E. 1991. *The enlightened eye: Qualitative inquiry and the enhancement of educational practice.* New York: Macmillan.

Engle, P. 1975. *The use of vernacular languages in education: Language medium in early school years for minority language groups.* Bilingual Education Series, 3. Arlington, Va.: Center for Applied Linguistics.

Erickson, F. 1986. Qualitative methods in research on teaching. In M. Wittrock (ed.), *Handbook of research on teaching,* 119–161. New York: Macmillan.

Erickson, F. 1990. Qualitative methods. In R. Linn and F. Erickson (eds.), *Quantitative methods/Qualitative methods,* 75–194. New York: Macmillan.

Fafunwa, A., J. Macauley, and J. Sokoya, eds. 1989. *Education in mother tongue: The Ife primary education research project.* Ibadan, Nigeria: University Press.

Fasold, R. 1984. *The sociolinguistics of society.* Cambridge, Mass.: Basil Blackwell.

Fergie, R. 1995. *Missions, mandarin, and minor: A study of church/state relationships in modern Papua New Guinea.* ms.

Finnegan, R. 1988. *Literacy and orality: Studies in the technology of communication.* Oxford: Basil Blackwell.

Fishman, Joshua. 1972. The sociology of language. In P. Giglioli (ed.), *Language and social context,* 45–58. Harmondsworth, England: Penguin Books.

Fishman, Joshua. 1980. Bilingualism and biculturalism as individual and as societal phenomena. *Journal of Multilingual and Multicultural Development* 1:3–15.

Fishman, Joshua. 1990. What is reversing language shift: RLS and how can it succeed? *Journal of Multilingual and Multicultural Development* 11(1 and 2):5–36.

Fishman, Joshua. 1991. *Reversing language shift: Theoretical and empirical foundations for assistance to threatened languages.* Clevedon, England: Multilingual Matters.

Fishman, Joshua. 1999. Sociolinguistics. In J. Fishman (ed.), *Handbook of language and ethnicity,* 152–163. Oxford: Oxford University Press.

Fishman, Joshua, ed. 2001a. *Can threatened languages be saved?* Clevedon, England: Multilingual Matters.

Fishman, Joshua. 2001b. Why is it so hard to save a threatened language? In J. Fishman (ed.), 1–22.

Fishman, Joshua, M. Gertner, E. Lowy, and W. Milan, eds. 1985. *The rise and fall of the ethnic revival: Perspectives on language and ethnicity.* Berlin: Mouton.

Franklin, Karl. 1975. Vernaculars as bridges to cross cultural understanding. In Kenneth McElhanon (ed.), *Tok Pisin i go we.* Kivung Special Publication No. 1. Port Moresby: Linguistic Society of Papua New Guinea.

Geertz, C. 1973. *The interpretation of cultures.* New York: Basic Books.

Giles, H., and P. Johnson. 1987. Ethnolinguistic identity theory: A social psychological approach to language maintenance. *International Journal of the Sociology of Language* 68:69–99.

Glesne, C., and A. Peshkin. 1992. *Becoming qualitative researchers: An introduction.* White Plains, N.Y.: Longman.

Goody, J., and I. Watt. 1988 (1968). The consequences of literacy. In E. Kintgen, B. Kroll, and M. Rose (eds.), *Perspectives on literacy,* 3–27. Carbondale: Southern Illinois University Press.

Grenoble. L. A., and L. J. Whaley, eds. 1998. *Endangered languages: Language loss and community response.* Cambridge: Cambridge University Press.

Grimes, B., ed. 1992. *Ethnologue: Languages of the world.* Dallas, Tex.: Summer Institute of Linguistics.

Hakuta, K. 1986. *Mirror of language: The debate on bilingualism.* New York: Basic Books.

Hale, K., ed. 1992. Endangered languages. *Language* 68(1):1–42.

Harris, S. 1990. *Two-way Aboriginal schooling: Education and cultural survival.* Canberra: Aboriginal Studies Press.

Harris, S. 1994. "Soft" and "hard" domain theory for bicultural education in indigenous groups. *Peabody Journal of Education* 69(1):140–153.

Haugen, E. 1956. *Bilingualism in the Americas: A bibliography and research guide.* Publications of the American Dialect Society 26.

Haugen, E. 1972. The stigmata of bilingualism. In A. Dil (ed.), *The ecology of language; Essays by Einar Haugen,* 307–344. Stanford, Calif.: Stanford University Press.

Haugen, E. 1985. The language of imperialism: Unity or pluralism. In N. Wolfson and J. Manes (eds.), *Language of inequality.* New York: Mouton.

Haugen, E. 1987. *Blessings of Babel: Bilingualism and language planning.* New York: Mouton de Gruyter.

Henze, R., and L. Vanett. 1993. To walk in two worlds—or more? Challenging a common metaphor of native education. *Anthropology and Education Quarterly* 24(2):116–134.

Hornberger, N. 1988. *Bilingual education and language maintenance: A southern Peruvian Quechua case.* Dordrecht, Holland: Foris.

Hornberger, N. 1994. Literacy and language planning. *Language and Education* 8(1 and 2):75–94.

Hunter, B., ed. 1994. *The statesman's year-book: Statistical and historical annual of the states of the world for the year 1994–1995.* New York: St. Martin's Press.

Jordan, D. 1988. Rights and claims of indigenous people: Education and the reclaiming of identity. In T. Skutnabb-Kangas (ed.), *Minority education: From shame to struggle,* 189–222. Clevedon, England: Multilingual Matters.

Krashen, S. 1991. *Bilingual education: A focus on current research. Occasional Papers in Bilingual Education, Spring 1991, 3.* Washington, D.C.: National Clearinghouse of Bilingual Education.

Krauss, M. 1992. The world's languages in crisis. *Language* 68(1):4–10.

Kulick, D., and C. Stroud. 1990. Christianity, cargo, and ideas of self: Patterns of literacy in a Papua New Guinean village. *Man* 25(2):286–304.

Kulick, D., and C. Stroud. 1993. Conceptions and uses of literacy in a Papua New Guinean village. In Street, 30–61.

Lacey, R. 1985. Journeys and transformations: The process of innovation in Papua New Guinea. *Pacific Viewpoint* 26(1):81–105.

Ladefoged, P. 1992. Another view of endangered languages. *Language* 68(4):809–811.

Lafanama, P. 1995. Why we say 'no' to SAP. *The National* [Papua New Guinea], August 9, 23.

Lal, B. 1995. Symbolic interaction theories. *American Behavioral Scientist* 38(3):421–441.

Lambert, W., and R. Tucker. 1972. *Bilingual education of children. The St. Lambert experiment.* Rowley, Mass.: Newbury House.

Larson, M., and P. Davis, eds. 1981. *Bilingual education: An experience in Peruvian Amazonia.* Dallas, Tex.: Summer Institute of Linguistics.

Lawrence, P. 1964. *Road belong cargo.* Melbourne: Manchester and Melbourne University Presses.

Leahy, M. 1991. *Explorations into highland New Guinea, 1930-1935.* D. Jones (ed.). Tuscaloosa: University of Alabama Press.

LeCompte, M., and J. Preissle. 1993. *Ethnography and qualitative design in educational research.* San Diego, Calif.: Academic Press.

Lincoln, Yvonne, and E. Guba. 1985. *Naturalistic inquiry.* Beverly Hills, Calif.: Sage Publications.

Lipka, J. 1994. Language, power, and pedagogy: Whose school is it? *Peabody Journal of Education* 69(2):71–93.

Malone, D. 1997. Namel manmeri: *Language and culture maintenance and mother tongue education in the highlands of Papua New Guinea.* Ph.D. dissertation. Indiana University

Malone, S. 1988. *Cooperation in change: Developing receptor-oriented innovation programs.* M.A. thesis. Fuller Theological Seminary, Pasadena, Cal.

Malone, S. 1997. *Cooperation, conflict, and complementarity: A study of relationships among organizations involved in mother tongue literacy and pre-primary education in Papua New Guinea.* Ph.D. dissertation. Indiana University.

May, S., ed. 1999. *Indigenous community-based education.* Clevedon, England: Multilingual Matters.

McLaughlin, D. 1994. Through whose eyes do our children see the world now? Traditional education in Papua New Guinea. *Papua New Guinea Journal of Education* 30(2):63–79.

McNamara, V. 1985. Papua New Guinea: System of education. In T. Husen and J. Postlethwaite (eds.), *The international encyclopedia of education,* 3753–3759. Oxford: Pergamon Press.

Meggitt. M. 1965. *The lineage system of the Mae-Enga.* Edinburgh: Oliver and Boyd.

Merlan, F., and A. Rumsey. 1991. *Ku Waru: Language and segmentary politics in the Western Nebilyer Valley, Papua New Guinea.* Cambridge: Cambridge University Press.

Merriam, S. 1988. *Case study research in education: A qualitative approach.* San Francisco: Jossey-Bass.

Modiano, N. 1973. *Indian education in the Chiapas Highlands.* New York: Holt, Rinehart, and Winston.

Moll, L. 1992. Bilingual classroom studies and community analysis: Some recent trends. *Educational Researcher* 21(2):20–24.

Mühlhäusler, P. 1990. 'Reducing' Pacific languages to writing. In J. Joseph and T. Taylor (eds.), *Ideologies of language,* 189–205. London: Routledge.

Mühlhäusler, P. 1996. *Linguistic ecology: Language change and linguistic imperialism in the Pacific region.* London: Routledge.

Myers-Scotton, C. 1993. *Duelling languages: Grammatical structure in code-switching.* Oxford: Oxford University Press.

Nongorr, J. 1995. On the down side. *The Saturday Independent* [Papua New Guinea], August 24, 11.

Olson, D. 1988 (1977). From utterance to text: The bias of language in speech and writing. In E. Kintgen, B. Kroll, and M. Rose (eds.), *Perspectives on literacy,* 175–189. Carbondale: Southern Illinois University Press.

Ong, W. 1982. *Orality and literacy: The technologizing of the word.* London: Routledge.

Ovando, C. 1990. Essay review: Politics and pedagogy: The case for bilingual education. *Harvard Education Review* 60(3):341–356.

Ovando, C. 1994. Change in school and community attitudes in an Athapaskan village. In J. Lipka and A. Stairs (eds.), Negotiating the Culture of Indigenous Schools. *Peabody Journal of Education* 69(2):43–59.

Papua New Guinea government, Australian Agency for International Development AusAID, and Asian Development Bank ADB. 1995. *Papua New Guinea education sector resources study.* Final report.

Paulston, C. 1986. Linguistic consequences of ethnicity and nationalism in multilingual settings. In Spolsky, 117–152.

Paulston, C. 1992. *Sociolinguistic perspectives on bilingual education.* Clevedon, England: Multilingual Matters.

Paulston, C. 1994. *Linguistic minorities in multilingual settings.* Amsterdam: John Benjamins.

Phillipson, R., T. Skutnabb-Kangas, and H. Africa. 1986. Namibian educational language planning: English for liberation or neo-colonialism? In B. Spolsky, 77–95.

Poplack, S., and D. Sankoff. 1984. Borrowing: The synchrony of integration. *Linguistics* 22:99–135.

Poplack, S., S. Wheeler, and A. Westwood. 1987. Distinguishing language contact phenomena: Evidence from Finnish-English bilingualism. In P. Lilius and M. Saari (eds.), *The Nordic languages and modern linguistics* 6:22–56. Helsinki: University of Helsinki Press.

Ramirez, J. D., S. O. Yuen, and D. R. Ramey. 1991. *Final report: Longitudinal study of structured English immersion strategy, early-exit and late-exit programs for language minority children.* Report submitted to the U.S. Department of Education. San Mateo, Calif.: Aquirre International.

Rand McNally and Company. 1994. *Cosmopolitan world atlas.* Chicago, Ill.

Rogers, A. 1992. *Adults learning for development.* London: Cassell Educational.

Romaine, S. 1995. *Bilingualism.* Oxford: Basil Blackwell.

Rubagumya, C. 1991. Language promotion for educational purposes: The example of Tanzania. *International Review of Education* 37(1):67–85.

Ruiz, R. 1984. Orientations in language planning. *NABE Journal* 8(2):15–24.

Schooling, S. 1990. *Language maintenance in Melanesia: Sociolinguistics and social networks in New Caledonia.* Summer Institute of Linguistics and the University of Texas at Arlington Publications in Linguistics 91. Dallas.

Schwandt, T. 1994. Constructivist, interpretivist approaches to human inquiry. In N. Denzin and Y. Lincoln (eds.), *Handbook of qualitative research*, 118–137. Thousand Oaks, Calif.: Sage.

Scribner, S., and Cole, M. 1981. *The psychology of literacy*. Cambridge, Mass: Harvard University Press.

Skutnabb-Kangas, T. 1986. Who wants to change what and why—conflicting paradigms in minority education research. In Spolsky, 153–181.

Skutnabb-Kangas, T. 1988. Multilingualism and the education of minority children. In T.Skutnabb-Kangas and J. Cummins (eds.), *Minority education: From shame to struggle*, 9–44. Clevedon, England: Multilingual Matters.

Skutnabb-Kangas, T. 2000. *Linguistic genocide in education—or worldwide diversity and human rights*. Mahjah, N.J.: Lawrence Erlbaum.

Skutnabb-Kangas, T., and J. Cummins, eds. 1988. *Minority education: From shame to struggle*. Clevedon, England: Multilingual Matters.

Smalley, W. 1994. *Linguistic diversity and national unity: Language ecology in Thailand*. Chicago: University of Chicago Press.

Smolicz, J. 1986. National language policy in the Philippines. In Spolsky, 96–116.

Spolsky, B. 1972. *The language education of minority children*. Rowley, Mass.: Newbury House.

Spolsky, B., ed. 1986. *Language and education in multilingual settings*. Clevedon, England: Multilingual Matters.

Spradley, J. 1980. *Participant observation*. New York: Holt, Rinehart, and Winston.

Stake, R. 1995. *The art of the case study*. Thousand Oaks, Calif.: Sage Publications.

Strathern, A. 1971. *The rope of moka: Big men and ceremonial exchange in Mt. Hagen, New Guinea*. Cambridge: Cambridge University Press.

Strathern, A. 1979a. *Ongka: A self-account by a New Guinea big-man*. New York: St. Martin's Press.

Strathern, A. 1979b. The self in self-decoration. *Oceania* 49:241–257.

Strathern, M. 1991. Artifacts of history: Events and the interpretations of images. In S. Siikala (ed.), *Culture and history in the Pacific*. Helsinki: Transactions of the Finnish Anthropoligical Society.

Street, B.,1984. *Literacy in theory and practice*. Cambridge: Cambridge University Press.

Street, B. ed. 1993. Introduction. *Cross-cultural approaches to literacy*, 1–21. Cambridge: Cambridge University Press.

Stringer, M., and N. Faraclas. 1987. *Working together for literacy*. Wewak, Papua New Guinea: Christian Books Melanesia.

Summer Institute of Linguistics. 1993. *Supervisors tokples education program.* Publicity brochure. Ukarumpa, Papua New Guinea: Summer Institute of Linguistics.

Summer Institute of Linguistics. 1994. *Developing elementary education in Papua New Guinea: The potential role of SIL.* Unpublished draft report. Ukarumpa, Papua New Guinea: Summer Institute of Linguistics.

Topping, D. 1992. Language and social change in the Pacific Islands. In A. Robillard (ed.), *Social change in the Pacific Islands,* 393–413. London: Kegan Paul International.

Troike, R. 1978. Research evidence for the effectiveness of bilingual education. *NABE Journal* 3(1):13-24.

Troike, R. 1984. Social and cultural aspects of language proficiency. In C. Rivera (ed.), *Language proficiency and academic achievement.* Clevedon, England: Multilingual Matters.

Vygotsky, L. 1978. *Mind in society: The development of higher psychological processes.* M. Cole, V. Steiner, S. Scribner, and E. Souberman (eds.). Cambridge, Mass.: Harvard University Press.

Waiko, J. 1993. *A short history of Papua New Guinea.* Melbourne: Oxford University Press.

Warakari, V. 1995. Taking stock of the state of the economy. *The Saturday Independent* [Papua New Guinea], October 7, 20–21.

Wari, P., and G. Roakeina. 1994. *Elementary school evaluation: Lessons from Milne Bay Trial.* Port Moresby: Papua New Guinea: Unicef and Papua New Guinea Department of Education.

Watson, K. 1994. Caught between Scylla and Charybdis: Linguistic and educational dilemmas facing policy-makers in pluralist states. *International Journal of Educational Development* 14(3):321–337.

Wong Fillmore, L. 1991. When learning a second language means losing the first. *Early Childhood Research Quarterly* 6:323–346.

World Conference on Linguistic Rights. 1996. *Universal declaration of linguistic rights.* Document produced at the World Conference on Linguistic rights. Barcelona, Spain. June 1996. (Information summary [on-line]. Available: < http://www.portal.comciemanconfdeng.html >)

SIL International
Publications in Language Use and Education

1. Reading Is for Knowing: Literacy Acquisition, Retention and Usage among the Machiguenga, by Patricia M. Davis, 2004.
2. "And I, in My Turn, Will Pass It On": Knowledge Transmission among the Kayopó, by Isabel I. Murphy, 2004.
4. Language Contact and Composite Structures in New Ireland, by Rebecca Sue Jenkins, forthcoming in 2004.

Publications in Sociolinguistics

8. Borrowing Versus Code-Switching in West Tarangan (Indonesia), by Richard J. Nivens, 2002.
7. The Dynamics of Sango Language Spread, by Mark E. Karan, 2001.
6. K'iche': A Study in the Sociology of Language, by M. Paul Lweis, 2001.
5. The Same but Different: Language Use and Attitudes in Four Communities of Burkina Faso, by Stuart Showalter, 2000.
4. Ashéninka Stories of Change, by Ronald James Anderson, 2000.
3. Assessing Ethnolinguistic Vitality: Theory and Practice, M. Paul Lewis and Gloria Kindell, eds., 1999.
2. The Early Days of Sociolinguistics: Memories and Reflections, Christina Bratt Paulston and G. Richard Tucker, eds., 1997.
1. North Sulawesi Language Survey, Scott Merrifield and Martinus Selsa, 1996.

For further information or a full listing of SIL publications contact:

International Academic Bookstore
SIL International
7500 W. Camp Wisdom Road
Dallas, TX 75236-5699

Voice: 972-708-7404
Fax: 972-708-7363
Email: academic.books@sil.org
Internet: http://www.ethnologue.com